HOME AND ALONE

DANIEL STERN

Published in the United States by Viva Editions, an imprint of Start Midnight, LLC, 221 River Street, Ninth Floor, Hoboken, New Jersey 07030.

Printed in the United States
Cover design: Jennifer Do
Cover Photo: Laure Stern
Back Cover Photo: Seth Gordon
Text design: Frank Wiedemann

First Edition.
10 9 8 7 6 5 4 3 2 1

Trade paper ISBN: 978-1-63228-093-0
E-book ISBN: 978-1-63228-121-0

*It is with deepest gratitude and love that
I dedicate this book to my parents, my children,
my friends, my colleagues, my fans,
and most importantly, my wife Laure.
Without each of you, this story doesn't exist.*

TABLE OF CONTENTS

INTRODUCTION

Hallelujah, I have finished writing my book! Wow, that was a lot of work. But finally, after all these months of toiling away at my computer, I am ready to begin. I am writing this introduction as an afterthought because when I started writing this tome, I had no idea what I was going to say, so I had no idea what I would be introducing. But now that I have completed this epic odyssey, I feel, at long last, prepared to write the first page. Isn't that the way it always is, in everything you do in life? In life itself? Just when you finally figure it out, it's over. Intelligent design, my ass.

First of all, thank you for buying or stealing my book. It has been quite a challenge writing it, and knowing that you care what I have to say enough to spend your hard-earned money on it, or even more impressively, risk jail time to read it, means the world to me. Despite the fact that the protagonist of this story leaves something to be desired, I hope you find a connection with this magnificent journey I have been on.

I have had a job since I was eight years old and if I don't have work to do, I go out of my mind. I *need* to be productive, and so I couldn't have chosen a worse profession than acting, where the average annual work schedule is on par with that of a shopping mall Santa. I have learned to make my own work. I wake up every morning with the same question—"What am I going to make today?" Some days it's money. I had a family very young and have been driven most of my life to make money and provide for them. But my need to create is something else and borders on psychotic. It really doesn't matter whether I am making a new TV show, a new sculpture, or a new chicken coop; as long as I feel like I've made something that day, I sleep well at night.

I hit sixty-five this year. That was a kick in the balls. My oldest child is forty-one, and I am a grandpa five times over. What the fuck? I've always been "the kid," the precocious teenager who moved to New York as a seventeen-year-old, at least ten years younger than all of my friends, the youngest dad at all my kids' school events. But you can't hide from sixty-five. No matter how I look at it, that circle-of-life conveyor belt keeps moving me along and there are fewer and fewer people in front of me every day, and so many more behind. I started hearing a voice in my head saying, "Whoa! Stop! Maybe it is time to stop making things for a minute and take a look at the crazy journey you have been on. It really could end at any time, and it would be a shame not to have taken the opportunity to try to gain some meaning and understanding of it all." So I started a list (which is one of my favorite things to do) of my life—What is the first thing I remember? What is the second? It was revelatory to lay it all out in front of myself and see how A led to B and B led to C. Of course, being me, I had to make a job out of it, so I decided to shape it into a book for me and my family, turning that list into chapter headings and doing a deep dive into each one. It settled my soul to put a little order in to my chaotic history and remember not only this journey of jobs, people, and events, but the feelings and emotions and thoughts that went with them. Being an admirer of good storytelling, I tried my best to be entertaining and funny, to find a moral to the story and share a little bit of knowledge or dare I say, wisdom, with the reader.

When Start Publishing said they wanted to put it into print, I jumped at the chance to do the work and try to actually write a book. I have been sitting *Home and Alone* for months now, and frankly, I am sick of myself. I hope you enjoy getting to know me, but I would recommend not reading this book more than twice because after that, I really start to get on your nerves. There has been no ghostwriter. I have zero typing skills, minimal computer skills, and a well-below-average knowledge of grammar, so it has been quite an English lesson for this high school drop-out as well (although I think I finally get where the punctuation goes when using a parenthesis.). I didn't want to pander to the reader by including too much stuff about celebrities, but my wife pointed out that I have been acting in the movies since I was twenty, so these people are not really celebrities, just my friends and workmates, and a large part of my life. Besides, none of these people think of themselves as celebrities. They are living inside their own heads just like the rest of us. Managing the power and ridiculousness of celebrity is something no one is trained for, and I have found it will reveal who you truly are, in a unique and distorted way. (And it sure does help when it comes to getting your book published.)

My personal mission of "Empowering Young People" has also been the message in some of my biggest family films, like the *Home Alone* movies, *Rookie of the Year*, and *Bushwhacked*, a message

I believe in because I was an empowered kid myself, finding my own unique path to a well-lived life. There is so much potential in each child—even artistic, dyslexic, little hippies like me—and our goal as parents and mentors is to help each kid discover who they are and how to make a life for themselves doing something they love and are good at. I am the living embodiment of that successful strategy, and my hope is that by sharing my story, I can inspire the feeling in the reader that, "Hell, if this guy can build a successful life, anyone can."

I have found myself in extraordinary places I had no place being in, working with extraordinary people who I had no business working with. I became a father when I was still a kid. I spent years making a salary of forty-five dollars a week and years making a salary of forty-five thousand dollars a week. I have found spectacular artistic satisfaction in my life in the movies, theater, and television, but have also found deep artistic satisfaction in my life as a bronze sculptor, cattle rancher, and lemon farmer, and mostly, in the creation of my family. I have tried to serve my community to the best of my abilities—coached my kids' sports teams, taught Media Literacy at the high school, and started a Boys & Girls Club which continues to serve thousands of kids to this day. I visited our troops in Baghdad, Iraq, during the chaos at the beginning of that horrible war. President Obama awarded me our nation's highest honor for volunteerism, one of the greatest honors of my life. My forty-five-year-long marriage, the incredible success of my children and now five magnificent grandchildren—I have packed a lot into my sixty-five years.

I am hoping the book gives people some laughs and they have fun going backstage with me on some of the movies, TV shows, and plays I have worked on. I try to convey my evolution from an actor into a writer and director. I share my development as a sculptor and why it is so important to me, as well as the importance of the work I have done with Boys & Girls Clubs, to whom I am giving all of the royalties from this book. I track my family and the amazing journey of parenting, as well as the peace and meaning I have discovered by becoming a real city slicker living on our farm and ranch. And I show off my skills at using a thesaurus, finding incredible alternatives to the word "incredible." So no more dawdling. Let's get to it. It is time for you to see what Daniel Stern is really like when he is *Home and Alone*.

BORN FREE

"You're writing a book? You can barely even read a book and you think you can write one? You think you are so important people will want to read all about *you*?" Ahh, nothing more inspiring than a mother's words of encouragement. You have a mother, right? You know how when you ask your mom about the day you were born and you expect to hear a nice story about the joy of seeing you for the first time and the instant connection she felt with you? When my mother tells the story about that day, August 28, 1957, she tells of one of the worst days of her life. Mom recalls that in the state of Connecticut, they put women under full anesthesia, Lord knows why. Mom evidently didn't react well to the drug and so when she finally came to, her first reaction upon seeing me was to throw up—a lot, according to her. She felt so sick that she didn't want to hold me for a while. And just as she was feeling a little better, she got the terrible news that her beloved doctor, who had just delivered me, went home afterwards and died of a heart attack. Yeah, not a great entrance on my part.

My parents' goal was to make me a fully independent person, as quickly as possible. By the age of four, my best friend and I walked through the streets of Philadelphia, on our own, the two-mile trip to my grandparents' house. I have Google mapped both of the addresses—our house and my grandparents' house—to see if my memories match in any way to what the reality is and, shockingly, I remember it pretty well. We had to cross Cheltenham Avenue, a six-lane thoroughfare with an intersection that brings together three different main roads, and I remember us being stranded on the center island, cars whizzing by on all sides. I have asked my mother repeatedly throughout the years, "What the fuck were you thinking!?"

"I knew you could handle it," is what she says to me. It was crazy to let such young children take off on their own that way, but on the other hand, I still remember it sixty-one years later, and it never fails to make me smile and feel proud.

John F. Kennedy took office in 1961 and my dad, being an inspired social worker called to serve by a great leader, took a job in the Kennedy administration, working at the Department of Health, Education, and Welfare on issues dealing with juvenile delinquency. He got a GI loan and bought a small house in Bethesda, Maryland, on Fairfield Drive, a tiny street with no sidewalks, and a stone's throw from the Bethesda Naval Medical Hospital, now known as Walter Reed Hospital, the Navy base where all American presidents receive their medical treatments. I went to Lynnbrook Elementary School, which was about a half a mile walk from our house. I was two years behind my sister and the teachers were already making it clear that I was not nearly as bright as she was, which was true. I had to go to the little building behind the playground for remedial reading and speech therapy. As far as I know they did not have a diagnosis of dyslexia at that time or place, but that is what I was suffering from. Once we got past "See Spot Run," I couldn't keep up at all. I loved when teachers read us stories but was humiliated when we went around the room and had to read out loud. But I also had a lot of successes. I was very good and quick at math. That made sense to me. I took up the trumpet in the band, and really excelled at that, getting the first trumpet seat even though I was only in fourth grade. We played kickball and football with the competitive ferocity of little gladiators, and I was good at sports, so that helped me have an identity as well. I was a very happy kid, and my thoughts were consumed by the same thing a dog might be focused on—playing with a ball of any kind and eating anything that was put in front of me. Our little brother was born and moved into my room. I loved having a brother, but I was six years older than him, and he was not as good at kickball as I had hoped he would be. At six, I took the train to Philadelphia by myself to visit my grandparents. At age eight, I got my first job, delivering one hundred newspapers for a dollar. I added a second paper route the next year, firmly indoctrinated into that atrocious child-labor racket of paperboys, where I would stay until I graduated high school.

Culturally, the world was going mad and sending my little brain all kinds of messages about love, peace, freedom, and equality. I didn't fully understand it, but I was obsessed with it all, especially the music and the comedy that was happening. My parents were into the folk music of Bob Dylan, Joan Baez, and Simon and Garfunkel. The famed folk singer, Pete Seeger, even came to our house a couple of times with friends of my dad's. We got our own little record player for the basement, and I spent my paper route money on 45s of the Beatles, the Rolling Stones, the Supremes, etc. We would memorize the words to the songs and then put on shows for each other in the basement, acting them out. In retrospect, I realize how seriously I took those shows, an indicator that I wanted to be part of telling stories, but I had no concept of anything called show business at the time. I just loved watching and listening to it all—*Get Smart, The Mod Squad, The Smothers Brothers*, Tom Lehrer, Bill Cosby, The Three Stooges, and Dick Van Dyke. Jerry Lewis actually made me throw up from laughing too hard at *Who's Minding the Store?*

I had a very typical American childhood in a typical American town, including some of the uglier sides of growing up in America. My parents had come to Washington to join a movement for equality and justice in America. Mom was teaching at a nursery school and Dad was dealing with changing the juvenile justice system, working with a racially and ethnically diverse group of exciting men and women on the same mission. We all went to the civil rights marches and anti-war protests, marching through the streets of Washington and into a few scary situations. My poor parents had to miss Martin Luther King's "I Have a Dream" speech because it took place on my birthday, but I'll never forget my dad stopping the birthday party and blaring the speech from the radio in our backyard. My parents had parties with their friends, and this kind of racial commingling didn't sit too well with our neighbors. Bethesda, Maryland, is located right on the Mason-Dixon line, and where we lived still had a very Dixie feel to it. No Blacks. No Jews. Segregated swimming pools and country clubs, and white supremacy and racism displayed everywhere with no shame or consequences. My sister and I were the only Jewish kids at Lynnbrook. For as much as we fit in, we were also freaks. We got our "Christmas presents" at Hanukah, we skipped school on the High Holy Days, and no one knew what the fuck was going on when we brought in our peanut butter and jelly sandwiches on matzoh at Passover. When I was about nine or ten, I had to start going to Hebrew school on Wednesdays after school and on Saturday mornings. (Just what I needed, more fucking school. And trying to learn to read another language, which is read backwards, when I couldn't even read English? Not going to happen.) We were The Jews. We were The Christ-Killers. We were The N-word Lovers. The kids really didn't know what half of it even meant and were only parroting their parents' fucked-up beliefs. Sometimes my friends would call me "a dirty Jew" and an "n-word lover" and, being a little kid who wanted to fit in, I dealt with that by calling other kids dirty Jews and n-word lovers. How fucked up is that? But I guess it was what I felt I needed to do to survive. Lines were being drawn, even among ten-year-olds. If your hair was long enough to touch your ear, you were a Hippie/Fag. If you went to a peace march, you were a Hippie/Fag. Puberty was coming. Kids were starting to smoke cigarettes and make out with girls, and I just wanted to play the next game and eat the next popsicle. The redneck culture of my friends in Bethesda was crashing into all of the lessons of equality, justice, multiculturalism, and peace that my parents were teaching me, and that the amazing pop cultural landscape was embracing. By the time I got to the end of elementary school, my survival instincts knew something was going to have to change. Luckily, it did.

Chevy Chase, Maryland, is where the Jews lived. That was the word on the street when I told my friends we were moving there the summer after finishing elementary school. It was only about a mile away and we were all still going to be going to the same junior high school and seeing each other every day in the fall, but I might as well have been moving to another country. I loved my friends there, but it was clear to me that I wasn't really going to end up on the same path as them. Besides, I was ready to let my freak flag fly a bit. I wouldn't get another haircut for the next four years.

A YOUNG JEW
ON THE MASON-DIXON LINE

J unior high was liberating. I still was an academic disaster, but now we had electives like shop, choir, art, and gym, and I was good at all of those things. There were so many new kids to be friends with—Jewish kids, Black kids, Latin kids and, most importantly, little hippies. David Rosenthal had the exact same schedule as me, every class, every day. Not only that, but David and I were starting at a new Hebrew school together, so we saw each other after school all the time as well, and that was where the real bond formed. Our bar mitzvahs were only a year away, so our class met three days a week. There were about eight or ten of us, all of us Little Jewish Hippies, being taught by Big Jewish Hippies, young college students living in Washington, DC, in 1969 with a passion for the teachings of Judaism. Three days a week they had us deeply engaged with Judaism and its relevance to the changes that were taking place in America. Judaism came alive as we debated the meanings of the Torah, the existence of God, the political landscape, and the cultural landscape. To have a group of Jewish friends was something I never knew I needed until I had it. The teachers took us on field trips to war protests in Washington and to the Orthodox Jewish community in Williamsburg, NY. The friendships in the group became very deep, and even after we all had our bar/bat mitzvahs, we stayed on into the Confirmation class, until we were about sixteen.

The music director at the school was a college kid named Eleanor Epstein, a true dynamo who taught music to kids from ages five to sixteen, all at the same time. She was from New York, loud, charismatic, and funny as hell. And she loved to put on shows. I had never been around the theater in any fashion or even gone to a play. I was way too shy to ever be in the shows, but I enjoyed the technical side, doing the lights and building the sets, and got that amazing feeling of camaraderie that comes only in the theater. David Rosenthal was a natural show-off and incredibly talented, and Eleanor gave him great shows to star in—everything from *The Tales of Chelm* to *Fiddler on the Roof*, where David was an outstanding Tevye at thirteen (and probably grew his own beard for the role, as he matured very quickly). He was my best friend, and I was so proud and amazed by him, literally shining the spotlight on his talent from backstage. But as he got the laughs and attention, my young competitive spirit was being challenged. It still looked terrifying to me to be in front of an audience and I really loved working backstage, but a seed had been planted.

The summer after seventh grade, my parents sent me off for six weeks to a canoeing camp in Northern Canada called Wigwasati that was owned and operated by my gym teacher, Mr. Wrightson. It was life-changing, being that far away from home for so long, paddling on lakes for weeks, hauling our own food, building tents, and carrying a waterlogged wooden canoe on my shoulders on a mile-and-a-half portage. I overcame challenges and did things I never thought I could, and I came back from there really ready for my bar mitzvah and the manhood that it represents. My haftarah was from Amos, and my dad helped me write a very powerful and political speech, with the words, "Let justice roll on like a river and righteousness like an ever-flowing stream" as a launching point for my statement on how I intended to live my life as a man.

David and I also took up hitchhiking as our means of transportation, and the world opened up to us. We would hitchhike to Georgetown to see old Marx Brothers movies, getting picked up by hippies in vans who would offer us Ripple Wine and pot. We'd hitchhike to folk festivals, peace marches, and to get back and forth to Hebrew school. It felt so empowering and grown up. In the summer, David and I, still thirteen years old, somehow talked our parents into letting us hitchhike up to Maine to visit one of the girls from Hebrew school, about a five-hundred-mile trip each way. We did the same trip two years later and there are enough stories in those trips to make an awesome Cameron Crowe movie. We got rides from truckers, hippies, and a couple of very creepy people. We slept anywhere we could—the back of a gas station, the woods along the highway. The airport police in Bangor, Maine, took pity on us and let us spend the night in their jail, eating dinner out of their vending machine. (They did not, however, even try to call our parents or ask us what was going on.) We broke into Tanglewood in the Berkshire Mountains of Massachusetts, and spent several nights in the storage room where they kept instruments and equipment listening to the concerts in the evening. These adventures gave me the confidence and independence to operate well in the adult world. I was flunking all of my classes, but I became great friends with my teachers, not just in school but outside school as well. I would hitchhike to their houses on the weekends for visits—Candy Means and her husband Howard in the suburbs, Mr. Wallace in Georgetown, and Mrs. Snyder at her rural home in Takoma Park.

I dreamed about dropping out and getting a job and my own place, but the only job I could get was still as a paperboy. I was now delivering *The Washington Post*, a very prestigious job in my mind, and supposedly the best-paying paper route. I had to get up at four thirty in the morning every day of the week, for three straight years. The guy who gave me his route also gave me his double-sided paperboy bag and a full-sized baby carriage to carry all of the heavy newspapers. It took me about two hours to deliver those seventy newspapers, each one placed inside the door. I would try to go back to sleep for a few minutes but then my mom would wake me to go to school. The real scam of paperboy human trafficking was the paperboy had to pay for the papers up front each month, out of his own pocket, and then at the end of each month, go door to door, at night, to collect the money from each customer and hope for a tip of some kind. I would end up clearing about twenty-five bucks a month. But I delivered the *Post* all throughout Watergate and got to read Woodward and Bernstein's articles before anyone else. I am glad I did it, but between the exhaustion from the job, the dyslexia, and the lack of structure at school, what little academic skill I had totally evaporated and I truly didn't care. My teachers took pity on me, and somehow I graduated junior high school.

Bethesda-Chevy Chase High School had just opened a new theater at the school and David Rosenthal jumped into the theater scene right away, getting the lead part in a Shakespeare play, and building a very cool reputation right out of the gate. I worked backstage with the manager of the theater, Mike Boyle, and ended up with an after-school job there, hanging lights, running sound, and cleaning up when they rented the theater for concerts and dance performances. The idea of being onstage as opposed to backstage was beginning to take hold, but with my lion's mane of knotted hair, I really couldn't imagine what possible role I could play or have the nerve to even try out for.

But during the section of English devoted to studying *Lord of the Flies*, I found an opportunity to write my own part. The book was so good that I made it all the way through, and then we watched the movie, which was absolutely riveting and inspiring. I asked the teacher if instead of writing a paper, I could write a musical play version of the book, and he said okay. That's right, *Lord of the Flies: The Musical* was my first dramatic effort both as an actor and playwright. I persuaded Mr. Boyle to let me use the big theater, since we would only be presenting it during the school day to our English class. I took songs of the day and changed the lyrics to fit the story. Cat Stevens's "How Can I Tell You That I Love You" became "How Can I Tell You That The Beast Is Within You" and the Spirit song "Nature's Way" captured the themes perfectly. I became obsessed with writing it and directing it, using my sound and lighting experience to make the music sound okay and the show look cool. And on top of it all, I played the lead role, even with my very long hair. I am sure it was horrible, but everything clicked into place for me. I felt myself begin to take flight, a flight that would last for the rest of my life, finding the deep joy of creation and collaboration in the telling of stories, and communicating with an audience through a shared imagination. I must have ended up reading the book fifteen times, which also was a first for me, and began to open my mind to the idea that maybe there was such a thing as a good book, after all my bad experiences with literature up until then.

The day came for us to present the show to our class, maybe forty kids in a theater that sat fifteen hundred. I can't remember if I was petrified or confident to start with, but by the time the performance was over and I took an actual bow at the curtain call, I was higher than I had ever been in my life. The adrenaline rush was enormous, and the dopamine hit from people treating me like an actor, like a "star," applauding and telling me I did a good job, was like nothing I had ever come close to imagining. I had been working so hard on the play that even my parents took note, and my mother actually took time off of work to come during school hours to watch the play. She had to get back to work afterwards, so it wasn't until I got home that I got to see her. This was the most successful thing I had ever done in school, and I was expecting my mom to have been impressed. And she was, just not in the way I had anticipated.

"So, what did you think?"

"Truthfully, I found it very sad."

"Sad? You mean the story was sad?"

"No. . . . You were sad. It was sad watching you."

"Why was it sad?"

"Is there something wrong with you?"

"What do you mean?"

"Why would you do that? Why are you getting up in front of people and showing off like that?"

"It was a play."

"I know it was a play. And you were in it, up there on the stage, showing off in front of everyone. I am seriously worried about you, that you feel the need to do something like that. Showing off like that just to get attention. We haven't been giving you enough attention and I have been feeling bad all day that you have been in so much pain and I haven't even noticed until it comes out like this."

Ironically, my parents love the theater. They had season tickets to Arena Stage in Washington for decades, went to New York to see the shows every year, and loved talking about the terrific plays and actors they saw. So I really did not see this reaction coming at all. They knew David Rosenthal was in plays and thought he was great, never mentioning what kind of cry for help he might be exhibiting. My sister's friends were in school plays and my parents might have even gone to see them. But me doing it was shameful. An embarrassment. Either an ego trip or a mental breakdown of some kind. Obviously, it still rings in my head. Who the fuck would say that to their kid in that situation? I have asked my mother on many occasions if this really happened and if that was her real reaction. She stands by all of it, and still feels it to a certain degree. I laughed her off, truly not hurt by what she said and maybe, in fact, a little sad for her, that she couldn't see the joy and awakening her son was experiencing because of remnants of the old Jewish shtetl mentality of never drawing attention to yourself. I had found my voice and my identity. My connection to the world of theater, first backstage and now as an actor and as a creator, was bonded for life.

For a Mother's Day present that year, I got a haircut. Not only did it reduce my mother to tears of joy, it was the perfect excuse to get out of the trap of my physical appearance and open myself up to try out for the prestigious summer stock theater program at our high school, run by our esteemed Mr. Dalla Santa, head of English and Theater. I got a couple of small parts, including one where I got to yodel my own song in *Leave It to Jane*, a campy 1920s-style musical. I was already over six feet tall and weighed about 120 lbs., and the sight of this pencil-necked geek yodeling got laughs every show. The next fall, I got the lead role in *Promises, Promises*, a Burt Bacharach musical in which I played a young businessman. It was a huge part, with nine or ten songs to sing, and I had to learn how to sing for real. This was before all of the wireless microphones they use now; I had to project my voice over the orchestra. I think I was pretty good in it. My parents came to see it, both of them nearly fainting from nervousness, but they ended up loving it, amazed at what I had done. WNET Public TV was doing a special series on the schools in the area, and we got to go to their TV studio and do two songs on television, which felt incredibly cool. The next summer, we had another high school do a joint production of *Fiddler on the Roof* with our school, directed by their theater director, Mr. Perialis. I really went for it at the audition, dancing and singing "If I Were a Rich Man" with abandon, and I beat out the star of their high school, as well as David Rosenthal, for the role of Tevye. That was a confidence builder and turning point. I had to actually act in that one, play a character that wasn't me, wear a beard and a costume that weren't mine. The show was really good, caught a buzz, and sold out the fifteen hundred tickets a night for its summer run of six shows. They decided to restage it in the fall, which was the beginning of my senior year, and we sold out again for the run. I was living the life of an artist—I'd built a potter's wheel in the basement, I was making metal sculptures in my metal shop class, acting, and singing in three different choirs—but I was flunking every non-art class. The guidance counselor told me I was going to have to go to summer school to graduate and it was only November. It was obvious what the next step had to be—I dropped out of high school and never went back.

To my parents' credit, they supported my leaving school. My sister was brilliant, in her second year of college and heading for a law degree, but they could see academics were not going to get me anywhere. They had to accept that I had some kind of acting talent, even if they didn't understand it at all. They had no concept of what a career as an actor would even look like, and neither did I. But I needed to find out, and soon, because like Big Ben, I was met with a near-hourly reminder from my mother—"I don't care what you do but you are out of this house when you turn eighteen." That gave me about eight months to figure out where I would be going.

GLENN CLOSE
IS MY WITNESS

I had a small window of time to try to figure out how to make money on my limited acting skills before I needed to move out and get a full-time job and a place to live. (At that point, Plan B involved finding an old school bus to park somewhere and live in, and getting a job at the car wash, which looked like fun.) It never crossed my mind to go to Hollywood or New York to be an actor. Not once. I didn't think of those as real places where real people go to try to "make it." The Arena Stage was, and still is, one of the premiere regional theaters in the country, but the dream of being an actor at Arena Stage was almost too big for me. Rehearsing in the daytime and performing a different play at night sounded very intimidating. Besides, sometimes they did Shakespeare plays and other classics, and there was no way I could ever be in one of those because I couldn't read them and I didn't understand what they were saying. Arena had an apprentice program, but even that seemed way out of my league, so I never even applied. My dream job was to get into Dinner Theater! Dinner theater is exactly what it sounds like—dining tables are set up around a center stage and the audience eats dinner during the play. Oh, and the actors are also your waiters. This was the only aspect of show business I thought I could probably fake my way through and actually make money as an actor—although at seventeen, I was much, much younger than everyone else there, so I knew my chances were pretty slim. I auditioned for a couple of shows but didn't get anything, although I did get the experience of seeing a dinner theater production of *Company* where the actors performed "The Ladies Who Lunch" while serving lunch.

The only relative I had even remotely connected to show business was a cousin of my mother's in Philadelphia named Sam Kressen. Sam was a dear and funny man, a jeweler by trade but a part-time local actor as well. His big claim to fame was that he looked very much like Ben Franklin, and in Philadelphia, that was a valuable thing. He played him in everything from local commercials and posters for the city to touring companies of *1776*. So now that I was considering being a professional actor, my mom drove me up to Philly to have a serious discussion with him about the profession. We went to his apartment for tea, and he told me everything he knew about show business, which I will share with you now.

1. You need to have a picture of yourself, and it has to be printed as an 8x10-inch photo. No other size will do!

2. Your best friend is the Yellow Pages! Look up agents, casting people, and theaters in it and then send them that 8x10 photo and tell them you want to be an actor.

3. Most importantly, the life of an actor is all about
   The Three Ds: Disappointment, Disillusionment, and
   Depression. You will be rejected every day of your life
   for one reason or another, and you have to learn to live
   with The Three Ds.

That was it. Not exactly the direction or opportunity I was hoping for, but it seemed to make a lot of sense to my mother, so it was worth the trip. A few weeks later, Sam got me an audition for the bus and truck company of 1776 that he would be touring with for eight months. A real audition! My girlfriend took my picture and we had it printed in the correct, 8x10 size. I went to the audition and did my best but did not get the part. Sam felt bad, and I did too. It turned out he was spot-on correct about Numbers 1 and 3 in his guide to an actor's life, eternal truths that still apply to this very day, even if the Yellow Pages did not turn out to be my best friend.

Mike Boyle, my high school theater director, recommended me for an apprenticeship to work on the lighting crew at the Washington Shakespeare Festival, a nonprofit organization that put on plays every summer on the National Mall in front of the Washington Monument. At my interview with the producers, I guess I told them of my experience working the lights at the B-CC theater or asked about the hours and the pay, but I honestly don't remember much of it at all. Just that one lucky moment, crystallized forever in my mind—that tiny little moment that changed everything. I had been teaching myself to play the guitar and had a habit of chewing on a guitar pick. As I got up to leave, the producers noticed as I put the pick back in my mouth and asked if I played guitar. Even though I only knew a few chords, I said yes, trying to seem cool and figuring they would never know the difference. A week later, I got a call saying that I had gotten the job. It would only pay one hundred dollars for two months of work, but it would be great experience to learn lighting from professionals and get my foot in the door with the producers. But when I reported to work on the first day I was in for the shock of my life. The producers met me with the news that I would not be apprenticing with the lighting crew; instead, they had cast me as an actor in the play! What? What the fuck was going on? They proceeded to inform me, "We needed someone who plays the guitar to be in the play, so instead of working on the lighting crew, you will be playing a servant who plays the guitar in the big wedding scene. Although it won't be a guitar, you will be playing the lute, a guitar-like instrument, because the guitar hadn't been invented yet. You will also be playing a few other minor roles, as well as helping with the props and changing the scenery between scenes. And when performances begin, you will also help seat people and hand out programs."

My jaw was on the floor. I was going to be in the play? I didn't even know what play they were doing, since I thought I was only going to be doing the lights. When they handed me a book, I started to sweat. When I saw that it was Shakespeare's *The Taming of the Shrew*, panic set in. I mean, I knew it was the Washington Shakespeare Festival, but I didn't think I would be involved in the Shakespeare part of it. I would have to actually learn Shakespeare!? I couldn't learn Shakespeare, because there was no way I could even read Shakespeare! To make matters worse, it turned out that this was the first day of rehearsal and we were all going to read the play out loud. I looked around and it was a room full of actors, no lighting people to be found at all. A fucking cold reading of a Shakespeare play, my worst fear coming true! I met the other apprentices, who had other small roles in the play and similar backstage responsibilities, but they obviously knew what their jobs were before they arrived. All of the professional actors and the director gathered in a circle to start the read-through while I furiously tried to find my little parts in this incomprehensible book. The actors began, and I couldn't understand a fucking word any one was saying. Absolute gibberish. An actual nightmare come to life.

The play progressed, my first scene came up, and I found my first line—"Aye, sir!" Hey, I knew how to say that. And I did. Later in the scene, my second line—"Aye, aye sir!" A little trickier, but I nailed it. The play moved on. I felt relieved that I had made it that far, hoping my part stayed in understandable English, as opposed to whatever language everyone else was speaking. I ended up with a couple more lines of a very similar degree of difficulty, and by the end of the read-through, I felt I could handle the job. The cast were all professional New York actors who had been brought in to do the show, so that meant full days of rehearsal and a chance to watch and learn what real actors did. This was going to be better than I ever could have imagined. The only hitch was going to be this lute thing. The lute? Well, I was so bad at guitar at that point that maybe I would have better luck with the lute. When I told my parents that I was in a professional Shakespeare play and that I would be playing the lute, the look of dismay on their faces is something I still remember, because I felt the same way.

It was the time of my life and the turn in my life I was looking for. The cast was a group of incredibly talented people, starting with the young, on-the-verge-of-greatness Glenn Close playing Katherine. Glenn is a force of nature, and my god, the way she spoke the language brought it to life in a way that even Dummy Dan could understand and love. She was funny and bawdy, with an inspiring confidence and a generous heart. Richard Greene, Roy Brocksmith, and other Broadway actors were all astonishingly great in the play, but more importantly to me, so accepting and encouraging of me as a young actor. I was glad my part was so small so that (a) I wouldn't be revealed for the uneducated idiot I was, and (b) with little responsibility, I mostly just hung out with everyone who wasn't in the scene that was being rehearsed. It gave me a chance to get to know all of these talented people who had moved to New York to be actors. They shared their experiences, what life was like, how you got jobs, found acting schools and apartments, and made it sound possible. They knew I had dropped out of school and was not a trained actor in any way, but they made me understand that there is a place in acting even for people like me. It isn't all Shakespeare, and no degree is required. I was making real friendships with real actors, who accepted me as an adult and an equal, even though I was just a seventeen-year-old puppy.

Especially one guy. Christopher Curry Root is a scatterbrained angel, sent from heaven to give me my life. He is an incredible actor and my lifelong friend. Christopher took me under his wing that summer, barely even acknowledging that he was twenty-six and I was only seventeen. Christopher was a bit of a bad boy with a dark sense of humor, his idol at the time being the sadistic main character from *A Clockwork Orange*, and his energy was infectious. I was hitchhiking or taking the bus to work most days, but when performances started, my folks let me use the car since I was getting home so late. Christopher and I would hang out after the show at the apartment he rented until very early in the morning, because we didn't have to get up until the afternoon to do the show the next night. I started to see the glory of the actor's life. "Hi-diddly-dee, an actor's life for me!" Sam Kressen did not mention any of this. I started thinking seriously about moving to New York, and so did my folks. We bought the *Village Voice* and looked up prices for apartments and acting schools, to see if maybe I could afford to try it for a while. As the final performances approached, Christopher told me that if I ever came up to New York, I could stay with him, and he gave me his address on a piece of paper. He said it rather casually but, with the countdown clock now down to one month, that piece of paper was my lottery ticket.

It had been an incredible summer of watching the actors, making friends, and learning the lute. The only thing that hadn't happened yet was getting my hundred dollars. The NY actors got their $253.35 paychecks every week, thank you Actor's Equity Union, but when I asked when the apprentices got paid, I was told it would be at the end of the run. The last Thursday of the run, the NY actors got their last paycheck, but we did not get ours. I asked why not and was told that it was from a different account, and we would be paid the next day. The next day, there were no paychecks for the apprentices, and I was starting to get a little mad. The math equation of our respective salaries was ridiculous if you looked at the fact that we had put in the same hours as everyone else. One hundred dollars for the whole summer worked out to about a dollar a day. I could almost make that on my paper route. I told the stage manager that we needed to get paid on Saturday because the show closed on Sunday, and I needed the money that I had earned. To put some teeth behind it, I said if the check wasn't there, I wasn't going to do the show. The other apprentices were not with me at all on this. They didn't care about the one hundred dollars; they wanted the experience and connections. But I needed the money and we had certainly earned it. When I came to work on Saturday, still no checks. I was pissed, but I didn't have the nerve to not do the show. At the end of that night, I restated my threat to the stage manager, saying the check had to be there on the last day or I would definitely not do the show. When I got to the theater on Sunday for the final performance, no check. I was shaking; I was so mad and scared of what I was about to do. I handed out programs and seated the audience for the final performance of the play and told the stage manager I was serious. I would start the play but if the checks were not there at intermission, I would quit. I had backed myself all the way down the gangplank and had nothing to lose. When I came off stage at intermission, of course there were no checks. So I said "No more!" and I went on strike right then and there. It was my job to change the set during intermission, as well as to open the second half of the show by coming out and playing the fucking lute I had learned, so they could not proceed without me. The intermission lasted about forty-five minutes, as the accountant was found, the checks were cut, driven over to the theater, and put in my hand.

I was shaking like a leaf, and the other apprentices were understandably trying to distance themselves from me in the eyes of the producer and stage manager. But Christopher, Glenn, and the rest of the cast were right with me, thinking it was ridiculously funny and brave for this seventeen-year-old kid to bring the whole thing to a stop. That was the longest forty-five minutes of my life. The audience was yelling, "What's going on?" and clapping to get the show started again. I went on stage to change the set for the second half and since I was the first person that the audience had seen in quite a long time, they started yelling at me, wanting to know what was going on. And I took the opportunity to tell them. Standing in the center of the stage, I delivered an impromptu monologue to explain exactly what had happened—that we had worked the entire summer for only one hundred dollars and they were holding that back, naming the producer and the accountant as the greedy, mean people who did this. I got a standing ovation from the audience. I finished changing the set and started the second half with my lute-playing scene, for which I got another standing ovation. My third standing ovation came at the curtain call. To add to the emotional craziness of the night, it was the final performance and time to say goodbye to the coolest people I had ever met and go back to my parents' house and my little life. Driving home, distracted with so many powerful feelings, I did not notice there was a police car following me, with their lights flashing, until I parked at my parents' house. In my second monologue of the evening, I blurted out how my entire evening had gone and apologized that I had been speeding or for whatever I had done. The officer took pity on me and let me go.

Two weeks later, and ten days before I turned eighteen, I was on a Greyhound bus to New York City, with my duffle bag, my guitar, four hundred dollars my parents gave me, and Christopher's address in my pocket. And all because I started chewing on that guitar pick. Amazing how things turn.

LIVING A
PAUL SIMON SONG

"When I left my home and my family
I was no more than a boy
In the company of strangers
In the quiet of the railway station
Running scared

Laying low, seeking out the poorer quarters
Where the ragged people go
Looking for the places only they would know"
—*PAUL SIMON "THE BOXER"*

I made the decision to move to New York quickly because I wanted to get out of Maryland before all my friends left for college, and to be able to tell them that I was doing something cool too. My parents insisted that if I went, I had to sign up for acting classes, to at least give the appearance that I was going for educational reasons. But beyond that, they had no idea where I was going to live, who I was going to see, or what I was going to do. They gave me four hundred dollars to get started, and I took the money from my savings account and got traveler's checks for safety. I stuffed my clothes and sleeping bag into the duffle bag I used at Wigwasati, grabbed my guitar and the piece of paper with Christopher's address on it, 21 West 86th Street, and walked out of my family home for good. My dad took me to the Greyhound bus station in downtown Washington and that was it—I was on my own, and would be for the rest of my life. Kind of like sending me out onto the mean streets of Philadelphia by myself as a four-year-old, only this time with a different message—don't come back. I was scared to death and already feeling homesick but, really, I had no other choice.

I am not sure why I didn't call Christopher to tell him I was coming before I left. Well, actually, I do. I was afraid he would tell me not to come. As it stood, legally speaking, the final offer on the table was "Come on by if you're in the neighborhood," and there was no reason to fuck with that. All I had to do was get myself to his neighborhood and he would be legally and morally bound to let me stay with him. The bus let me out at the Port Authority on West 41st Street and 8th Avenue, a very sleazy part of town in 1975. With "my suitcase and guitar in hand," I still remember the feeling of hitting a wall of humanity, and just being swept up in it like a school of fish. There were buses that went to the Upper West Side, but they were so crowded and I had so much stuff that I decided just to walk the two and a half miles. Eighth Avenue was crazy, lugging that duffle bag and guitar, being jostled by the crowd, surrounded by hookers, porno theaters, three-card monte games, and food carts. But at 59th Street, it turned into Central

Park West, which was a whole other world I was seeing for the first time. I made my way up to 86th, turned left, and there was Christopher's building, with an awning that read The Brewster Hotel. I went through the revolving door and up to the clerk behind the desk, asking if Christopher lived there. He told me he did, gave me his room number, and up the elevator I went. I don't think I had peed since I left my parents' house that morning and my bladder was close to bursting, so barging in on Christopher was not the only reason for my anxiousness when I knocked on the door.

Bruce McGill is a daunting motherfucker. He is from Texas and is built like a bull. He is an amazing character actor you have seen in movies and TV for decades, from *Animal House* to *My Cousin Vinny* to *Ali*, playing bikers, cops, judges—any character whose intention is to intimidate, because he is a formidable guy. He opened the door to Christopher's apartment with a look that said, "I am in the middle of a lot of things and who the fuck are you?" I wasn't sure if I had the right apartment because Christopher never mentioned anything about having roommates.

"Is Christopher here?"

"No."

"Oh. Is this his apartment?"

"Yes, but he's not here."

"Do you know when he'll be back?"

"Maybe in a week or two. Who are you?"

"I'm Daniel. . . . A week or two?"

"He is upstate shooting a PBS movie. What do you want?"

"Oh. Uh, well, I met him in Washington this summer and he said I could stay with him if I ever came to New York and so I came."

"He said you could stay here?"

"He did but I didn't know he wasn't going to be here. Could I please come in? I really have to pee."

"You want to come in and pee?"

"Please?"

"Alright."

And that was it. Bruce said I could sleep on the couch until I found a place to live, even though he had never even heard of me before that moment. Bruce, Christopher, and John Heard all shared the apartment, and took me in like the lost dog I was. I was stoned for the first time in my life within minutes of my arrival. Everyone was in their mid to late twenties, and having a seventeen-year-old in their midst was kind of like having a pet. The Brewster Hotel was a cheap place for young actors to live and there was a constant party going on. I finished my first day in New York at four o'clock the next morning, at their favorite bar, the Tap A Keg, drunk off my ass, and then passed out on the couch. I knew I was home.

They were all working actors, going to auditions, arguing with their agents, and checking their messages at the telephone answering services that everyone had back then. I think Bruce was in *Hamlet* and Heard was doing *Streamers*. Christopher came back to town but moved in with his girlfriend, Patricia Richardson, so I was able to stay at the Brewster a little longer. I signed up for a beginner's scene-study acting class at HB Studio, a very good acting school run by Uta Hagen and Herbert Bergoff. I struck up a conversation with a talkative stranger in the lobby one day, commiserating about trying to find an apartment in the city. He was also new to town and staying at the YMCA. At that moment, as luck would have it, the actress who had played Bianca in *Taming of the Shrew* came into the lobby and gave me a very warm greeting. She was surprised that I had actually moved to New York and told me that there was an apartment available in her building on West 75th Street and Broadway. The talkative stranger, John Nichols, and I decided we would be roommates on the spot, got on the subway, and went straight to the building to talk to the landlord, who was a very kind old Jewish man. He said we could have the place, a two-room apartment, and when we asked how much the rent was, instead of telling us, he asked what we could afford. We told him we could pay one hundred dollars each, and he gave us the keys. John got his stuff from the Y and I got mine from the Brewster, and we met back there later that day. There was an abandoned building next door, which was some kind of whorehouse/drug den. John and I ventured in there and found two mattresses, which we dragged up to the apart-ment. There was no electricity, but there was heat, water, and gas, and we started living there that night. We eventually found a card table and some chairs, but to save money, we didn't get electricity for about four or five months, just lived by candlelight at night. My dad stopped by when he was in town on business and tried to put up a good front, but I could see he was worried about the safety of the place. It was a barren crash pad, like Ratso Rizzo's place in *Midnight Cowboy*, and I loved it.

I was out most of the time anyway. The lifestyle of an unem-ployed actor in New York fit me like a glove. Playing frisbee in Central Park in the day and going to the Tap A Keg at night, my friends all so much older and cooler than me but accepting me as a fully-fledged, functioning adult. Their apartments had actual furniture, their girlfriends were beautiful and kind, and they fed me more meals than I could ever count. There was a little outdoor newspaper stand at our corner where I could pick up some money watching the stand and selling papers when the owner needed a break. Christopher's circle of friends included Doug and Tay Cheek, who lived in a loft in Chelsea and had a young daughter. The whole gang was my family, the best big brothers and big sisters any eighteen-year-old kid could ask for, feeding me, taking me to plays, and teaching me guitar. I went to auditions that I found in the trade paper, *Backstage.* They would post real jobs for actors, in regional theaters, industrial films, off-off Broadway, chorus parts, and student films—anyone who needed actors. I stood in lines at the cattle calls and got to take my swings and see how the game was played.

At HB Studios, it was time to sign up for the next semester of classes. I had a chance to audit Herbert Bergoff's class, sit in the back, and watch the elite actors in the school do scene work with this legendary acting teacher. I still don't know why, but when he finished the lecture at the beginning of one of his classes and the first team of actors was preparing for their scene, Herbert looked into the shadows of the last row, pointed to me, and said, "Come down here and sit next to me." After a confused, paralyzed beat, I made my way down to his table at the edge of the stage and sat down next to him. He told me I was going to be able to see much better up there and really get a sense of what he was talking about. I told him I was grateful, although I had never even spoken to him and had no idea why this was happening. Herbert then stood up in front of the class and, being the great actor he was, made a grand gesture of taking a dollar bill out of his pocket. "I am going to give this young man a dollar. He looks like he could probably use it, but I am giving it to him as an investment. Because I think great things are going to happen to this young man and that he has a real future. You are all a witness that he has accepted this investment and I now own a piece of his talent." The class laughed as he gave me the dollar bill. I sat through the class, pretending to pay attention, but I was so surprised by this random act of validation that I couldn't focus on anything else besides the dollar bill in my pocket. At the end of the class, I offered to give it back, but he insisted I keep it. I wrote home to my parents telling them the story, trying to create the illusion of progress. I thought about framing that dollar, but I needed the money, so I spent it at some point. But the confidence booster he gave me, for whatever his reasons, has lasted all this time.

I signed up for Austin Pendleton's acting class. Austin is an incredibly talented actor, director, and acting teacher as well. I knew it would be challenging, but my confidence was growing. Since I was the new kid in the class, and so much younger as well, I spent the first month or two just watching. It was a very serious class. The actors were good, and the way Austin gave them notes and direction was always so exciting and insightful. I saw how the actors made their adjustments to their performances, using the same words but with very different intentions, completely changing the meaning of the scene. And then one day, I finally got my chance to get up in front of the class. As a homework assignment (the good kind of homework), Austin had told us to be prepared to recreate three minutes of our life onstage. No dialogue or plot or story, just exist on stage and behave in as natural a way as you can. I guess I wanted to appear cool and hip in front of my older classmates, so I had decided that my three minutes would just be me hanging out in the living room, where I would roll a cigarette and just smoke it. When I got to class, I started to get really nervous, especially when I watched all of the other actors before me and realized I HAVE NO IDEA WHAT I AM DOING! I AM A TOTAL FRAUD! When Austin called my name, my heart jumped out of my chest. I got on the stage, pushed a couch and table to set the scene, put my tobacco and cigarette papers on the table, and began. I thought I would calm down once I started, but that didn't happen. I started to hyperventilate and walked around the stage, trying to catch my breath. I could feel how red my face was turning, and I was so upset with myself for choking the first time in front of all these great actors. I decided to just get to the part where I roll the cigarette. Do you know how hard it is to roll a cigarette when your hands are shaking like you are inside a fucking blender? I could barely roll a joint on a good day, but under these conditions it was going to be absolutely impossible. The rolling paper was shaking, the tobacco was flying, and my ego was being crushed. I tried to gather myself and make a second attempt at rolling the cigarette, but the guy in *My Left Foot* would have had a better shot at accomplishing that at that moment. I was also getting a real good lesson of just how long three minutes can be. I was near tears by the time Austin said that the time was up. But to my absolute astonishment, the class broke out in applause, and Austin said how terrific I was and how real that felt. He said, "What was going on in that scene? What three minutes were you recreating?" I saw a way out of this fiasco, and I took it, lying my ass off. "Well, I was almost hit by a bus on Broadway the other day. It really scared me and I was pretty shook up and so this was the three minutes when I had just gotten back to my apartment." Given my meltdown onstage, that scenario made perfect sense and Austin bought it hook, line and sinker. "Well, I have no notes. That was just great." When I took my seat in the class, I didn't feel invisible anymore. I had totally fooled them. Oh, wait, isn't that what being an actor is? To try to totally fool people? I was good at bullshitting. I majored in it at high school. I thought, "Hmmm. I might do well at this."

I am not sure if I ever did another scene in Austin's class or not, because within a short time, Austin offered me my first professional acting job. He was directing a prestigious play by Robert Lowell called *Benito Cereno* at the American Place Theater on West 46th Street, starring Roscoe Lee Browne as a slave on a slave ship. Austin gave me the part of a sailor on the ship. I guess he had heard about my work in *Taming of the Shrew* because my character in this had the exact same dialogue—two or three "Aye, aye, sirs!" and maybe an "Over there!" or a "Halt!" He took a chance on me—I didn't even have to audition. I was making forty-five dollars a week as a real actor in a real play in New York, eight shows a week. At the same time, I landed the lead role in a play at St. Clements Church, which was a very respectable off-Broadway venue at the time, and it was also located on West 46th Street but over at 9th Avenue. They arranged the rehearsal and performance schedule so I wouldn't have to miss any shows at the American Place, but I would have to run from one theater to the other some days to be there in time. The play was terrible, but the director was very cute and became my girlfriend for a while. My mom came up and saw both plays and she got to meet Roscoe, who charmed the pants off her and told her what a talented actor I was. She knew Roscoe from television and his validation made my career seem legit in her eyes.

When those plays ended and I stopped getting paid, I had to take a job at a pharmacy on East 71st Street, delivering prescriptions and cleaning the store, but that was the last straight job I ever had. Before long I went to another audition from *Backstage*, to be the understudy for David Mamet's first New York play, *Sexual Perversity in Chicago*, at the famed Cherry Lane Theatre in the Village. I auditioned for David and got the job, which also included changing the sets, buying and setting the props, running the sound, and being an usher, and it paid forty-five dollars a week. The play, starring F. Murray Abraham, was a huge hit. I understudied Peter Riegert, who was dating Bette Midler at the time, so there was an electricity around the theater, and it felt like a pretty prestigious play to be involved with. To save money, I downgraded my living conditions, moving out of the shithole with John and into a closet in the apartment of a couple I had met. An actual closet. I brought the single mattress from the whorehouse up the five flights and put it on the floor of their hallway storage closet, and could only partially open the door in order to get in the room. But I only had to pay seventy dollars a month instead of one hundred dollars, and that way I could pad my bank account for the lean days that would surely come. I understudied for six or eight months, rehearsing the play once or twice a week, but Riegert never missed a show. When he finally announced he was leaving, I hoped they would ask me to step in, but they gave the part to the guy who was the understudy before me. Being the prideful idiot I was, I quit the job. I needed the money very badly, but it would have been too hard to be the understudy to the guy who was the understudy, some kind of bizarre actor purgatory.

Anyway, I was kind of a working actor. I did another off-off Broadway play. Doug Cheek cast me in a children's TV show called *Vegetable Soup*, which was actually a groundbreaking show on PBS at the time, with a diverse cast and a progressive message. I got paid a couple of hundred bucks, which meant a few more months of rent. Then one day, I got an audition down at HB Studios Playwright Center, the theater connected with the school that develops new plays. The play was called *Almost Men*, which sounded perfect because that was just about where I was in my personal life—nineteen and almost a man. The play had already been in rehearsal for three weeks. Evidently, there had been five other actors who had been cast in the role before me—one broke his leg, a couple got paying jobs—and with the opening only ten days away, there was a bit of stress in the air when I came in to audition. The play is about four high school students from Texas who go to New York City on an adventure. It was an excellent play, very funny and natural dialogue, and mine was the lead part, playing the playwright when he was a teenager. The actors, director, and writer were all in the middle of rehearsal when I came into the theater, but stopped to do my audition. I had no idea that by the time that little play ended, I would be ready to take the next step toward becoming the kind of man I wanted to be, with a life as well as a career, with a wife, children, furniture, a car, and a community and all of the things that have happened since that day. Standing onstage to audition with me was a beautiful woman, wearing a very sexy outfit, who played the hooker-with-a-heart-of-gold in the play. But wait, that's no hooker. That's my wife!

MEETING LAURE

Laure Mattos. Even writing it now, her name makes my heart skip a beat. Since we met that day, our lives have been bound together, and will be until the end of time. She is, and always was, smart, tough, beautiful, righteous, curious, hardworking, fun-loving, adaptable, compassionate, and overflowing with opinions and love. And you get all of that in the first five minutes that you meet her.

I guess I gave a good audition. I know Laure and I had chemistry right off the bat, and the production was somewhat desperate, so I ended up with the part. Rehearsal started immediately; the starting gun had been fired and I dove in. Once again, I was the nineteen-year-old kid and the other actors were all in their mid-twenties, with theater degrees and apartments and lives, including Laure. The rehearsals were fun and intense. Everyone else already knew the play and the staging had been pretty well blocked, so they focused on getting me up to speed. The part fit me perfectly, the cast was absolutely outstanding, the director really great, and there was a loose atmosphere, with a penny-ante poker game going at all times. Laure was one of only two women in the cast and she loved being as tough as all of the twenty-something men, a little flirty but mostly using her humor and smarts to be one of the guys. A bunch of us would take the train home to the Upper West Side together after rehearsal and go for drinks to talk about the play, so there was no opening to act on the attraction that was happening between us, but I got the feeling that after opening night that would change. And boy, did it.

The opening went incredibly well, and we were all flying high. Laure was having the cast party at her apartment, and we all splurged on cab fare from the Village all the way to West 84th Street. Laure and I were jammed in close, the adrenaline of the evening definitely pumping. We got to her apartment and, holy shit, was it nice! Big living room, nice kitchen, separate bedroom. And everything so classy. Artwork, carpets, knickknacks, books, appliances, and tons of food she had made herself. The party kicked in, the cast and crew fired up from our great opening and mixing with some of Laure's other friends who were there as well. I was mingling, but most of my attention was focused on getting close to Laure and perhaps even kissing her. So you can imagine my surprise when at one point in the evening, I worked my way into the circle of people she was talking to and got introduced to her best friend, her old roommate, and her husband. . . . I'm just going to let you sit with that for a moment.

No need to go into too many details of our incredible court-ship, but by the evidence that Laure and I are still together after all these years, it is clear that my man-musk was too powerful to resist. (Or maybe I am remembering the smell of the never-cleaned sleeping bag from Wigwasati that I had been sleeping in for five straight years.) She was married for four years to her boyfriend from college, an actor who made his living as a successful waiter at a high-end restaurant. They had had a real wedding and had made a nice home, but obviously there was something missing if there was room for me to come into her life. Our affair was secret at first. I wanted her to leave him but, of course, I had nothing to lose and she had everything. I was living in a closet, on a mattress on the floor, in a sleeping bag. I had a few hundred dollars in the bank and I was nineteen years old, six years younger than her. But we were madly, madly in love with each other and there was nothing that was going to keep us apart. We knew we were meant to be with each other, even though it didn't make much sense on paper, because we had a sign from God. The New York City Blackout of 1977. We had snuck off to our favorite Chinese restaurant that night and were in the middle of a great meal when it all shut down. We finished by candlelight and then wandered through the crazy streets on the Upper West Side, the energy of that night amazingly electric, especially considering there was no electricity. We went back to her place until I had to go, but we both knew we were going to be together forever.

Laure needed space to figure out how to end her marriage in the best way for her, her husband, and their families. I went back to my parents' house and I couldn't shut up about her. I put her 8x10 resume picture on the mantel in the living room to show everyone the love of my life. My brother was afraid her husband was going to murder me. My mother assumed there must be something wrong with her if she was in love with someone like me. My dad thought she was beautiful. Interestingly, the one thing her family, her husband's family, and even my family could all agree on was, "Why Danny?"

She and her husband parted ways amicably, and soon I moved in with her. Laure only came to my closet room one time, drunk after a party she was at with Al Pacino (who I think had hit on her), and proved her love for me by getting naked with me in the petri dish that was my sleeping bag. It made sense for me to move in because I was going to her place a lot, and now she was responsible for the whole three hundred dollars a month rent. So goodbye to my closet and hello to a real apartment. But also, goodbye to my seventy dollars a month and hello to one hundred and fifty dollars a month.

The other life-changing thing that came out of *Almost Men* was that I got an agent. Mary Sames lived at the Brewster and was a junior agent at a small agency. Christopher and Bruce convinced her to come see the play, and she signed me. I got a real resume picture taken and started going to a few auditions. I got a good part in a play at Manhattan Theatre Club and finally got my Actors Equity card when I understudied a play at the Public Theater, which led to the holy grail for every actor at that time— unemployment checks! Free money every week. Not a lot, but I loved it. Stand in line and get free money. I hit that cash cow every time I qualified, and it kept our heads above water. John Heard had just done his first movie and was starting to take off. Bruce got a film too, and Christopher was on Broadway; there was a code among them about having a career with integrity. There were cool places to work and cool people to work with, and I wanted to have a career like that too. I had a network callback to play the role that Jeff Conaway played in the legendary *Taxi*. But doing television in those days was very low class in the New York acting world, and you wouldn't be taken seriously as an actor if you were on a sitcom. I remember being at dinner with Laure and Heard and Christopher, all discouraging me from selling myself short, even though I had nothing and could've made real money, and I turned it down. In hindsight, what a stupid fucking idea that was!

Laure was working in telemarketing because it paid pretty well and had flexible hours, but she was very bad at it. Her big break came when she landed the understudy role in a Broadway play directed by the legendary Hal Prince. Laure knew Hal because she had worked in his office as an assistant when she first got to New York and was there during some of his greatest collaborations with Stephen Sondheim. Unfortunately, the play was terrible and, after an all-expense paid tryout in Philly and a few good Broadway paychecks during previews, the play closed two days after opening night.

I began to lose my mind living at her apartment. I loved living with her and sharing our lives, but the apartment was making me crazy. The walls were so thin, and I believe a tap dancer and her dog lived directly above us. The rent was expensive, my unemployment eventually ran out, and I had very little savings left at all. She went back to telemarketing but hated it, and wasn't so sure about being an actress anymore either. And we were surrounded by the furniture and dishes and rugs that were from her wedding and marriage with the other guy. In July, we found an apartment on West 78th Street that was cheaper and talked our way into it, even though we weren't really qualified to get it. We needed the first month's rent and another month in security, which we got by selling all of her stuff except the essentials (I had nothing to sell except my sleeping bag, and there were no takers). When we moved in in August, we realized why the rent was so cheap. It was on the third floor, right on Amsterdam Avenue, a pothole-filled thoroughfare full of trucks clanging and people fighting. And one block away was the fire station. It was insanely noisy and the trauma of that really fucked with me ever being able to get a good night's sleep. But we loved it. It was ours. We were in it together, fully. This shitty apartment is where we would get married, have our first child, and entwine our lives together for eternity. We were more in love than ever. The only question was, "Where is next month's rent coming from, because we are literally out of money?"

Hark, is that an angel? I believe it is.

BREAKING AWAY, AKA MY FIRST PORNO

Now that I had an agent, I was getting an audition or two for movies, but hadn't landed anything. When I got an audition for a new film called *Bambino*, I showed up to an office at the ICM agency without a script or even the scene I would be auditioning with, so I was filled with anxiety because it sounded like it was going to be a dreaded "cold reading." I was taken into an office where a very handsome and dignified English gentleman was in the midst of an intense phone conversation. This was Peter Yates, the supremely accomplished director of classics like *Bullitt*, *The Hot Rock*, and *Friends of Eddie Coyle*. I gestured that I could wait outside but he gestured back to have a seat, so I did. When the phone call ended, Peter sat down with me and explained the premise of the movie, that it would shoot in Indiana, and the role I was right for. I don't remember saying much of anything, just quietly dreading the moment when he would hand me the audition material and I would embarrass myself by trying to read it out loud. But that never happened. Instead of giving me just a scene to read, he handed me the whole script and told me to come back at the end of the week and we would read it then. I left confused, relieved, and excited to have a chance to actually study the script before my audition.

The script was written by the remarkably gifted Steve Tesich and would go on to win the Academy Award for Best Screenplay for the retitled *Breaking Away*. I had only read one or two screenplays at that point and had no idea the talent it took to write something so funny, true, meaningful, and relatable. I just knew that the story felt like me and my friends at the end of high school just a few years back, all of us having to break away from each other and our families to start our own lives. The part was a character named Cyril, who was terrible in school but a funny kid who just wants to hang out with his friends and play sports, and who felt completely like me. I had forgotten to ask which scenes I would be auditioning with, so I got familiar with the whole script to be ready for anything. I went back to the same office at the ICM agency at the time of my appointment but to my surprise, I was redirected to the conference room. The room was packed with people, a huge table in the middle, and chairs lining the walls. Everyone was mingling like it was a party, and there was an enormous buffet laid out against the windows, which overlooked all of Manhattan. I had my dog-eared script in my hand, mentally preparing myself to do my audition, only to be thrust into a fucking cocktail party. I had no idea what was going on and must have looked a little stunned. Peter quickly came over and welcomed me, explaining that we were going to all sit around the table and read the whole script. He pointed out the other actors around the room, the writer, and studio executives, and told me to help myself to the buffet. This was the best audition this starving actor had ever been to. I filled a plate with as much as I could load without being gross and found a seat at the conference table, and we read the script. The part of Cyril had some fantastic jokes and I got lots of laughs, and I nailed the emotional scenes as well because I had had the time to really learn the part. After it was over, everyone went back into party mode, thrilled at having just heard the future Oscar-winning script read out loud for the first time. I got nice handshakes from people and said hello to some of the actors, but mostly I was filling the pockets of my jacket with as much food as a could get. I mean it was free food and Laure and I were really down to our last nickels. Peter made his way over to me. "Daniel, you did great. Just terrific. I will see you in LA." "Great. Thank you." That was the whole conversation. I didn't know what else there was to do or say so I probably stuffed some pickles in my socks and left.

Riding down the elevator, I was in shock from the whole experience, but those words kept ringing in my ears. "I'll see you in LA." What did that mean? There was a phone booth right at the corner of Columbus Circle and I called Laure immediately. I told her what had happened—the table read, the food, and those words, "I'll see you in LA," and she said, "I think you just got a movie," which I had. Peter Yates had just changed my life forever. We had no money—like, none. Now I would be making eight thousand dollars, more money than I had ever dreamed of making. I would be in the union and have health insurance, unemployment insurance. I would fly in an airplane for the first time, and in First Class no less. I would be starting out my film career with a great part in an Academy Award-winning film, and I would find a mentor and a friendship with Peter that would last for the rest of my life.

I called my parents to tell them the amazing news. "Guess what? I just got cast in a movie! It's called *Bambino*."

Swear to God, this was my mother's reaction: "*Bambino?* What is that, a porno?" I could take the rest of this book to dissect that comment, to try to understand why that would be her reaction. Was it the title that threw her? Was it the idea that only the lowest form of moviemakers would hire me? Did she think I was that much of a stud that I would be qualified for such work? She still has no justification for that knee-jerk reaction. Even when I finally explained to them that I was going to Hollywood to be in a 20th Century Fox film, they were skeptical, and not until the movie came out did they believe that any of what I said was true. I, too, had trouble dealing with such good fortune. I loved acting and I loved being able to make money for Laure and me but, in what would become a recurring theme throughout my life, it turned out I hated leaving home. Surprising, considering how fearless a traveler I was as a teenager, but then again, the home Laure and I had created together was the home I had always dreamed of, and it tore me up to leave. Stamped in my memory is the night before I left, crying like a baby on the sofa, and Laure hugging me and rubbing my back telling me everything was going be fine. I was scared to death of going on an airplane, of being away from her, of going to strange unknown places, and of acting in a real movie. But I did it. I got on the plane and spent a week in LA "prepping" for the film. The costumer loved how "natural" my own clothes looked—my old T-shirts and shorts and Chuck Taylors—and we went and bought replicas of my own stuff which she would distress to make them look as bad as mine. We were supposed to rehearse but never did. They gave me some cash for per diem but I didn't know anyone in LA and needed to save every penny, so I just waited in my hotel room for a week until it was time to fly to Bloomington, Indiana, to start filming.

That's when I finally met the rest of the cast—Dennis Christopher, Dennis Quaid, and Jackie Earle Haley—my new best friends. They had all been in some movies already, but Jackie was the only actor I knew of, from his standout role in *Bad News Bears*. We hung out at the motel getting to know each other for a few days before shooting and fell into an easy friendship, one that has lasted our whole lives since then. The first scene we filmed was a fight scene in a bowling alley, us against the college jocks, which ends when I throw a bowling ball through a plate glass window, and I got my first chance to watch stunt people in action. Holy shit! It looked like what I had fantasized as a kid, people throwing themselves onto tables that would break away, smashing bottles over each other's heads, punching, being punched, smashing shit. And then when the take was done, they set up and did it again, with the prop department bringing out more shit to break. Like a newborn colt, I was taking my first steps in my new world of being on movie sets, learning the rhythm of a shooting day. The army of trucks, the walkie-talkies, the jargon, and the strict line of command gave a militaristic order that made you feel shit was getting done. I got reprimanded for trying to help carry camera equipment and again when I tried to move one of the chairs for the actors. The movies are not an "everyone pitch in and help" type of job. Everyone has very specific responsibilities and needs to be in control of their domain so they are prepared to jump on a very fast-moving train. They don't need me to suddenly be moving their shit around. My job is to be prepared to perform the scene after everyone else sets the table.

My part of the fight scene didn't shoot until the second half of the day, so I had a little time to get my legs under me and try to get past the imposter-syndrome feelings that we all feel at the beginning of a big, new undertaking. But just as I was beginning to convince myself I was no longer "Danny Stern from Bethesda" but, instead, "Daniel Stern, Movie Actor," reality came calling. Two very familiar faces suddenly came into view, riding bicycles and calling my name. I was confused at first because *Breaking Away* had a lot of bicycles in it and it could have been people who worked on the movie. But it wasn't. It was two of my best friends from Bethesda, KC and Tim, guys who I hung out with in high school literally every day but who I hadn't seen since I left for New York. They had always loved taking long bike trips together and were spending their summer vacation from college riding across the country. They had called my parents and found out what I was doing and decided to put it on their itinerary. So fucking strange that it timed out for them to land at this very moment, just before my very first shot on my very first day of my very first movie. I was caught completely off guard and didn't know the rules, whether they could come on the set or eat the snacks, and so we just stood right there for about twenty minutes. I felt awkward and guilty that I was not up for an impromptu hangout with my old best friends. My new, pretend best friends were all playing pretend fight on a movie set and that was where I wanted to be. They didn't really seem to want anything more than to just say hi, and it was a crazy feeling to watch them ride off, literally watching my old life fade away and my new life begin. Even though it threw me at the time, I love that it happened. God works in mysterious ways sometimes, but this lesson had the subtlety of a sledge-hammer—your past informs your present, so learn to understand it as a source of knowledge and strength. When it was my turn, I picked up my fake bowling ball, fought off those college jocks like a champ, and when the time came, put the bowling ball right through the sugar-glass window on my first take, getting a nice round of applause from the crew. Cherry popped.

Since it was my first movie, I had no idea what an extraordinary filmmaking experience I was having. The Oscar-winning script was as solid as a rock, the perfect blend of comedy, action, heart, and romance. Peter's gentle directing style got incredible performances from all the actors, including an Oscar-winning one for the super-talented Barbara Barrie. The quarry where we shot our swimming-hole scenes was a natural wonder, and the town of Bloomington felt like Bethesda. Laure came for a week to celebrate my twenty-first birthday and became fast friends with everyone. Jackie was a celebrity wherever he went and was so humble and kind to his fans. Quaid was already being a movie star, buying a mint-condition 1954 Chevy from a local and practicing his preening. His girlfriend was there the whole time and the two of them had a severe case of PDA, to the point of ridiculousness. He convinced me to open the accordion wall between our tiny dressing rooms to make one slightly bigger room, but I was forced out of the room on more than one occasion when they would start making out, with the three of us sitting on the one couch we shared, actually laying up against me. (I need to shower just remembering it.) And Dennis Christopher was working his ass off, as he was in almost all the scenes, and training on his bicycle in his down time. I got more comfortable in front of the camera, although when I see it now, I can see how Peter used my shyness and the awkwardness of my inexperience to create a very sympathetic character, which was maybe his plan from the first time I walked into that initial meeting at ICM.

When the filming ended and we got back to New York, Peter continued to mentor and support me. He invited me to the editing room to learn how the film was really put together, where I got to watch him experiment with different pacing, different performances, different music, and all of the post-production elements that a director uses to tell exactly the story they want to tell. He and his wife, Virginia, had Laure and me over for dinner at their apartment in the famed Dakota building often, and we fell in love with their kids, Toby and Miranda. They were the definition of a classy English family and loved Laure's sophistication (she had spent her teenage years in Spain and Manila when her father served there in the Foreign Service). And we got to meet all of their amazing friends from England—Michael Caine, Peter O'Toole, Jacqueline Bisset, and Roger Moore.

Peter also introduced me to his agent at ICM, the legendary Sam Cohn. Sam was not only Peter's agent but also represented Woody Allen, Meryl Streep, Robert Altman, Nora Ephron, Bob Fosse, Jackie Gleason, Arthur Miller, Paul Newman, Mike Nichols, and the list goes on. So when he asked me if I would like to be a client at ICM, with him overseeing my career, I jumped at the chance. I felt bad to leave Mary Sames, but she understood, considering Sam's status as the biggest agent in the business, and we stayed good friends. Obviously, Sam had too many important clients to really pay attention to my career, but he became a dear friend to both Laure and me when we started spending time with him and the Yateses. He was an avid tennis player with a membership at the very fancy West Side Tennis Club in Queens, and he took me to play once or twice a week. The other old men there were various Captains of Industry and even though I was a total novice at tennis, I was a six-foot-four-inch, athletic, twenty-one-year-old kid, and we kicked ass in doubles matches. Then we would all have lunch in the beautiful Club Room and head back to the city. Sam was a very eccentric man. He loved to eat paper. Not only did he have a box of Kleenex next to his desk to munch on, but on more than one occasion, he would tear off pieces of a script or a contract that was on his desk and his assistants would have to make new copies to sign.

It took a year for *Breaking Away* to hit the theaters, and in the meantime, I was anxious to work more. Laure and I had barely escaped financial disaster when I got started getting paid for *Breaking Away*, with only days to spare, and my only "career plan" was to try to make more money now that I had my Screen

Actors Guild card. Strangely, I had started off my film career by landing a leading role, so it was a bit of a step backwards to take a bunch of one-scene parts, but they each paid a few hundred bucks and there was no way I could say no. Luckily, each one not only paid the rent but also gave me a chance to work with the caliber of directors that Sam was encouraging me to work with.

I did a one-line part in Alan J. Pakula's *Starting Over*—a scene with Burt Reynolds—and I got four hundred dollars, which Laure and I used to buy our first television. I had a horrible day shooting a one-scene role in a cool-at-the-time movie called *A Small Circle of Friends*. I played a kid going for his induction into the draft of the Vietnam War, who tries to appear mentally unqualified by tying a ribbon around his dick when he is going through his physical, and the whole day was spent hiding my junk, pressing myself into the locker just like I did in junior high school gym class. I brought home another four hundred dollars and a bit of PTSD. I got a small part in a film with Jill Clayburgh called *It's My Turn*, where I played a brilliant college math student. The director wanted me to do some "character research" and had me take the train to Princeton and sit in on some very heavy-duty math classes. It sounded good in theory, and it felt cool to be introduced to all those brilliant students as an actor doing his homework for his big new film, but the truth was I couldn't understand anything and could barely stay awake. I came away from that job with eight hundred dollars and the knowledge that I am *not* the kind of actor who knows how to do any real homework or research on a character.

I was still a total unknown, waiting for *Breaking Away* to come out, but Sam Cohn got me an interview with Woody Allen for his new movie *Stardust Memories*. I idolized him (and still do). As a teenager, I must have seen *Take the Money and Run*, *Sleeper*, and *Play It Again, Sam* ten times each, hitchhiking to

Georgetown just about every weekend to the art house theaters. David Rosenthal and I even saw him do his stand-up act at Shady Grove (Jim Croce opened for him) and we laughed for weeks about him "being breastfed by falsies." So the fact that I was meeting him was almost beyond comprehension. The casting agent led me into a darkened office where Woody was sitting in a high-back chair, barely visible in the shadows. He was extremely uncomfortable, mumbled in vague terms about the movie for maybe a minute or two, and then the casting agent led me out. Of course, I was over the moon when I heard I got the job, but the problem was I had no idea what the part was or what the movie was about. I was very anxious because I wanted to do my best for my idol and had no idea how to prepare. They told me Woody was very secretive about his films so just to be patient about getting a script. The night before I was to shoot, there was a knock on our apartment door and an envelope slid under it. Sure enough, it was from the production. But there was no script, only one page—the scene I would be shooting with Woody the next day. I was to play a young actor who was trying to give his resume to a famous film director (played by Woody). I practiced all night, trying to think of good ways to do the scene. In the morning, I brought in my real resume and some pictures from plays I had been in, including Tevye in *Fiddler on the Roof.* Woody let me improvise and loved the Tevye reference. It was like living a dream, to be doing a scene with my biggest idol, and I was on cloud nine. Later that week, I got word that Woody liked me and wanted me to come back and do a second day of shooting. The night before I was to do my second scene, I stared at the apartment door like a dog waiting for the mailman, waiting for the knock and my scene to be slid under the door. Nothing. Morning came, and I went to the set. I got into my costume and had coffee, still not knowing what I was supposed to be doing. I finally got called to the set and Woody greeted me warmly. I thanked him for inviting me back and told him I had not received my page, so I wasn't sure what the scene was, and he apologized. He opened his own, personal script and turned to the scene but instead of giving me the whole page, he tore out just the one line he wanted me to say at the bottom of the page. I still value that scrap of paper more than two of my children.

My other idol growing up was Paul Simon. I love every song he has ever written and know every one by heart. I taught myself to play the guitar from his epic songbook, and felt my life was basically his songs come to life. "The Only Living Boy in New York," "Duncan," "The Boxer," and "Homeward Bound" were coming of age stories that hit me as hard as Holden Caulfield did in *Catcher in the Rye*. Paul was making a movie called *One-Trick Pony* that he wrote about his life as a musician. Sam Cohn represented the director and amazingly, I got cast again with no audition. The part was to play a Hare Krishna zealot who hassles Paul Simon at the airport, which was a big thing at the time. I really wanted to nail the part, even getting the official prayer book, *Bhagavad Gita*, to try to do some "character research," although once again I failed miserably in that regard because the book was incomprehensible. The Hare Krishna all had shaved heads with little ponytails in the back, so even though it was a small part, I thought doing a character that looked so different would show some "range" in characters I could play. I flew to Cleveland to shoot the scene. The scene took place at night in the airport and so when my plane landed, I was already on the set, and they took me directly to the makeup trailer. I was disappointed to find out that I would not be having a shaved head with the little ponytail in the back. The director had decided my character was a Hare Krishna who was trying to *not* look like a Hare Krishna, so he was covering his shaved head with a bad wig. I ended up looking ridiculous, my head covered with a bald cap topped with a black polyester wig, but there was no time to fix it because I was imme-diately escorted to Paul Simon's Winnebago. Paul met me with such warmth, and I was so beside myself to be sitting there with him that nothing else mattered. His brother Eddie, another great musician, was hanging out in there too that night, and I spent the next twelve hours going back and forth from Paul's trailer to the set, doing the scene and then hanging out with Paul and Eddie. Paul treated me like a friend and made me so comfortable that it wasn't until we wrapped at dawn, said our goodbyes, and I took off my costume that it dawned on me how ridiculous I had looked the entire night in front of someone I looked up to so much. I got back on the earliest flight out of Cleveland and was back home, with two thousand dollars and a dream realized, having never left the airport. Years later, Laure and I were walking up Columbus Avenue when a limousine stopped right in front of us and Paul jumped out. He gave me a big hug, told Laure what a great actor I was and how much fun we had had, told me how much Eddie liked me and that he hoped we could do it again sometime, and then he got back in the limo and drove away. It made me feel so good not only that he recognized me without the stupid wig-over-bald-cap look but that he actually took the time to stop the car and tell me all of that. His talent is only surpassed by his menschi-ness.

By this point, Laure had wisely decided to stop pursuing her acting career and shift her focus to become a chef, at which she was immediately brilliant and successful. And finally, after a year of waiting, *Breaking Away* opened in the theaters and was a hit with the critics and audiences. It was only playing at a couple of theaters in New York, and I remember Laure and I standing across the street from one of them, watching in disbelief as audiences lined up around the block to see it. I was in a hit movie right out of the gate, soon to be Oscar-nominated. If I was just starting out now and got a great part like Cyril in *Breaking Away*, my agents would probably help me to map out a "career," hire a publicist, and choose my next projects carefully to build my brand. But at the time, none of that entered my mind. I'd had a good start, but really my only career goal at this point was to have one.

COCAINE COUPONS

Once *Breaking Away* came out, I started to get auditions for good parts. The most exciting shot I got was for the role of Conrad in *Ordinary People*, Robert Redford's directorial debut and another absolute masterpiece of a film. I got flown out to Hollywood to do a screen test. This was a ground-shifting event for me. The only time I had ever heard about "Hollywood Screen Tests" was in the old "Hollywood Movies About Show Business" I might have seen as a kid, and now I was flying in an airplane for maybe the third time in my life, in First Class, going to meet with Robert Redford and do a Hollywood screen test for what was obviously going to be an extraordinary film. Literally living the dream.

I worked very hard on the part. I even read the book—the whole book, start to finish, which took a long time for old Dyslexic

Dan. I met with Redford before the test and we talked for a long time about the script, the part, the book. He must have known how nervous and excited I was, and took all the time necessary to put a green actor at ease. He wanted me to succeed, after all. That's why he flew me out there. And he also wanted to get a feel for who I was as a person, how I would be on the set, and how I would handle it all. We went onto a small set with a skeleton crew and did take after take as he gave me great notes and I did my best to make the adjustments. Anyway, I did not get the part and was crushed. I had so clearly imagined myself in the part, as well as the leap I would make in The Biz. It was a good wake-up call, letting me know that my story was not going to be "the kid from nowhere gets a Hollywood Screen Test, shows his amazing acting skills, lands the part of a lifetime, and the doors of Hollywood Heaven open wide." And when I saw the movie, I knew there was no way I could have played that part. In the vision that Redford had for that film, there is no one who could have played that part except Timothy Hutton. He gave an unbelievably beautiful performance that won the Academy Award, deservedly so. I felt good that I had at least been in the running, got to take my swing and be taken seriously for such a serious part. I mean, I had a Hollywood Fucking Screen Test with Robert Fucking Redford! Not bad.

John Schlesinger was one of the premiere directors in the world at the time, having directed *Midnight Cowboy*, *Sunday Bloody Sunday*, *Marathon Man*, and other iconic films. So when he cast me in his newest film, *Honky Tonk Freeway*, I felt I was taking a huge step in my career. Unfortunately, I had no way of knowing that his best days were behind him and I would be participating in one of the biggest flops in American film history—luckily overshadowed by an even bigger flop which had come out a few months earlier, the infamous *Heaven's Gate*. The script didn't seem that great to me, but what did I know, I had only read about five film scripts at that point (plus the one-and-one-sixteenth pages of Woody Allen's movie) and was not going to question the legendary Schlesinger. The movie was a huge ensemble filled with amazingly talented actors like Hume Cronyn and Jessica Tandy, William Devane, Teri Garr, and Beverly D'Angelo. All of the characters are taking the same freeway to the same final destination for some ill-conceived finale at a big hotel or something, and I played a hitchhiker named Spanky, who was a coke dealer and got rides in various characters' cars. With so many characters, I didn't have all that many scenes, but the ones I had were okay. In my pathetic Method acting attempt to create a memorable character, I decided to get my ear pierced with not one, but two earrings, and grow my hair out into a ponytail. My ear got infected right away, probably because I had it done at the pharmacy in the neighborhood, and the holes in my ears are still with me today, a forever reminder that for an actor like me, there is only madness to the Method. The movie was supposed to be a comedy, and even though we all were trusting Schlesinger's track record to make it come together, the scenes all felt pretty lame. There were spectacular stunts being performed—car crashes, explosions, a water-skiing white rhinoceros—but the main source of entertainment on the set was cocaine.

The movie was a five-month shoot in Florida and Los Angeles and seemed shady from the beginning. My salary was fifteen hundred dollars a week, just over minimum, but the living expenses, the per diem, was two thousand dollars a week, which was paid in cash. So each week I was handed twenty one-hundred dollar bills to pay for all of my expenses. That is way too much cash to be carrying around, especially in Florida, and I just squirreled it away in a sock in my duffel bag. This was 1980, and cocaine was rampant. I had never tried it because I could never afford it, but on this movie, everyone was doing it—the director, producers, actors, prop guys, drivers—carrying around little vials with tiny spoons attached, filled with white powder, and whiffing it up all day long. I was playing a coke dealer in the movie, and there were scenes where I was supposed to snort the stuff, for which the prop department provided ground-up B-12 vitamins, but the real stuff was as available as the coffee at the catering truck. A gram of coke cost one hundred dollars, and the hundred-dollar bills everyone was getting for their per diem were soon referred to a "coke coupons." I cashed in a few of mine, but I was still way too poor to be burning up my money that way. My gram would last a week or two while most people could snort theirs in one good night of partying.

One day, one of the head honchos called each actor into his office, one at a time, for a private meeting. When I went in, he had a grave look on his face. "I know there is a lot of cocaine flowing around on the set and I am very concerned. I hear there might even be an undercover NARC on the set and that would be very bad for the movie and the production. So you need to be very, very careful. I am not saying you are doing coke or not but please, if you are, I want you to promise me that if you want to buy coke, you will only buy it from me. That way you know it will be good and safe." Not quite the ending to the lecture I was expecting, but eye-opening. Maybe the coke sales were funding the film? Who the fuck knows, but it was crazy.

And it turned out Schlesinger was one of the biggest abusers. He was an abusive man, anyway. He was nice and wanted to be liked by all of the actors, but he was absolutely terrible to his crew. He was semi-closeted gay and had a lot of gay men working around him, but treated them worse than anybody else on the film. The first assistant was a great guy named Michael, but John would only call him by the humiliating nickname he chose for him, "Cunt," said with such an ugly bite I can still hear it today. John might have made one of the best movies I have ever seen in *Midnight Cowboy*, but he had a total lack of understanding of our movie or comedy in general, and was incredibly unprofessional and cruel. He ended up working the rare water-skiing white rhino to death, literally, refusing to stop doing takes with the poor animal until it finally had a heart attack and died. The ASPCA was on the set after that, and it is one of the few movies that cannot claim "no animals were harmed in the making of this movie."

And he almost killed me too. I had a scene where my character is sitting on the hood of a school bus, snorting coke. It was the end of the day and the last shot on location in Sarasota before the whole crew had to pack up everything and move to Fort Lauderdale, so tension was already high and everything was being rushed along. They brought me onto the set, I got up on the hood of the bus, and John yelled, "Action" as quickly as he could, before we had even rehearsed the scene. I had to stop the scene because I didn't have the prop vial of cocaine to snort and John got pissed. He started calling everyone "cunts," screaming for the prop department to hurry up and get me the prop. But the prop guys were either in the truck packing up or getting high, or both, and couldn't be found, further enraging John. He finally yelled to his assistant, "Cunt, get me my briefcase!" The assistant brought John his briefcase, from which he pulled out his own little vial of coke and handed it to me. "Here, use this! Now let's shoot this piece of shit and get the hell out of here." At first, I thought, "Cool." Not only would this satisfy my hope to be a Method actor and be more "real," but I was going to get some free cocaine and save my "coke coupons" to take home when the movie was over. But I almost didn't make it home, because with everything so rushed and the crew scattered, the crane with the camera kept fucking up as it came zooming into my face for a close-up. We did take after take, each time John getting more pissed, and each time me taking a big whiff of cocaine. I finished his first vial, so he gave me his backup. I must have done fifteen hits, one after another, and my heart started racing like it never had before. I didn't want to die, but I also didn't want John to yell at me. They finally got a usable take, John yelled "Cut and wrap!" and everyone launched into packing mode to hightail it to Fort Lauderdale. I smoked a pack of cigarettes and didn't sleep for two days.

Sam Cohn opened a new restaurant and market in East Hampton that summer called The Laundry and hired Laure to run the market. Laure lived in Sam's guesthouse, right on the beach, and was having the time of her life working with food and living in a million-dollar house. We missed each other so much but were both too busy to be able to visit. We talked on the phone but could both feel ourselves drifting away. Five months is a long time, and we were both living in worlds the other one knew nothing about. The final sequences of *Honky Tonk Freeway* shot in Los Angeles. To save money, I stayed at the Tropicana, the cheapest motel I could find and as sleazy as you can imagine. I was robbed there, someone breaking into my room while I slept, but luckily, they only took the wallet from my pants and not the huge roll of hundred-dollar bills in the sock in my duffle bag. By this time, *Breaking Away* had been nominated for a bunch of Academy Awards, including Best Director, Best Screenplay, and Best Picture. Peter and Virginia Yates came out for the ceremony and invited me over to their suite at the four-star Beverly Wilshire Hotel to have champagne and caviar with them beforehand. When the limo took them to the awards show, I went back to the Tropicana and watched the Academy Awards sitting on the end of the flea-infested bed. Steve Tesich won for his screenplay and Barbara Barrie won for her acting, and it was incredibly exciting. When it came time for the Best Picture award, they showed a clip from each of the nominees. To my absolute astonishment, the clip they showed for *Breaking Away* was my biggest scene in the film, a sweet and funny monologue about how my father loves when I fail so that he can be sympathetic. I was stunned as I watched myself on the television, and even though another movie won, I felt as proud as if I had just won an Academy Award myself. Laure called me within seconds and we both screamed in amazement and joy. My parents called and none of us could believe that they had shown my biggest scene at that crucial moment. One of the biggest thrills of my life.

Honky Tonk Freeway finally ended. I flew home with my huge wad of cash. It had been so long since Laure and I had seen each other, and so many things had happened to each of us, that we were both a little anxious about seeing each other again, hoping we still had our connection after five months apart. That first night we went out to our neighborhood bar, the Dublin House, a very old-school Irish pub, for a drink. We sat in a booth in the back room, which we had to ourselves. Any awkwardness was gone within minutes, and we sat and drank and talked for a couple of hours, falling in love all over again. I mean, really falling in love, harder than I ever knew I could. In fact, my love for her exploded so much that at the end of that first night back, I surprised us both when I asked her to marry me. I had no idea I was going to do that, no ring or anything like that, only pure, overwhelming love. She said yes, and six weeks later we got married in my parents' backyard in Chevy Chase with just our families and a few friends present, catered by the same people who did my bar mitzvah and paid for in hundred-dollar bills.

SHREVIE AND FRIENDS

Laure and I getting married took a lot of people by surprise, including us. I had just turned twenty-three, and even though all my New York friends were ten years older than me, none of them had even gotten close to getting married, and as my high school buddies had just graduated college, marriage was the farthest thing from their minds. Sam Cohn loved Laure after working with her all summer, but even he told me not to get married, that it would be a distraction from my career. Laure had already been married and divorced, and her parents were rightfully skeptical about her trying it again so quickly, especially with a mostly unemployed actor six years her junior. My brother and sister were both confused by it. My dad was smitten with Laure and my mom thought she was great, although they did have a long talk with her to try to talk her *out* of it, because they thought she could do a lot better than me. But there was no doubt that Laure and I were destined to make our own family together. Peter and Virginia Yates threw us a wedding party at their home in the Dakota and had us invite all of our weirdo New York actor friends, none of whom had ever been inside the historic building. It was eye-opening to see how out of place my friends were inside such a classy apartment, with beautiful trays of hors d'oeuvres and fine china and the Yates's kids and the feeling of a substantial home. Laure and I looked up to the Yateses so much; they were role models of what we were striving to be, and they gave our marriage an auspicious beginning.

Which is why it was such a perfect time to land the role of Shrevie in Barry Levinson's first film, *Diner.* Whereas *Breaking Away* was a coming-of-age film about how childhood friendships get tested by the diaspora that occurs at the end of high school, *Diner* was a coming-of-age story about how childhood friendships get tested when everyone starts getting married. Barry saw me in a really good play I was doing, *How I Got That Story,* and asked me to come in and meet. There was no audition; we just sat and talked for a half hour about the movie. The script was great, and the part was perfect for me at that moment in my life. Shrevie was the first one married among his friends and so was I. The movie took place in Maryland (where Barry had grown up too) and we knew all of the same sports trivia about the Colts and the Orioles. I got the part and was in Baltimore before I knew it, sitting in a hotel room reading the script out loud for the first time with some of the best actors and best people I have ever gotten to work with—Paul Reiser, Steve Guttenberg, Kevin Bacon, Tim Daly, and Mickey Rourke.

Barry Levinson has got to be the coolest cat to ever get behind the camera. It was his first film to direct and he had written the script. You would think he would hold on tight to his vision and his words, but his vision was about recreating the friendships and the world he grew up in—about hanging out, making each other laugh, riffing on each other's bullshit, talking about girls—and we soon realized that Barry had cast each of us for our bullshitting prowess. We were all young men who knew how to hang out in a bar and kibitz the night away, which is what is at the heart of the *Diner* story. From the very first reading of the script he had us improvising, Barry telling his assistant to jot down some of the ideas we came up with. And it only got more loose as we started filming the movie. In the scenes we did with other actors, we stuck to the script pretty closely, although Barry always had an extra line or joke for us to try. But when it was just the guys, most of the script went out the window. He knew the film he wanted to make and was determined to make it, even though no one had ever made a movie that way before. There were about three or four weeks of night shooting where we did all the scenes of us hanging out in the diner. We would go to work when the sun went down, stay up all night improvising the hanging-out scenes, smoking cigarettes, and eating the prop food, and when the sun came up, we would go back to the hotel restaurant, order breakfast and Bloody Marys, and hang out again, with even more bullshitting and cracking each other up. We'd go to bed at ten in the morning and wake up at sundown to go to work again. It was absolute heaven! So many fucking laughs, but here are two I will never forget.

There is a scene when Guttenberg's character is giving his off-screen fiancée a quiz about Baltimore Colts trivia to see if she is worthy of marriage. Steve thinks she will flunk the test and has a line where he wonders, "Do you think she'll go down for the count?" When Reiser improvised the response, "No, but I heard she blew the Prince," we laughed so hard and for so long that they had to shut down shooting for the night, because every time that line came up in the scene, we started laughing all over again.

Reiser is as sharp as a razor and his quick-wittedness kept us all on our toes.

Steve, Tim, and I were all solid actors, but Kevin Bacon and Mickey Rourke were movie stars, even then. They had the animal presence and magnetism that defines all the biggest movie stars I have met, insisting on operating at their own rhythm, which can create moments of electricity that are priceless on film. But sometimes marching to your own drum in a scene can create moments of absurdity too. In one scene, Mickey's character, a gambler, is in the diner having a conversation with his bookie, a guy named Bagel. Mickey's character comes over to the table where the rest of our gang is sitting and tells us, "Bagel heard about my basketball bet," to which we respond with some things like, "I hope you win" and "That's a lot of money." In trying to create a really interesting line reading, Mickey threw in a few extra punctuations marks, which totally changed the meaning, so that when he came over to the table, he said the line this way—"Bagel, heard about my basketball bet?"—as if Bagel was sitting at our table, which obviously he was not, and he was asking him if he heard about his bet. The scene came to a grinding halt and Barry explained to Mickey that Bagel is the guy he just came from, who heard about his basketball bet and now he is coming over to tell his best friends that "Bagel heard about my basketball bet." Mickey nodded, and we began take two. Mickey started at the table with Bagel, walked across the diner to our table, and delivered the line the same way: "Bagel, heard about my basketball bet?"

We lost our shit laughing. "Bagel isn't here! He's there, at the table you started at. That actor there is Bagel. None of us are Bagel. We are Shrevie, Fenwick, Eddie, Modell, and Billy! No Bagel here. You are telling *us* that *he* heard about your basketball bet!"

"Okay, I get it now," said Mickey. Take three, I swear to God he did it one more time. I don't know if he had not read the script or he had just practiced the line so much one way that he couldn't stop himself from saying it that way, but to this day, when the rest of us get together, "Bagel, heard about my basketball bet?" will still make us giggle. One night, I made the mistake of clashing with Mickey over the use of the single land-line phone we were allowed to use on the set. I wanted him to get off the phone because he was taking too long, and evidently, he wanted to put me in a headlock. Well, we both got what we wanted. Lucky for me, the fight was broken up quickly because Mickey is a beast—he went on to have a second career as a prize fighter.

Diner was one of the best creative experiences I ever had on a film, and the whole cast are still dear friends to this day. But the game-changer at the time was that I made thirty-five thousand dollars, which was a mind-blowing amount of money and made us able to afford to have a kid. The news of Laure's pregnancy was another shock to friends and family, but Laure and I were more in love than ever, now bound together in a way that we didn't anticipate. She couldn't wait to be a mom and I couldn't wait to be a dad. I had so much time on my hands between projects and wanted to put my energy into something real instead of wasting time living the unemployed actor's life of Frisbee and smoking weed. Sam Cohn told me I had to be picky and patient in my career choices and that getting married and having kids leads to "selling out," and he was right. I still had standards—no TV shows, no commercials, only good directors—but at only twenty-three with a kid on the way, I was in no position to turn down anything in the ballpark.

I got offered a role in my third Jill Clayburgh film, *I'm Dancing as Fast as I Can*, in which I played a young man in a mental institution who has an affair with Jill's character after she is admitted to the facility. One of the best and one of the worst film experiences of my life happened to me filming that movie.

The worst thing happened my first day of shooting. The movie had already been shooting for a few weeks when I got to LA to do my part. My first scenes were supposed to be on the mental hospital grounds, but because it was raining outside, they decided to go to the "cover set," an indoor scene set aside for just such a situation. Unfortunately, the cover set was the scene where Jill and I are in bed making love. I had been dreading this scene ever since I read the script, but it was scheduled for the end of the shoot, and I figured I would be comfortable with Jill and the crew by the time it came up. The day's schedule was already screwed with the change of locations, so they hustled me right up to the set. I walked in, clothes wet from the rain, and saw the situation. There was a bed with Jill Clayburgh in it, wearing a sexy nightgown. There was a camera mounted directly above, looking straight down on it. There were lights shining and a crew of about fifty men and women surrounding the bed. The director, who I had never met, came up to me and introduced himself, and told me the scene. "The scene will be you fucking Jill Clayburgh. Ready? Okay, let's go. Get in the bed. We are running very late!" Get in the bed? This was my worst dream coming true before my very eyes. I was standing in my cold, wet clothes in the center of a room full of strangers who were waiting for me to strip naked, get in the bed, and start fucking Jill Clayburgh while they watched and photographed it. And somehow, I did it. I reintroduced myself to Jill, who unbeknownst to me thought I was great as her student in *It's My Turn* and had them cast me in this. She joked about how sorry she was that we had to start with this scene, while I stripped off my wet clothes down to my tighty-whiteys and crawled under the sheets, freezing cold. The director quickly gave us his choreography—first kissing, then her on top of me, then me on top of her, etc.—and said it was time to remove my underpants. I was numb not only with hypothermia but with the out-of-body experience of acting out an actual nightmare in real life. My memory of the scene is quite hazy. Jill was a good sport. I think my balls finally thawed out from their initial raisin-like state into something more along the lines of a date or a kumquat. I had my butt up to the camera, pretending to pump away, although I probably looked more like a walrus making its way across the sand and back into the sea. Thankfully, we will never know, because I was cut from the movie.

The best part of making that movie was that Joe Pesci was playing a fellow inmate at the mental hospital and we became good friends. Even though this was a serious drama, Joe and I loved making each other laugh, a precursor to our future partnership. Joe put me on the floor with laughter one day when he walked over to the ping-pong table in the therapy room, took the huge roll of maps his character was walking around with, put it up to his nose like a straw, and pretended to sniff up the entire white line down the middle of the table. We still laugh about it. It was also the first time I stayed at the Chateau Marmont hotel, living in the bungalow next to my old friend, John Heard, who was shooting *Cat People* at the time. Having my big brother there was a blast, and the hotel ended up being my home away from home for years to come. Just goes to show that you never know what magic mushroom might grow out of a pile of cow shit.

Laure was very pregnant by the time I got into my first action movie, *Blue Thunder*, starring Roy Scheider. Sam Cohn had gotten me eighty-five thousand dollars for the part, which was almost triple anything I had ever made before, so Laure quit her job and for the first time was able stay on location with me. She was gorgeously pregnant, and this was our last hurrah at being footloose and carefree. We would swim in the pool at the Chateau, go to nice restaurants and explore LA, all while making money and being in a movie. It was a time of perfection. The movie was easy and fun. Flying in helicopters, crashing helicopters, doing a few stunts too. I played a rookie cop who gets killed, and I got to do a whole sequence of being chased by a car with my hands tied behind my back before getting run over. So fun! Roy was a client of Sam's, and Roy's wife Cynthia was the editor of *Breaking Away* who I got to know when Peter Yates took me into the editing room, so Roy and I were very comfortable with each other right off the bat. I knew Roy was a great actor and a huge movie star, but what I did not know was that he was a sun-worshiper, with an almost religious fervor. We wore one-piece flight suits as our costume and Roy had nothing on underneath his except a Speedo bathing suit. He kept a chaise lounge nearby at all times, as well as a reflector pan to hold under his chin, like you have seen in cliché movie scenes with rich movie stars sunning themselves. Whenever the crew had to set up for another shot, Roy would strip down to his Speedo, lie on his chaise lounge, flip open the reflector pan, and bake himself in the sun. It seemed funny when we were shooting on the Warner Brothers lot, but it was kind of weird when we were on location. I will forever remember the image of Roy sunbathing on one side of the chain-link fence and on the other, a crowd of South Central LA residents staring at him and yelling questions about *Jaws* or *The French Connection*. *Blue Thunder* was also the only time I was ever stoned on a movie set, although it was by accident. They had wrapped me for the night, and I had smoked a joint with the prop guys when the director realized he had forgotten to get a shot and asked me to come back to the set. All I had to do was walk up to my apartment, put the key in, and go inside. It sure seemed simple enough, but my heart was pounding and my guilt raging at being so unprofessional, so it took a few takes for me to get it right. Making movies is all about creative precision and focus, and being stoned never felt more wrong.

We came back to New York when the film was done and had money to buy a crib, do Lamaze classes, and get ready for the baby. I was in midtown when I called from a pay phone to check on her, and Laure said her water broke. I raced home and we gathered the baby bag, but when we got outside, I could not get a cab to save my life! Our doorman, Sammy, who still is a dear friend to this day, was an auxiliary policeman in his spare time and he was as nervous as we were about getting across town to the hospital while Laure was starting contractions. Sammy locked up the building, got his car, put his blue flashing light on the roof of it, and sped us across Central Park with his horn honking the whole way to Lennox Hill Hospital.

Life changed that night. I watched Laure go through labor and finally understood the near-mythical strength and power that women have that men can't even begin to conceive of. At the moment of truth, when the baby's head first popped out, the doctor let me reach in, grab the shoulders, and pull the baby out the rest of the way. I held the baby up, facing his mother, saw his balls hanging between his legs, cried out "It's a boy!" and put him on Laure's chest. The whole thing was utterly miraculous. I went to the coffee shop downstairs, got Laure some food, and we sat and stared at Henry until Laure was ready to go to sleep. I met my best friends at a bar where we drank and celebrated until dawn. I went back to the apartment and shot a little Super 8 film of myself, which to this day I have never had the courage to watch. I have been a father since that moment, and having our children is the most powerful, profound, religious, meaning-giving experience of my life, with nothing else even a close second.

Diner came out a few weeks later to an outstanding critical response. Another underdog film like *Breaking Away*—the audience and critics fell in love with it (and continue to hold it in high regard). The *Diner* boys and I did some publicity for the film, and we had a blast hanging out again, amazed that all the improvising we had done was actually in the movie! They were so excited and awed that I now had a child, and had tiny little T-shirts made saying "Hank," "Dr. Stern," and "Bird Jr." I was only twenty-four years old, but I had it all. A wife and child, a budding career, incredible friends, an apartment, and even a little money in the bank. The tricky part of "having it all" is that in order to keep "having it all," you have to work your ass off or else you end up "having it all turn to shit," which is something I always try to avoid.

CALIFORNIA
HERE WE COME

W hen *Blue Thunder* came out, I was invited to go on *Late Night with David Letterman* to promote the movie. I was such a fan of the show and Dave was a fun and funny interviewer. A day or so before I was to appear, I got a call from the producer asking what I wanted to talk about on the show. I told him that we could talk about whatever Dave wanted to talk about. He told me that is not the way it works. He wanted me to tell him stories of things that had happened on set, anecdotes about my career or my life, and then they would pick the ones they thought were funny and have Dave ask me about them. I had no idea that was how it worked and had to come up with something funny and interesting enough for Letterman on the spot. I told him something off the top of my head, but there was dead silence on the other end of the phone, followed by, "Anything else?" I tried again, same reaction. I was getting desperate and realizing just how uninteresting a person I am, and getting the feeling that if I didn't come up with something immediately, I might not be appearing on the show after all. I have no idea why I said it, but the words, "My uncle is a helicopter pilot," came out of my mouth, trying to pick up the theme of *Blue Thunder*.

The producer perked up immediately. "That's fantastic. What did he think of the film? Did he give you any tips?" I have no memory of the lie I spun for him, but it was enough to get myself off of that disastrous phone call and onto the show. Walking into the Ed Sullivan Theater, I couldn't believe any of it was happening—me on Letterman in the theater where I saw the Beatles play on TV. The producer came into my dressing room and told me that Dave loved the stuff about my uncle and was going to go with that story. I feebly tried to guide him back to one of my other scintillating stories, but to no avail. Sure enough, when I sat down Dave's first question was about my uncle, the helicopter pilot. Although I have not often been compared to George Washington for my unflinching truth-telling, the old adage, "Honesty is the best policy," really came into play that night. Instead of trying to make up a fake story about a fake uncle, I told Dave and his audience I had lied. I told them how I had panicked when the producer asked me for funny stories because I did not understand how talk shows work, that I thought they were real conversations, not discussed beforehand and written on cue cards. Dave thought this was a fucking riot, and the whole segment turned out to be Dave loving the chance to go completely off script. Boy, did I pull that one out of my ass or what?

I wanted to keep making money. I took a terrible movie, a remake of *Samson and Delilah*, having to say phony biblical dialogue: "I anoint thee with this oil of hyacinth, on this day of days and this night of your nights," which I still cannot get out of my mind. We shot it in Durango, Mexico, and I had to ride a horse, which was as foreign to me as being in this new country. I nearly bit the dust when the asshole who was supposed to teach me to ride put me on a horse bareback and with no reins, slapped the horse on the ass, and yelled "Hold on!" I barely clung to this wild animal's mane while it raced across the dry plains of Mexico until it finally threw me off. (After that, I did my horseback riding scenes sitting on a tall ladder with wheels on it, being pushed by underpaid locals.) I did a movie called *Get Crazy*, a weird little film about the Fillmore East concert scene with Malcolm McDowell, Lou Reed, some awesome punk rock bands, John Densmore of the Doors, Dion, and Ed Begley Jr. The movie was silly, and I was terrible in it, but Laure, Henry, and I rented a house from Scherrie Payne of the Supremes, which included a swimming pool and a disco room, and we had the time of our lives. Laure and Henry went back to New York a couple of weeks before the movie ended. It was the first time I had been away from them, and I felt the punch in the gut of "life on the road when your family is at home." It was bad enough before, being away from Laure, but with the baby in the mix, it was nearly unbearable. Henry and I were buddies in New York; we played all the time, going to the park, restaurants, food shopping—and being in a movie didn't hold a candle to those simple pleasures.

When I got home, we had enough money to buy an old VW Bug and started driving out of the city so we could all experience nature a bit. We eventually rented a small cabin in Woodstock for two hundred dollars a month, and it gave us an entirely new lease on life. I had grown up a little hippie and so had Laure, and we were realizing that this was the dream we wanted to be living: getting back to the land in the ultimate hippie village. We spent more and more time in Woodstock, and it started to make New

York seem claustrophobic. We still loved our friends, but we were our own family now, and our role in the group was changing.

One of the gang, Shep Abbott, wrote a script called *C.H.U.D.* Doug Cheek found a producer who would let him direct if he got John Heard and me to star in it, since we both had a bit of a movie career going. John didn't even read it before he said he would do it. I read it, but there wasn't really a part for me, so I said I would do it, but I had to write a part for myself to play. It is a story about homeless people who live underground and get poisoned by a secret toxic waste dump in the sewers. I decided to play a social worker who, like my real-life hero, my dad, fights for justice for the marginalized. So I invented The Rev. I rewrote the script from top to bottom, giving myself a great part, the hero who kills the bad guy in the end, and Doug was wide open to all the changes. We hired our friends and family in the cast and crew, including Laure as the first victim in the opening scene. We spent the summer filming in the sewers of NYC, and we were all in creative heaven. I got to go into the editing room as much as I wanted and for the first time helped make a movie from start to finish. The producer had the final cut, of course, and added some really terrible, cheesy monsters for the C.H.U.D.s, so the final product was kind of disappointing. But it was one of the best learning experiences of my life, and the movie has held on as a cult classic. I have even met people with C.H.U.D. tattoos on their bodies, which is nuts.

I was working on good films, but their success was hit and miss. I got to work with legendary director Sidney Lumet on *Daniel*, performing a page-and-a-half-long monologue as a 1960s revolutionary lecturing Tim Hutton's character, but it was eventually cut out of the film. I had a great part in a mediocre movie based on a very good play called *Key Exchange*, although the worst part of the film was that I had to do another nude scene, which went better than the two previous ones but was still absolutely traumatizing. Disney decided they were going to bring back "the short," popular when movies first started showing in theaters in the 1930s and 1940s, a short film that plays before the film you came to see. Their first effort was a short film called *Frankenweenie*, about a dog who is killed and brought back to life by his young owner. A young animator named Tim Burton wrote and directed it, his first film. I am so proud to have been able to teach Tim everything he knows about filmmaking in our short time together and I accept his gratitude for my guidance. Seriously, he was a genius right out of the gate, shooting in black and white, with strange camera angles and an extraordinary set built on a soundstage. Such a great little film; but after we shot it, Disney basically abandoned the idea of showing shorts, and decided to focus instead on taking over the entire world.

One of the hottest plays at the time was Steppenwolf's production of Sam Shepard's *True West* at the Cherry Lane Theatre, imported from Chicago, which starred John Malkovich and Gary Sinise. I got an offer to be in the replacement cast and said yes immediately. The play blew me away. It was wild, animalistic, violent, absurd, and dark, and sparked laughs like I had never heard before in the theater. The play is about two brothers, one a meek Hollywood screenwriter and one a violent and dangerous drifter, trapped in a house and a fight for survival. Gary not only starred in but directed the play as well. I assumed I was replacing him as the intellectual writer, but when I got to the theater for the first day of rehearsal, Gary told me I would be playing Lee, the psychopathic brother, and that he was staying in the show to play it with me. That was a mind-fuck and took me a minute to wrap my head around it, but it turned out to be one of the greatest roles I ever got to play. The audiences went crazy for the show, and I got to act in a way I never had before, playing a larger-than-life character by finding the truth of that character and taking the audience along for a crazy ride. Gary was brilliant, and when he eventually left, the understudy, Jere Burns, took over the role. He and I became dear friends and brothers and knocked the shit out of each other, eight shows a week. We did the show for three or four months, and Jere and I were wild animals onstage by the time the producers brought in Tim Matheson to join the play and replace Jere. When Tim finished rehearsals with my understudy and had to get up on stage with me and an audience, I think I scared the shit out of him. He felt I took the violence on stage too far, scratching his face too hard with the toast and strangling him too hard with the telephone cord, and maybe he was right. I definitely made people fearful. He and I lasted about a week, and then one day I came in to do the show and was met by two security guards and the producers. They told me I was fired and said to get my stuff from the dressing room and leave. I was tired of the show anyway, and the fact that they thought they needed security guards to escort me out was an acting badge of honor I still take pride in, in some fucked-up way.

Laure got pregnant again, and we needed to move to a bigger apartment, but this time we could afford to buy instead of rent. We found a little two-bedroom on 87th Street for eighty-five thousand dollars. I was nervous about having a mortgage and wasting money on paying interest, so we took all the money from our savings and paid for it in cash. (Since then, I have bought every house, every car, and paid every tuition with cash, never wanting to be in debt to anyone, ever.) I loved owning it and felt like I was investing in myself when I painted it, put in a new kitchen counter, and got our first dishwasher. Two weeks before the baby was born, Laure's father died, completely unexpectedly. The juxtaposition of the grief from that loss with the joy of the newborn baby still lives with us today, all these years later. Laure dealt with it with her iron will, keeping the pain and sadness of losing her dad at bay, knowing she had to focus on bringing this new life into the world safely and with joy. I got to see her go through labor all over again. The same doctor was with us and again, when the baby's head popped out, he let me reach in, grab the shoulders, and pull the baby out. I held the baby to show Laure and I saw the little balls hanging down between their legs, just like with Henry, and announced "It's a boy!"

Laure and the doctor looked at me like I was crazy, and said, "It's a girl, you idiot. Look again." Sure enough, I had missed the call, mistaking the baby's engorged labia for testicles. (I still feel like a dummy about that one.) Sophie entered our lives that day and changed our world forever. She was a very different kid than Henry. She hated the noise and action of the city, and we started spending more and more time in Woodstock, where we were all much happier. More space, more nature, more focus, and more time together.

My only guiding principle for my career was, "work with the best film directors," and so far that had served me well. Woody Allen asked me to play a fun character, a famous rock star shopping for art, in his new film, *Hannah and Her Sisters*. The scene was with Barbara Hershey, Michael Caine, and Max von Sydow. I had met Michael Caine through the Yateses and knew Max from the Samson movie, so I felt very comfortable playing an arrogant asshole in the scene with them. This time, Woody was friendly, hanging out in the trailer with me, talking trash about other actors, being funny. He was so meticulous in setting up a huge, intricately choreographed master shot that we didn't have time to shoot one frame of film before we broke for lunch. Woody invited me to join him at a fancy restaurant along with other actors. Just Max Von Sydow, Woody Allen, Michael Caine, Barbara Hershey, and Daniel Stern at a table. Talk about imposter syndrome—I spent the meal having a complete out-of-body experience, with the phrase, "One of these things is not like the other," running in a loop inside my mind. It felt like a huge milestone to be included in the troupe of New York actors that Woody Allen called on to be in his films, my talent recognized by my idol.

The city was driving us crazy with two kids—taking them to the park, playdates, day care, living in four little rooms. Woodstock life was so much easier, so after a year or so, we decided to sell our apartment and buy a house in Woodstock. I figured it was only a two-hour drive from Manhattan, so I could come down for auditions. Our apartment was already worth one hundred and twenty-five thousand dollars and we sold it immediately. We found a beautiful, woodsy house on twenty acres in Woodstock for the same amount and opened escrow on it. We were excited and scared, but the school seemed good, and we could finally commit to our dream of raising our family in a small-town community. Laure and I went to dinner with one of my agents to tell her the news. She said, "What are you, retiring?"

I said, "No, I want to keep working, of course. But we just can't live in an apartment anymore with two kids. We need a house with a yard so they can go outside and play without having to go to the park or a play date. We need a house!"

To which she replied with these fateful words—"They have houses in Los Angeles," and stunned Laure and me into silence. The thought of moving to Los Angles had never even entered our minds. "They have houses in Los Angeles *and* they have show business. What are you going to do in Woodstock?"

Laure and I went home that night and talked it through, unable to refute anything my agent had said. But we had already sold our apartment, so we were committed to moving. We were luckily still in the window where we could get out of escrow on the Woodstock house, and we did. I spent five days in Los Angeles and found a house to rent in an area called Beverly Hills Post Office, and we told the moving company to take our stuff there instead of Woodstock. Within a matter of weeks, we were living at the top of a canyon, at the end of a dead-end road, with a swimming pool, deer eating in our backyard, sheep grazing on the side of the hill, in a house that the famed singer Lola Falana once lived in, and seeing Fred Astaire drive his Rolls-Royce up our canyon road when we went into town for supplies. No wonder we fell in love with California so deeply.

DRIVING ROBERT REDFORD
AT ONE HUNDRED
MILES PER HOUR

T he move to California changed everything. Henry and Sophie each had their own bedroom. And a playroom. And a dead-end street to play on. Henry started preschool, and we dove right in. The beauty of it was that there were not only houses in LA, but also work. Within a week, I got offered the lead role in a comedy called *The Boss' Wife*. The script was mediocre, and from my point of view, if they were asking me to be the lead actor, that meant (a) it had been turned down by all of the really good comedic leading men, (b) the director/writer was a tall, goofy Jewish guy who saw themselves in me, and (c) it was not going to be a hit movie. I hated to turn down work, so I told my agent I would do it only if they paid me the outrageous sum of two hundred thousand dollars (the most money I had ever made was eighty-five thousand dollars). Knowing they would never go for it, I threw the script in the garbage and felt good about my integrity.

When my agent called with the news that they had agreed to my terms, I had to fish the script out of the garbage, the cover now stained with baby food and peanut butter, the perfect symbol for the stain one gets from doing things just for the money. The movie was actually fun. Christopher Plummer played my boss (obviously a low point in his amazing career), and Martin Mull and Fisher Stevens became my friends as well. There was, once again, an awkward sex scene I had to do in a shower with a beautiful and wonderful model/actress named Arielle Dombasle. What made this one especially uncomfortable is that we did the scene in some makeshift set in a weird warehouse in the desert of Palm Springs, and as we shot it, ripping each other's clothes off while making out furiously, we began to notice that our clothes were turning a very dark brown from the disgusting water they had rigged to the shower. They stopped filming to try to fix it, but they couldn't figure out the problem, so we just shot the scene in the rusty water. I went home to Laure feeling dirty in so many ways.

Things got back on track when I got the part in one of my favorite movies, *Born in East L.A.* Cheech Marin wrote, directed, and starred in it as a Mexican American who gets trapped in Mexico without his passport and has to sneak back into America. I played a "coyote," a human trafficker and a real asshole who lives in Tijuana and smuggles people across the border. *True West* had opened me up to finding the fun of playing a bad guy, but this was the first time I got to try it on film. The part fit like a glove, and we had a blast filming it, improvising and making each other laugh a lot. The toughest part was being away from the family. When I had a day off, I would hitch a ride in the van that drove the actual film back up from Tijuana to LA to be developed. The poor driver had to do that three-hour drive twice a day. There were a couple of times he was so tired that he started to fall asleep behind the wheel and let me do the driving—which was a big deal, for a Teamster to let one of the actors drive.

I will gladly bet you ten-to-one odds on ten dollars, dear reader (or listener, if you are enjoying this epic work as an audiobook), that you have never seen Robert Redford's *Milagro Beanfield War*, one of the sweetest movies I have ever seen, let alone been in. And instead of sending me the ten dollars you now owe me, go buy, rent, or stream this movie. It is a great American story about a town of people whose anger at their lost land and lost rights comes to a boiling point when a farmer, his field dry because the water rights to his land have been taken, illegally taps into an irrigation pipe and his field begins to flourish. The town is inspired and rises up against the land developers and, like all good movies, righteousness wins the day. It is lyrical and funny and human, with incredible performances by Christopher Walken, Melanie Griffith, Sônia Braga, Rubén Blades, Chick Vennera, my old friend John Heard, and on and on and on. Watch this film! My agent got a call offering me the part of Herbie, a social work student who comes to the town of Milagro to do some kind of study but ends up joining the town in their fight against the land developers. Redford remembered me from my *Ordinary People* screen test and offered to put me in the company of one of the classiest troupes of actors ever assembled. My agent explained the "favored-nations" deal, that we would all be in New Mexico for five months and everyone would get sixty thousand dollars. The prestige of the film, working with Redford at last, and being so flattered that he had cast me alongside these other actors made me very proud and excited, but the "five months in New Mexico" part was a bit of a problem. When my agent conveyed my reservations, Redford stepped up to the plate for me again. Even though it was favored-nations, he had them include in my contract an airplane ticket every week so I would be able to go home and see my family. He was so thoughtful and generous, and off I went to New Mexico.

It turned out to be one of the greatest experiences of my life. Five months is a long time and the friendships I made were deep. Rubén Blades was a force of nature. I could barely compute the breadth of the life he was living—a phenomenal musician, political activist, an icon in Panama who was considered presidential material at the time, and a brilliant fucking actor on top of it all. So knowledgeable, and so fucking funny too. We saw each other for years afterward, but have since lost touch. (Rubén, if you're reading this, call me.) Having my dearest friend John Heard on the set, who had taken me into his home and life from my first day in New York, was so sweet, and we got to hang out like old times. Sônia Braga lived next door to me and fed me lots of meals. Such a loving friend. I was a Mets fan, and that was the year that they won it all, with the spectacular Billy Buckner misplay, and I watched every inning of it in amazement, cheering loudly in my little room. I loved Chick Vennera, who played the central character of the farmer, Joe Mondragon. He had the weight of the world on his shoulders as a relatively unknown actor who Redford had chosen over Cheech Marin. I was rooting for Cheech when I found out he was up for the role, but Redford had a vision for the film and Chick was the person he saw. And he was right. After my near miss with *Ordinary People*, I know how Cheech must have felt not getting the part, but in the end, it is right there on film to see—each of Redford's artistic choices coming together to create a masterpiece. One of the sweetest parts for me in the film was my character's relationship with an old man in town, a man who speaks with angels and who takes me in. He was played by an amazing actor, Carlos Riquelme, who had a long career in the Mexican film industry. He gave such a tremendously funny, smart, sly, and innocent performance, and was such a loving person.

One fateful day, I had a big scene with Carlos. His character lived in a hut, and he was teaching me a prayer or something. It was a very good scene, and I was excited to finally get to do an intimate scene with him and get a chance to work closely with Bob (yes, I knew him well enough to now call Mr. Redford "Bob"). With so many characters and storylines, you really savor the moments when you get to do your thing. We rehearsed and started shooting and it was going well but at some point, Bob seemed a little annoyed with me. (He was not really annoyed at all, but that's how it felt, because I wanted to be perfect.) We were between takes and I was just waiting for the next setup, not doing anything. And I think that was the problem—I wasn't doing anything. Bob came over and asked me something that still rings in my ears today.

"Do you know what lens we are on?"

"What?"

"Do you know what lens we are on?"

"Um, no."

"So how do you know how to perform the scene, if you don't even know what the camera is seeing?" He came up close and framed my face with his hands, mimicking a close-up. "Are we here?" he asked.

"I don't know."

"Are we wide?"

"I don't know. Why?"

"Because it is a totally different performance if the camera is seeing you here or here or here. If I am on a fifty millimeter from this distance, then I am seeing your whole body. Your body language, the scene, the atmosphere. But when I come here, on a one hundred and twenty millimeter, I am right on your face. You have to bring the whole performance into just right here. And I might come closer, right into here." He framed just my eyes. "You have to carve out your performance for each shot, each take, and know what you are trying to do each and every moment for that particular shot. That is part of your job."

I felt embarrassed, but also incredibly challenged. And I immediately got what he meant. It was the best film acting lesson I ever got, and the best directing lesson as well. It changed the way I have approached my work since then, understanding what each shot is, what the audience is seeing and feeling at all times, and using the framing of each shot to show a slightly different side to the character and story. I have passed Bob's lesson on to many young actors myself. That's what makes Bob "Robert Redford." He is a master filmmaker both in front of and behind the camera, and he knows how to connect to an audience like no one else. Watch his performance in *All Is Lost*, a film with only one character, no dialogue, and shot under the toughest conditions imaginable. His artistry is on full display in that film, and his lessons are still with me in a very deep way.

I think he felt bad about challenging me, because as we were wrapping for the day and I was getting in the van to go back "home" to the condos, Bob came out to his car, the beautiful Porsche 911 he drove to work every day. He was kind and told me what a good job I had done in the scene, and I got to thank him for guiding me through it so well. I must have commented on how cool his car was, because the next thing I heard was, "Do you want to drive it?" It was one of those moments in my show business life where it feels like I might have lost consciousness, or have awakened in Oz. Before I knew it, I was behind the wheel of a Porsche 911, just me and Bob, speeding down the mountain road at eighty miles per hour.

I could tell he had second thoughts almost immediately.

Followed quickly by third, fourth, and fifth thoughts. But he was determined to really let me experience this engineering marvel and challenge me for the second time today, in a wholly unexpected way. The way home from the set is on the High Road to Taos, a spectacularly beautiful, twisty mountain road from Taos to Santa Fe, and I drove it so fucking fast! It was completely exhilarating! Very intimate, these race cars. There were only two seats in the whole car. Just me and Bob in a tuna can, screaming down the High Road to Taos. Bob looked like any dad might, white knuckles gripping the door handle, feet pressing through the floorboards, and a forced smile plastered on his face, which did not conceal the terror and nausea I could see coursing through his body. But he kept encouraging me to go faster, explaining the aerodynamic theory about how in a Porsche, going faster into the curves actually helps push the car into the ground and hug the road. Or something like that. (My knowledge of cars is basically pedals and steering wheels.) I like to go fast but not do anything dangerous, but this was a once in a lifetime chance, and anyway, to quote Rain Man, "I'm an excellent driver." Shifting up and down, Bob taught me how to listen to the engine, roaring so perfectly, running up the rpms so high. The car hugged the road like there was glue on the tires. It felt like one tiny, wrong tug on the wheel would send us flying off the side of the mountain. But he told me to push it, and I did. I have to say, that was a lot of pressure. Not only were our lives on the line, but one wrong flick of the wrist and I would forever be known as the idiot who killed Robert Redford. Not the legacy I was hoping for. At the bottom of the mountain, there was a good long stretch of straight highway and for the first and only time in my life, I drove a car at a hundred miles an hour. I have never forgotten how sick he looked, and it still makes me laugh. He never did invite me to drive it again, but I was able to bring this American (and personal) treasure back to my condo parking lot, safe and sound and beating the vans with the cast by about a half an hour (I win!). Robert Redford is an artist and a talent of the highest magnitude and, on top of that, has done enormous things in his epic life for the environment, the film industry, promoting art, Native American culture, and on and on. And I just want it to be known that a lot of that would not have happened if I wasn't such an excellent driver, a God Behind the Wheel. You're welcome, world!

Crazily, a year or so after the shoot, the film was finished and premiered at the Cannes Film Festival, 1990. I was in Rome, in the middle of shooting a terrible underwater monster movie that starred Peter Weller, a major flop called *Leviathan*. Peter's character in our movie was similar to his *RoboCop* character, only stiffer and less human. I played the part of "Six Pack" (obviously nicknamed for his beer consumption, not his ab muscles), a disgruntled underwater miner with a weird hairdo and a ridiculously bad facial hair configuration. I got a call inviting me to the Cannes Film festival for the opening of *Milagro*. It was going to be me, Redford, Sônia Braga, and Melanie Griffith (cue "One of these things is not like the other" again). Like the idea of a Hollywood Screen Test, the Cannes Film Festival was something I had only vaguely heard about in movies I'd seen about Hollywood. I stayed at the Carlton Hotel, right on the French Riviera, and it was a crazy show-business atmosphere of actresses, producers, financiers, paparazzi, and swag. I did a bunch of interviews to publicize the movie, and all my expenses were paid by the studio, so I was having the time of my life. The day of the premiere, I was told to report to another hotel, a much nicer hotel, where Bob, Sônia, and Melanie were staying. I was waiting in the lobby when they suddenly appeared, on the move with an entourage of security. They pulled me in with them and off we went. Let the chase begin.

Bob was the biggest, handsomest, coolest movie star and director on the planet, and this was the center of the publicity machine. It was like being with the Beatles. They took us on a freight elevator, through the kitchen and an underground tunnel to a parking garage. The four of us got into a limo. As soon as the limo left the garage, the chase was on. Racing in a harrowing fashion through the streets of Cannes, paparazzi on motorcycles butted up against the window trying to get a photograph. It was quite terrifying—not only the physical danger, but to get a small glimpse at what Bob's life was like. He is such a humble, thoughtful artist, and so successful, and this is the price? Just insane. Weirdly, I feel like I got the tiniest taste of Princess Diana's final moments and really, thank God we came out alive. The driver was insanely good (although Bob knew my driving skills, so I hope he was comforted that I was ready to jump in if needed). We left the narrow roads and screeched into and through another underground lot. I had no idea where we were or where we were going. When the car finally stopped and we got out, we had somehow landed right at the red carpet, with hundreds of photographers snapping our picture. We climbed the red carpeted stairway to a platform and turned to see a sea of tens of thousands of people, fans, chanting and cheering in a deafening roar for Bob and the beautiful Sônia and Melanie. And there I was, somehow right next to them all, in a terrible rented tuxedo and my Six Pack style, saying to myself, "You'd better enjoy this because this will never ever happen again." And I was right; it never has.

Now what are the chances of having two death-defying car rides with the worldwide legend, Robert Redford himself, and living to tell the tale? Crazy, right?

KEVIN ARNOLD
TEACHES ME TO READ

*T*he *Wonder Years* was a game changer for me in so many ways.
Neal Marlens and Carol Black had written a brilliant pilot script,
and I was asked to audition for the role of the Narrator, the older
Kevin Arnold who was telling the whole story. The producers
wanted to cast the part of the unseen character without the bias
of seeing the actor doing it, so I went to a recording studio and
recorded it anonymously. It was a huge part, so much dialogue,
but it fit me like a glove. A kid in the 1960s, the exact same age as
I had been, living in a suburb that felt like Bethesda and my junior
high school, with neighborhoods where kids played football in
the street and eighteen-year-old brothers were being shipped off
to Vietnam. Written with such fondness, humor, and insight, this
narrator had observations into my own childhood that helped me
understand myself a little more. When I got to the final scene of

that audition, talking about walking through the neighborhood at night, seeing families through their windows and the blue lights of people's televisions, I was transported back to Bethesda, walking the neighborhood at night collecting my paper route money from my neighbors. I connected with the character so much that I felt like I just had to get the job. And I did. By the way, it turned out that Carol Black was my age and grew up in the town next to Bethesda, Silver Spring, Maryland. Like I said, it fit me like a glove.

It came time to make the deal. There really was no precedent for this type of part. The offer was low, about four thousand dollars an episode, but I didn't care about that much. I only asked for two things—to have freedom to continue to act in movies without the show interfering with that, and to be able to direct the show. They agreed to both. The only thing left to negotiate was my billing. It was a cast of unknowns so, having a bit of a reputation already, I could've been the first one billed, but that wouldn't make sense since Fred Savage was really going to be the star of the show. I could have been the final person billed, with a fancier credit like "And Daniel Stern as the Narrator" or "Daniel Stern as Adult Kevin Arnold," but both of those made it feel like my character was separate from the story and I didn't want to mess up the show's integrity. I thought it was important for the audience to just listen to my words and not think about me; just like at the audition, the unseen character played by an unknown actor. So, much to my agent's disbelief, I decided to take no billing at all. Just let my voice speak for itself . . . and Kevin Arnold.

Since I was going to direct an early episode, I shadowed the director of the pilot every day to get a feel for the style he was creating, as well as to get to know the actors and crew. Interestingly, they hired an actor to stand off camera and read the narration during the scenes, to give the actors the right timing to fill up those silent moments. Very smart idea, although weird to hear someone else doing my part. I gave the script to my brother, who by this point had moved to LA to be a television writer. I knew he could write this show, which was basically our childhood, and before we had even finished the pilot, David had written a brilliant future episode. Being on the set and in the editing room also gave me a chance to become friends with the producers, Neal and Carol. They were perfectionists, and I must have re-recorded different sections of the pilot at seven or eight different sessions. The show turned out to be amazing, and not only did the network pick it up for a series, but they also decided to premiere the show in the best TV slot possible, right after the Super Bowl. I gave David's spec script to Neal and Carol, and they wisely hired him, as he went on to write some of the show's best episodes and has had a sensational career himself. Narrating, directing, still a free agent for films, and with my brother working on the show—it was the perfect gig.

I would swing by the writer's room sometimes to see David and Neal and play basketball during their breaks. One day, I happened to mention that I had been offered a movie that was going to shoot in Africa. The script wasn't that great, and I wasn't going to do it, but it would be awesome to go to Africa. Neal was worried that it might mess up the scheduling of the recording sessions for the show, and I reassured him it wasn't going to happen (and it didn't). But evidently Neal was not reassured, because my agent got a call the very next day informing him that I was fired. Ouch! Even though my contract explicitly said I was free to do any other movie I wanted to—and that I hadn't even taken the movie— Neal had second thoughts and decided to get rid of me before the pilot aired. What a two-faced asshole he turned out to be. I was devastated. I loved the show, I loved my part, and I was very upset about losing my directing opportunity too. And it made it awkward for my brother who, of course, had to stay in this break-through job. The show premiered after the Super Bowl, with the very talented Arye Gross now narrating the story instead of me. I was bummed watching it and kind of pissed off because I had gotten fired for no good reason whatsoever, with Neal Marlens taking something I said so off-handedly, as a friend hanging out, to stab me in the back.

But then a crazy thing happened. The very next day, my agent got a call from the studio asking to rehire me. To this day, I still have no idea who brought me back, but somebody thought that whatever I was bringing to the role elevated it to a different level, and that I was an important member of the cast. It worked out beautifully. They tripled my salary, gave me bonus payments each time I had to re-record in the studio, guaranteed me three directing jobs per season, and reiterated the terms which allowed me to take any other job I wanted, anywhere in the world. I pretended there were no hard feelings toward Neal because my brother was working with him, and I would work with him closely while directing, but I never trusted him again. He is a very small man, with an enormous chip on his shoulder, and I think the fact that I am a foot taller than him makes him very competitive with me. That little fucker separated my shoulder when he blindsided me with a vicious hit during what was supposed to be a very casual game of touch football. He and Carol created a brilliant show and hired an outstanding writing staff and terrifically talented actors, but he really couldn't handle the pressure of producing great tele-vision every week. I was very happy when he left after the first season and Bob Brush came in to helm the show through all of the following seasons.

I absolutely loved directing. Fred, Danica, Josh, Olivia, and Jason were fantastic young people. I loved them like my own children and directed them that way too. Dan Lauria and

Alley Mills, top-notch actors, played the parents. I loved leading the crew and trying to get the best out of each person. The director is the conductor, aware of what note every instrument is playing, making sure they are all in harmony as they bring the score/script to life, and directing *The Wonder Years* was like leading the most talented orchestra in the world. I directed ten episodes, and it was like getting paid to go to film school. I grew in confidence on the set and loved the discipline of having to meet tight schedules and find creative solutions within those limits. And I loved working with actors, watching them.

When I first had to audition actors, I would hide in the back of the room, embarrassed to be the director, on the other side of the casting game. Knowing how much each actor wanted/ needed the job, I felt bad they had to go through the humiliation of auditioning, when each one of them is overqualified to begin with. But over the years, I realized that the actors are having fun—enjoying their chance to perform, putting themselves on the line with an outrageous choice of characterization, willing to take directions and help bring the story to life, picking up their instrument and seeing if they fit into this orchestra. After years of feeling like acting was a self-aggrandizing profession for egomaniacs, watching actors audition and perform, exposing their deepest feelings for our entertainment, education, and enjoyment, finally made me realize the nobility and importance of the acting profession.

I loved watching Fred and the gang grow up. They all had high academic ambition and were wrapped up in their on-set school, coming out to do their scenes but really thinking about whatever the hell they were studying in there. Fred went to Stanford, Danica is a brilliant mathematician who has written math books, Josh is a lawyer, and on and on. They have great parents who helped them navigate the minefield of being child actors. For my money, being a child actor is a lose/lose situation for a kid. Either you try and fail, personally rejected by the powers-that-be, which can really take a toll on a young ego, or you are in a hit TV show or movie, and then you have to deal with the consequences of fame, money, puberty, and all the rest of it in the public eye. *The Wonder Years* kids and their families dealt with it as well as any I have ever seen.

My salary kept going up and up, although not that high by today's standards, but it was easy money. And when I was shooting a film, I was getting two paychecks at the same time (sweet!), going into recording studios in Chicago, Reno, San Francisco, Rome, or wherever I was on location to record for *The Wonder Years*. When I was doing *City Slickers* in Santa Fe, I had to get the narration out fast for broadcast and couldn't find a recording studio in time, so I had the sound guy from the film come over to the house I was renting, and we recorded it there. It was a very echo-y tile house, so I actually recorded it on my bed, in my pajamas, with the blanket over my head to deaden the sound and a flashlight to read the script. When we sent it in, they loved the quality of the recording and wondered what studio we used. Go figure. The other unforeseen bonus to the job was I was suddenly hot in the commercial voiceover world. The Madison Avenue commercial people are a whole other breed of human, and trying to please those executives can be a trying experience. When I recorded a commercial for Burger King, I must have said, "The winds of change are blowing with a sandwich made a whole new way," about six thousand times, in every possible inflection, before that idiot director finally thought it was perfect. What the fuck does that even mean? It was a hamburger, for fuck's sake!

But maybe the most life-changing thing about my wonderful years on *The Wonder Years* was that I actually learned to read. I had already gotten a little bit better at reading from reading more and more scripts. I even ventured into reading books for fun every so often, once I discovered Harry Crews and Elmore Leonard, although they still took me a while, fighting through my dyslexia. The years of reading *The Wonders Years* stories out loud, week after week, year after year, vanquished my fear of reading out loud, of the dreaded "cold reading," a fear I thought I would never overcome. I can now pick up any book or script or article and read it cold, almost flawlessly, with meaning and understanding. I have no idea how I do it, except that so many times I was handed a new rewrite of a *Wonder Years* script and had to read it cold, with meaning and understanding, so my brain learned how to process the information and make it come out of my mouth, while keeping me and my fears out of the way. I am still flabbergasted and proud every time I do that.

Narrating the show was the opportunity of a lifetime. Every script was great, and I loved my part in each one. Every week I got to tell my story to America. Sure, I was playing Kevin Arnold, remembering his stories. But his stories always felt like my stories—my first kiss, bad teachers, great teachers, my older sister, being a hippie, the music, and on and on. My connection to the show was bone-deep and the connection the show had with audiences, and still has, makes me deeply thankful to have been the voice of this seismic cultural experience.

The show ended after six years, one short of where I think it should have ended. If Kevin had had one more year, we would have watched him graduate high school and deal with the final coming-of-age rituals that happen at that time. But for whatever reason, they pulled the plug. It was a late decision, and the writers had to try to write a decent finale in a very short time, with no chance of the real groundwork being laid in the shows leading up to the last one. But like the true champions they were, they wrote a beautiful final script, wrapping up stories, giving glimpses into the future and saying a heartfelt goodbye to the audience that had been with us the whole time. In the final moment of the show, the premise of the whole series, that Kevin Arnold is now an older man telling the story of his childhood, comes into play for the first and only time. Suddenly there is another voice on the narration track, the voice of a child talking to the Narrator, interrupting his story-telling and asking him to come outside and play. I don't remember whose idea it was, but that very last day, I brought my son Henry to the studio and he read those lines, playing the unseen son to my unseen character. Like I said, from the very first time I read it, *The Wonder Years* always felt like it was really my own personal story that I was telling every week, and having Henry there bringing it to a close was almost more than I could handle. The recording session lasted much longer than usual because I kept crying in the middle of the reading, so sad to see it end and so proud of what we had accomplished.

ENTER JOE ROTH

Life was very full at this point. California started to feel like home. With the money from the New York co-op and the movies, we bought the rental house in Beverly Hills Post Office. Henry and Sophie consumed our lives, driving them back and forth to each of their schools, play dates, sports teams. When Henry was five, I signed up to coach the T-ball team in the Beverly Hills Little League, loving teaching those little boys and girls the game and soaking in their innocence. (Throughout their childhoods, I coached all of my kids' baseball and basketball teams.) The joy increased exponentially when our third child, Ella, was born. At her birth, we had a different doctor in a different hospital, but I felt the same awe when I got to pull her out by the shoulders and announce her arrival, "It's a girl!"—which was the right call, because she was, in fact, a girl. (Two out of three ain't bad.) I was only thirty-one and had a ton of energy, which was needed to put the time and focus into raising three very different kids, each with their own needs and at very different developmental stages. Laure had become the greatest mom, wife, and partner in the world, and kept our lives organized and our bellies full. And while the kids were young, we decided that instead of me leaving everyone at home when I got a movie out of town, everyone would come with me. When Laure was a teenager, her father was in the foreign service and was stationed in Spain, Malaysia, and the Philippines. Every time the family moved, Laure watched her mother find a house to live in, schools to attend, stores to shop at, and cultural experiences to learn from for the kids. Who knew that all of that would come into play in our lives, but she was built for this. Working on good films and bringing my family with me was my deepest dream come true.

Joe Roth is one of the most brilliant movie producers and executives ever to participate in show business—starting his own company, Morgan Creek, then running 20th Century Fox, then Disney, Revolution, and on and on. I didn't even think about who had those executive positions at this point because my boss was always the director, and I didn't need to please anyone but them. Morgan Creek was producing some of the best films around, but Joe decided to take a break from producing and to get behind the camera and direct a sweet little film called *Coupe de Ville*, another terrific coming-of-age story of three brothers on a road trip needing to readjust to life with the news that their father is dying. I really liked the script, and the part was a tough Air Force pilot, the oldest brother and disciplinarian, very different than any role I had ever gotten to play. Joe and I met, and he gave me the part. He had loved the coming-of-age movies I had been in, *Breaking Away* and *Diner*, and I think wanted to capture some of that feeling in this movie. We shot the film in Florida and South

Carolina, and Laure packed us all up and moved us into houses and neighborhoods in both places, even finding summer camp for the kids. Not only did Joe and I hit it off right away, but Joe's wife Donna and Laure became fast friends. They were in the same boat as us, with a newborn baby, finding housing, shooting the film, and we all became friends for life during that time. Joe was a really good director, very encouraging and focused on the nuances of each character. He had a clear vision of the film but was also open to letting the actors own their characters and improvise. Maybe a little too open.

It was a comedy, but the storylines were filled with conflict, which the cast was more than capable of creating. It was an intimidating joy to do scenes with the hyper-talented Alan Arkin. He played my father, and watching the subtlety he brought to everything he did was like getting a masterclass acting lesson in real time, forcing me to find the simplest truth in each and every beat of a scene. And off camera, his humility as a person and an artist were life lessons in themselves. My younger brother was played by Arye Gross, the actor who had temporarily replaced me on *The Wonder Years*. Arye and I became fast friends, had a great time doing our scenes together, and really bonded over dealing with the actor who played our youngest brother, Patrick Dempsey. Patrick was an up-and-coming young star, handsome and funny. He had done a couple of teen comedies, but he acted like he was a major movie star. He was probably around twenty-three, and he had recently married his acting coach/manager/guru, Rocky, who was about twenty-five years older than him, and the two of them set out to undermine the director and take over the film. I have worked with arrogant actors, but I have never seen anything like this. Rocky would be on the set, and after we did a take, instead of coming over with the rest of us to talk to the director about adjustments he might like to make in the scene, Patrick would beeline to Rocky, who would whisper her notes to him. It was incredibly disrespectful, but Joe didn't want to cause a problem with one of his lead actors, so he tried to manage the situation rather than confront it. Rocky's notes to Patrick seemed to be all about how to draw attention to himself at every moment of every scene, even if that meant not doing the dialogue, taking other people's lines, doing extraneous physical business to distract, and whatever else the two of them came up with in their fucking little confabs. I got tired of that shit real fast and told him so. He said his character was a clownish person and he was just playing it to push my character's buttons, which would be fine if that was what the director asked us to do. But this had nothing to do with the collaboration that needs to take place on a film set and everything to do with ambition and self-aggrandizement.

I finally lost my shit one day. The movie is called *Coupe de Ville* because the three brothers are driving their father's prized car across the country so he can have it back before he dies, and my character is the one who does all the driving. The picture car was a beautiful and rare car and, both as the character and the actor driving it, I had to take really good care of it. We were shooting a scene of us driving down the highway, talking about something or other, and Patrick was riding shotgun. In one of the stupidest improvisational moments in film history, Patrick slides over to me, pins my foot down on the gas pedal, and tries to wrestle control of the steering wheel from me. The camera crew was driving right beside us, filming from an open truck, and this putz risked crashing into them, running us all off the road, and killing people. I slammed my elbow into him to get him off of me and he finally slid back to his side of the bench seat. I pulled the car over, went around the car, and pulled him out. I think he scared himself, or at least knew he had crossed a line, but still tried to laugh it off as just "improv." The crew pulled us apart before a real fight began, but I made it clear I wasn't going to play that way anymore. From then on, Joe took more control of things, Rocky was not allowed on the set, and Patrick got moved to the back seat. Assholes.

Joe and I really bonded over it all. When we got back to LA, our families were still seeing each other regularly. He knew that I was interested in directing, and when he decided to shoot an additional scene to open the movie, which had younger actors playing the three brothers, he asked me to come to the shoot and help him direct the child actors, since I had experience doing that from *The Wonder Years*. I offered absolutely no help whatsoever, but it was flattering to be respected in that way. And this was just the beginning of the influence Joe had on my career and my life. Joe was not only editing the film, but secretly negotiating to leave his own company and take the job of running 20th Century Fox. Only a couple of months later, I was in Chicago shooting a film, and Joe had taken the reins at Fox. He called me up one day with very exciting news: "Hey, I just bought your movie." That movie was *Home Alone*.

"SO WHAT IS
JOE PESCI REALLY LIKE?"

I wish I had footage of myself the first time I read the script for *Home Alone*. I was alone in the house, lying on the sofa in the living room, and it was the first time I read a script that made me laugh so hard that I got stomach cramps. John Hughes's screenplay was a masterpiece, the perfect family Christmas story. He thought of some of the best physical comedy gags ever and he wrote them with such specificity, shot by shot, that it was like watching the movie already made. It would be a riot to see what I must have looked like reading it—rolling off the sofa in laughter and then tearing up when the neighbor saves the day and the family reunites—like a crazy person going through every emotion in the world by himself in a room. From page one, I started to see myself in the role of Marv Merchants. I absolutely loved physical comedies when I was a kid—Stooges, Chaplin, Keaton, Marx

Brothers, Bugs Bunny—but that kind of comedy had fallen out of favor, and John's script was brilliant in bringing that lost art form back to the big screen. By the time I put the script down, I was determined to get that part!

I can't remember what scenes were used for the audition, but I met the director, Chris Columbus, in the National Lampoon offices at Warner Brothers. I listened to Chris's vision for the film and then did the scenes a few times. He seemed to like what I did, but when I was driving home, I felt disappointed in myself. I replayed the scenes in my head, and thought about the vision Chris had talked about, and I suddenly understood exactly how I should have played it. I pulled over, called my agent, and asked them to call Chris and ask if I could come back and try it again. My agent assured me that wasn't necessary, but I insisted, and I stayed on hold until he got the okay that I could go back to Warner Brothers and try it again. So I did. Chris told me later that he had already decided to cast me and there was no need to come back, but I didn't know that. I wanted to give myself my best chance to be a part of something very original and laugh-out-loud funny. And it was a good chance to really try to play Marv for the first time and lock in with Chris and John's vision of the film.

My agent made the deal, the same as I had gotten on *Coupe de Ville*, three hundred thousand dollars for six weeks of work. I was very happy with the deal but feeling anxious and guilty about leaving the family behind; it was too much to ask Laure to move us all again. Just before I was about to leave, I got a call saying they had redone the shooting schedule and they would now need me for eight weeks instead of six. They were asking me to add on 33 percent more shooting time, so I asked if they were going to raise my salary the same amount, and they said they were not. My agent said to just do it anyway, that when you get to this pay level, you commit to the project, and the weekly salary doesn't matter. But I was still in the blue-collar work paradigm of getting a daily or weekly rate for one's work and I didn't think it was fair, since the deal had been set for a month or so. My guilt at leaving my family further clouded my thinking, and I ended up making one of the stupidest decisions in my show business life—I backed out of the movie. They hired another actor, and he and Pesci started rehearsals in Chicago. I still had *The Wonder Years* directing and acting work, but I realized quickly what a mistake I had made and was kicking myself for letting my pride get in the way of doing something I deeply wanted to do. The gods somehow intervened (and when I say "gods," I mean Joe Pesci), because after a couple days of rehearsal, I got the call that they wanted me back in the movie and that they would honor the original contract and make the schedule six weeks. By that point, I was so full of regret that I would have done it even if it took six months to shoot!

Within a day, I was sitting in a restaurant in Chicago with Joe and Chris, laughing, drinking beer, and talking through the film. Chris wanted us to be as scary as we could at the beginning of the film so the audience would feel a real threat to the kid, and who better to scare people than Joe Fucking Pesci. Joe said he was going to make up a cartoon language for when Harry gets angry and frustrated, which Chris loved. Marv was always the dumber and sillier one, so I was looking for my way to play against Joe. In Stooges talk, Joe was Moe, and I was a cross between Larry and Curly. It was so fun to work with the costumer to find just the right look—the coat, sweater, and shoes—and with the makeup artist to figure out just what kind of damage an iron was going to do to my face. We shot on location at the house that has now become a tourist destination spot but at the time was just a nice house in a nice neighborhood, with the locals hanging out on the sidewalk right there with the movie crew. It was winter in Chicago, so it wasn't pleasant, but it was perfect for creating the look of the Norman Rockwell Christmas that we were going for. Joe and I started with a few of the scenes parked in our van, plotting our fool-proof strategy, and it was a nice way to break the ice, but the fun began when we actually started to try to break into the house.

This film had absolutely no special effects. Everything in it really happened, relying on great camera work, great props, and great stunt people. The first physical comedy scene I shot was Marv going down the outside stairs to break into the basement. Kevin, that little devil, has made the steps icy, sending Marv falling and sliding down the stairs on his back. We started shooting the scene. I walked to the top of the stairs, scanned my surroundings, took my first step onto the icy stairs, slipped, and fell backwards out of the shot and onto a nice soft landing pad behind me, just off camera. We did a few takes and got some funny ones. Then they set up for the stunt of Marv actually sliding down the concrete stairs. Leon Delaney, my brilliant stuntman, took his place at the top of the stairs, Chris said, "Action," and I watched in painful amazement as Leon threw himself up in the air, landed hard on his spine at the top stair and proceeded to slide down the entire flight of concrete stairs on his back, landing in a heap at the bottom. Holy shit, it was something to see, so painfully funny, and the whole crew applauded loudly—and set up for take two. Leon did it again, and then again, each time adjusting to Chris and the stunt coordinator's notes to "Jump a little higher," "Slide a little bumpier," and "Keep your face hidden," until they got it exactly how they wanted it.

I vividly remember sitting with Leon that night between takes and asking him, "Doesn't that hurt?"

"Fuck yeah, it hurts."

"So why do you do it?"

"Because I have two girls in college and Daddy's got to pay the bills . . . and besides, it's really fun." It started to dawn on me just how far we were going to take the physical comedy, that it really was a live-action cartoon. They moved the camera to the bottom of the stairs for the shots of me sliding down the last few stairs, getting up, and breaking into the house. Leon gave me his body pads, apologizing for how sweaty they were (even in freezing weather). They felt good to have on, ready to take a hit like I was wearing football pads, and I decided to go for it as best I could. I slid down enough stairs to get good momentum to crash land on the bottom landing. I thought it would be fun to make it super slippery when I tried to stand up, and I had the set decorators grease the landing to make it easy to slide around. At one point, I brought my slip-and-slide to an abrupt end by sliding my feet out to the side to brace myself in the narrow stairwell, channeling a Roadrunner cartoon, the way something chaotic comes to a sudden, frozen, comic halt. It was a small beat but felt just right, and the crew and Chris loved it. The scene was really funny, and I now understood how this movie was going to work—Leon would do the big stunts, but I was going to have to keep up my end of the bargain and bring this cartoon to life when it was my turn in front of the camera. Joe's stunt double was Troy Brown, a former rodeo rider who was tough as nails. I watched him and Leon do such dangerous things that any other normal human would end up in the hospital if they did them— falling from the staircase after the paint cans to the face, climbing across the rope in the backyard and then crashing into the side of the house—but because of their professionalism, they not only survived but thrived in their craft.

There were so many fun gags to play—the nail in the foot, glass Christmas bulbs crushed into my feet, paint can to the face, iron to the face, BB gun to the face (my face took a beating!)— it's hard to pick a favorite because I loved doing them all. John had written each one so vividly, and the way Chris and the cinematographer shot them brought them to life just as I had imagined. I knew just what Marv was supposed to look like in each shot, with each lens, just how Redford had taught me, although in a very different milieu. The prop department was genius, creating such realistic props that it made you feel like each gag was really happening. Christmas bulbs made of sugar crunching under my feet made me feel the pain that poor Marv was feeling. Driving a rubber nail into my foot and feeling a foam iron smash me in the face are as close as I ever want to get to having those things really happen, but what an opportunity to get to play it out in such a funny and safe way. The worst I ever got hurt was doing one of the simple scenes. It was a perfect comic frame, sticking my big face through the doggy-door and right into the camera, with a big shit-eating grin, only to get shot in the face with a BB gun and have to pull my head back out again. The problem was that my nose is so fucking big that not once, but twice, I clipped it on the frame of the doggy-door when I was pulling my head out and gave myself a bad bloody nose. It's those little ones you think are simple that will get you every time.

But the weirdest one had to be the scene when I have a tarantula crawl on my face. The day came to shoot that scene and I assumed the genius prop department would come up with a realistic-looking tarantula, but when I got to the set, the prop was just a rubber bug, no mechanics for it to move or crawl. That's when they brought in the "Tarantula Wrangler" and introduced me to a very large and scary-looking spider. The wrangler explained to me that they had done some tests where he had let it crawl on his face and nothing bad happened, so it was probably safe. I asked how he trains a tarantula and he said that they are not really trainable, but as long as I didn't make any sudden moves, I should be fine. He explained where the poison is located on the spider, how it bites, and how long you have to live once you get bitten. He told me that they could remove the poison, but that the tarantula would then die. I said I understood, but if the tarantula bit me then *I* would die, so maybe we should think about removing the poison. But I could tell that was not going to happen. The scene had me lying on the floor, not noticing the spider crawling up my body until it eventually crawls across my face, at which point I scream with fear. I was concerned that when it came time for me to scream in the scene, that might scare the tarantula and cause it to attack me, but the wrangler brushed off my concern, telling me that spiders can't hear. I guess that could be true, since as far as I know, spiders don't have ears, but this question had never come up in my entire life. I was going to have to hope for the best. Before the camera rolled, they had it crawl around my face, just to get it used to the terrain, and I started to get comfortable with it. By this point in the filming, I was loving the challenge of each individual stunt and gag, and ready to take a few chances. Once I got comfortable, I could really let it rip. They rolled the cameras and released the tarantula onto my face. It just walked around randomly but any time it got into a good camera position, I was ready to go. The crew squirmed, watching it go in my mouth and all over my head, and that only made it more fun. I wanted the scream to sound like the woman being attacked in the shower in the movie *Psycho*, and I think I got pretty close. Once we got those shots, we moved on to the equally dangerous part where Pesci beats me with a crowbar. Joe had a rubber crowbar, and I had a pad protecting my stomach, but he got me good a couple of times on unprotected areas. Quite a badge of honor, to have been beaten by The Man himself. God, did we have fun!

There were only a couple of scenes where Joe and I got to act with Macaulay, and he was as sweet a kid as he appears in the movie. Chris was so great with all the kids, directing them so that they felt they were doing a great job, making them feel safe, keeping things simple, giving them line readings, and acting out for them so they could mimic him and clearly know what he wanted. John Hughes didn't really spend much time on the set, trusting Chris completely—and probably spending his time writing all the great scripts that came after this one. We didn't have scenes with any of the cast except Macaulay, but we did get to cross paths with everyone and watch them work—Catherine O'Hara was a hero and great in the film, Kieran Culkin was just as funny at age seven as he is now, and John Candy's improvisations had everyone rolling on the floor with astonished laughter. But the biggest treat was that John Heard played the dad. An amazing twist of fate that the stranger who took me into his home my very first day in New York and I would now be doing our third movie together.

I rented a little apartment outside of Winnetka and ate at the Wendy's next door just about every night, barely able to take care of myself on the road. I missed my family so much, but it was frustrating trying to talk to the kids on the phone because, frankly, they were boring as hell. In person, we talked and played and did homework, but on the phone, everything was a monosyllabic answer. They wanted to get back to real life, not answer questions from a disembodied dad on a phone call. At some point during the shooting, Warner Brothers decided the budget was getting too expensive and wanted to unload the movie. I got that call from Joe Roth, who had been running 20th Century Fox for less than a week. He saw the footage of what we had shot and scooped up the movie, seeing the potential the film had. I finished my six-week stint and was glad to get home to Laure and the kids and our friends—and started looking for my next job, with no idea that the film I had just put in the can would become the worldwide cultural phenomenon that it has become.

THE SECRET OF MY SUCCESS? . . .
GETTING FIRED!

I loved our sweet little house on Highridge Drive in Beverly Hills Post Office. I was so lucky to have found this little oasis. It was a last-minute decision not to move to Woodstock, which was going to be the cure for the claustrophobia and pressure caused by living in Manhattan for twelve years, and our house on the top of the canyon felt like we had moved to the country. But our little, secret, natural hideaway had been discovered by rich assholes bound and determined to make it theirs, and in doing so make it not little or secret or natural or a hideaway.

Some pretentious prick bought the house next door and started doing major construction to transform a modest house into a palace, including drilling pylons right next to our house to support the upper deck swimming pool he was putting in. It drove me insane. Pastureland a block away, where sheep used to graze, was plowed over to build Beverly Park, now one of the most exclusive gated communities in the world, home to Sylvester Stallone, Eddie Murphy, oil barons, and such. We started looking around LA for what would be the equivalent of Woodstock, a couple of hours outside of town where we could buy a house in nature, with a lot of space and privacy. We looked in Ojai and Santa Barbara, but they were too expensive and had already been discovered by the pompous glitterati anyway.

Laure's family had a tiny, nine-hundred-square-foot summer cabin in the middle of a national forest in Lake Tahoe that we got to use for a couple of weeks each year, another little, secret, natural hideaway, with no entitled assholes in sight. The water was pristine and icy, and we spent every day at the beach, playing and swimming with the kids. This year in particular was fantastic. Our kids started hanging out with some other kids on the small beach, and Laure and I got to be friendly with their parents and grandparents. We had cookouts and got to know each other and told them of our desire to move out of LA. One of the families was from a place called Half Moon Bay, a small town right on the beach, an hour away from San Francisco, with good schools and modest prices. It sounded like the perfect town for us but was probably too far from LA to move to. But I decided to take a peek at it on the drive home, and the amazingly generous people from the beach gave us the keys to their house so we could spend the night there. Since it was going to be a lot of extra schlepping, Laure and the girls took a plane home, and Henry and I drove the loaded-up Chevy Suburban to Half Moon Bay. It was spectacular, with a Pacific Ocean beach with huge rock formations. The farms on the hillside were like out of a painting. We drove through the neighborhoods, by the little league field and the elementary school, and I could really envision raising our family there. The house we stayed in was in a very nice, suburban-feeling neighborhood, and Henry and I went to dinner that night at a place called The Distillery, right on the water. We decided to eat on the outdoor porch, with the waves crashing and mist overtaking us. It was an incredible night with Henry, but I was really wishing Laure was there so we could have shared the absolute romance of this day and night.

The next morning, we packed up for the drive to LA, and as we passed through town, I spotted a real estate office and decided to pick up one of those real estate listing magazines to bring home to Laure, just so we could fantasize about it together. I spoke to a very nice realtor there. The prices for homes with land were so affordable compared with Ojai and Santa Barbara, the schools were great, and it was so easy to get to the San Francisco airport and get a plane to LA if you had to. She told me of a house in an even smaller town a few miles up the coast called Moss Beach. This house was on seven acres, overlooked the ocean, and was seven hundred and fifty thousand dollars. She asked if I wanted to go look at it right then, since I was there, just to see, and that is what we did. Moss Beach was a tiny town that consisted of one block with a bar, a pizza place, and a video store, all a person really needs. We drove up the hill above the town to a dirt road and took that small road until it came to a dead end and some impressive-looking gates. The gates opened, and an incredible, tiled villa and guesthouse laid out in front of me, with the Pacific Ocean right below. We went inside, and it was like out of a magazine—huge windows, professional kitchen, bedrooms galore, and an interior courtyard, complete with swimming pool. There was a sauna and steam room, but my mind was officially blown when I got to the "his and hers" bathrooms and the "his" bathroom had a urinal. Who ever heard of having a urinal in your house? It all made me laugh, especially the thought that all of this could be had for seven hundred and fifty thousand dollars. I called Laure from a pay phone and told her I thought I found our new house. We talked about it all week and flew up the next weekend so she could see it. She was blown away by it too, and we felt our vision of living in a small town in the countryside with a bit of land was finally within our reach. We bought it the next day and started making plans to move in time for the kids to start the new school year there, which was only about six weeks away.

I was prepping for directing an episode of *The Wonder Years*—scouting locations, casting, scheduling—when I got a call to go in as soon as I could to audition for a new Billy Crystal movie called *City Slickers* because Rick Moranis had just dropped out and the movie started shooting very soon. I got the script delivered to my house that night. Like *Home Alone*, the script was absolutely perfect, full of great characters, inventive, truthful, insightful, action-packed, and with fall-on-the-floor laughs. The character was Phil, a sweet, self-loathing guy with a terrible wife, who had so many good moments of comedy, heroism, and friendship over the course of the movie. By the time I finished the script, I wanted this one a lot. I went in the next day and, holy shit, there was Billy Crystal! And a bunch of other people who I would end up knowing well but at the time were a blur because, holy shit, I was going to read the scenes with Billy Crystal! I knew this character very well, the jokes were natural to me, the rhythms perfect, and the audition felt like a home run. Sure enough, I got the job. It was shooting in Colorado and New Mexico in ten days, but I needed to start right away with horseback riding lessons at a ranch in Griffith Park, because so much of the movie takes place on horseback. My agent got me four hundred and fifty thousand dollars, a surprising and enormous leap in salary. The tough part was it was going to take three and a half months to shoot. I was in almost every scene, so there would probably be no time for any trips home, and it was right when we were supposed to be moving to our new house in Moss Beach. But I had to say yes, and I had to say it fast. The producers at *The Wonder Years* were great and said of course to take the job and that I could direct a different episode when I got back. The nice thing was that they agreed to replace me with my first assistant director, who would finally get his break to make the leap to being a director. Before I knew it, I was in Griffith Park staring at TJ, who had been chosen to be my horse in the movie.

Horses and I do not get along. I have already told you of my death-defying horse-riding experience on the set of *Samson and Delilah* in Durango, Mexico. The only other time I had been on a horse was when Laure and I were on our honeymoon trip to England. We took a very freaky side trip to the Moors, land of ghostly spirits (check out my episode of the TV show *Ghost Stories*), but it got dangerous when the owners of the inn we were staying at gave Laure and me their trail horses and sent us on our way. The horses were very old and slow, and I started to relax, letting go of my PTSD. Laure was a natural on the horse (and is now an accomplished rider), and it all felt right out of a postcard or TV commercial—young lovers on horseback, sun shining, flowers blooming. But things changed rapidly when, from out of nowhere, a helicopter came tearing across the landscape, flying as low as a crop duster, and buzzing right over us. Both of our horses reared up on their back legs, something they probably hadn't done in fifteen years. I held on for dear life and watched my wife hold on for hers. The horses bolted, galloping across the moors. Luckily, they were old, so they ran out of gas after a couple hundred yards. We got off those fucking horses, walked them back to the bed and breakfast, and drank whiskey with the weirdos in the bar until our nerves calmed. The point being, horses and I don't get along.

TJ was different. TJ was a real movie horse. He had done a lot of movies, maybe more than me. His trainer was Jack Lilley, a legendary horseman and stuntman. I told Jack my bad experiences and fears, but he didn't care. He knew I *had* to learn to ride because the movie started shooting in a week and the first scenes were on horseback. Billy, Rick Moranis, and Bruno Kirby had all been training for months to prepare for the riding, and I had a lot of catching up to do. Jack basically took me on a pony ride, leading TJ around the arena and teaching me the fundamentals of how the gas pedal, brakes, and steering wheel work on these things. I held on tightly to the horn of the saddle and Jack kept telling me to let go, because "You can't ride like that," but my survival instincts were on high alert. Eventually I got the reins and walked TJ around the arena by myself. Well actually, TJ walked me. All I had to do was hold on. They had picked the mellowest horse in the stable, and he knew just how to handle me. It's supposed to be the rider who is the leader, in control and command of his horse, but every horse I have ever been around can read me easily and knows they are in charge of the situation, and TJ was no different. TJ was a pro. He knew his job. Jack and his trainers would tell TJ to do something, and he would do it. He broke into a trot when Jack clicked his tongue and stopped when he raised his hands. I moved the reins to guide him through a figure-eight pattern, but he already knew what he was supposed to be doing. My first-day confidence was building. I got a tiny glimmer of how this could work, although knowing all the herding of cattle, stampedes, and galloping that were written into the script, I was still very intimidated. But not as intimidated as when Billy and Bruno arrived at the arena.

Billy and Bruno had done *When Harry Met Sally* together, playing best friends, and the friendship stuck. Billy and the writers, Lowell Ganz and Babaloo Mandel, had written the part of Ed especially for Bruno. So just like the story, these two best friends were living their fantasy, getting horseback training from the best in the business and making a real Western movie. We kibitzed for a few minutes, and then they hopped up on their beautiful horses, already saddled by the wranglers, and took off. I watched them gallop and trot, even ride backwards. I watched them herd and rope cows. These guys had been training a lot and were proud of all they had accomplished. They tried to encourage me, but I obviously had a long way to go.

I was no better the second day than I was the first, which is to say ridiculously bad, especially considering the riding challenges that were coming up very quickly. The director, producers, and writers came out to Griffith Park to watch and work that day and I got to know everyone a bit more. The one issue seemed to be that I looked a little too young. We were all supposed to be having a mid-life crisis. Billy and Bruno were both ten years older than me, and everyone felt I didn't look "mid-life" enough. I tried on some glasses, which helped make me look a little older, and that seemed to solve the problem.

When I went for riding lessons on the third day, they had a makeup trailer in the parking lot. Billy and Bruno were doing tests on the progression of how dirty they should get over the course of the film. Evidently people were still a little nervous about how youthful I looked because the makeup folks tried some aging makeup on me. They put lines around my eyes, which I thought looked pretty fake. They tried more lines on my forehead, which looked even worse. But it hit an absurd level when they said they wanted to try a bald cap on me. I said I didn't think that was going to work. They agreed, but insisted I try it, just to show the producers. They squeezed a terrible-looking bald cap over the top part of my head, leaving my hair on the sides and the back showing. I guess they were going for the classic Larry David look, but with the aging makeup on my eyes and forehead, the look was much closer to Bozo the Clown. While Billy and Bruno were trying on their sexy, dirty cowboy look, I was looking in the mirror, horrified and embarrassed, thinking how terrible it would be to ruin such a wonderful script and movie by looking like I came straight from Ringling Brothers. The producers knocked on the door and said they wanted to speak with me, so I stepped out of the trailer to show them how ridiculous this look was. They agreed it was not the right look but said that was not what they wanted to talk to me about.

"We don't know if you know this, but the reason Rick Moranis left the film was that his wife has been diagnosed with a very serious form of cancer and Rick left to be with her."

"Oh my God, I had no idea."

"Yes, it's terrible. The thing is, he's changed his mind. He wants to come back to the movie. He and his wife decided it would be best for Rick to keep working and carry on with life. And so he wants to come back and be in the film."

"Oh, okay. So I guess I'm out?"

"We are so sorry. You would have been great. And thank you for being so understanding."

"Sure, I understand."

I mean, what was I going to say? It was such a loaded situation. It was so embarrassing to be fired on the spot with no warning and for no offense, and having the bald wig and clown makeup on felt like the perfect, humiliating costume to receive the news in. I couldn't even go back in the trailer. I grabbed my stuff and got in my car, where I pulled off the bald cap, wiped off my face, and drove home.

The first thing I did was call the folks at *The Wonder Years* and tell them I had been let go and wanted to come back and direct the episode I had left. The first AD and producers were mensches and said of course, because they knew how much it hurt to have the movie fall apart and how important it was for me to get back to work rather than stew in my own juices. I went back to work the next day and dove into prep again. In some ways, it was a relief. I had been about to ditch Laure and force her to pack up the whole house, move the family to the new house in Moss Beach, and start the kids in a new school all by herself. Now we could all start that new life together.

Two days later, I was at home when my agent called and said that Rick had changed his mind and was dropping out of the film again. They wanted me back. I was stunned, exhausted, and thoroughly confused. My agent said we might be able to get more money, but that was not the issue.

"The issue is I am back directing, which I love, and I can't be so flaky and leave again. It was wrong to leave Laure with all the responsibility and logistics of the huge move, especially since the whole thing was my idea to start with. And besides, I have my stupid pride. It was so embarrassing the way the firing happened that I don't really feel like going back. I have many other commitments and I am exhausted, and therefore please tell them that I pass, that I am not going to just pack up everything at the drop of a hat and leave my responsibilities." I hung up with my agent and felt the real weight of how tired this rollercoaster had made me. I went into the bedroom and fell asleep. To this day, I remember it as one of the deepest and most energizing naps I have ever had.

When I woke up, I realized what a stupid decision I had made! My pride had made me shortsighted, just like it did when I left *Home Alone*. What an opportunity I was throwing away—an incredible part, the best actors, a ton of money, experiences I would never have any other way—and my wife was willing to shoulder unfathomable burdens to see that the family was taken care of while I pursued these dreams. I came out of the bedroom to messages on my answering machine from Billy, the director, the producers, and my agent, all begging me to reconsider. I was already planning to beg them to take me back, so it was nice to be begged as well. I called everyone back, told them what a great nap I had, that I was an idiot, and that I couldn't wait to get started. I once again backed out of my directing job at *The Wonder Years*, which was embarrassing, but the First AD couldn't have been happier. The next day I packed up my stuff and had a very nice panic attack and cry, with Laure and the kids comforting me and telling me that everything would be fine. I took a small plane to Durango, Colorado. Upon arrival, the teamster driver didn't take me to the hotel or the production office, but instead drove me into the beautiful mountains outside the town. I was met by Jack Lilley, a few other wranglers, and TJ, saddled up and ready to go. The sun was setting as Jack led us on a trail ride into God's country, TJ surefooted and steady on the tight mountain trails, and me holding on to the saddle horn for dear life.

RIDE 'EM, COWBOY!

It was a great way to start the film, shot out of a cannon into an unknown situation, needing to do things I had no idea how to do and wanting to not only survive but succeed. After all, that is exactly what *City Slickers* is about, and my character, Phil, is probably the least prepared of all the friends. The first scenes we shot took place in the middle of the movie, in the thick of the shitstorm, having completely lost control of the cows, who escape into the woods, and which we must somehow capture and drive back to the main herd. I was on TJ's back, riding chaotically through a forest of trees, herding a hundred cows while a rain machine blasted a torrential downpour. Billy had an amazing horse named Beechnut who he could get to do all sorts of tricks— walking backwards, sideways, cross-stepping stuff. (They bonded so much that he kept Beechnut after the movie was over.) Bruno was also quite comfortable in the saddle. Mickey Gilbert was the stunt coordinator on the film. He had become a Hollywood legend when he doubled Redford in *Butch Cassidy and the Sundance Kid*, jumping off the waterfall in the iconic scene of that movie. I had worked with Mickey on four films already—*Honky Tonk Freeway, Blue Thunder, Milagro Beanfield War,* and *Coupe de Ville*—and I loved and admired him. He knew I liked to play and have fun doing stunts, and I knew I could trust him with my life and he would never put me in danger by asking me to do something he didn't think I could do. On the wide shots, and shots where we had to gallop, Troy Gilbert, one of Mickey's sons, doubled for me, but I was doing a lot of the riding myself. They all knew I had no idea how to ride, but Troy would rehearse TJ for each particular shot so by the time I got on his back, I just had to hold on and let TJ do his thing.

Ron Underwood was the perfect director for the film. He had a great eye for real-feeling action that made room for the characters and the comedy to shine through. He is a kind and reasonable man, and maybe most importantly, collaborative. This was Billy's vision from the beginning. He developed the script, wrote it with Lowell and Babaloo, executive produced the movie, starred in it, and was intimately involved in all aspects of the film, including hiring Ron. So Ron was very respectful of Billy's input, but not to the point of being a pushover. He had a firm hand on the set and was very organized, leading the crew with great humor through mud and rain and cow shit to get every scene shot and every moment covered with no stress. Billy and he would talk after each take, maybe watch video playback, and make sure everyone was happy before we moved on to the next shot. We got through those first tough days with no problems—until the dailies came back.

It was a tradition at the time to screen dailies almost every night after the shoot. The cast and crew were invited to watch the footage so that everyone could see what had been shot and the director and crew could make adjustments. They served food and beer, and it was a great way to unwind together and enjoy new friends outside of work. So about three days into the shoot, we all gathered in the production office for the first day of dailies. Two astounding things happened.

The first is that it turns out that on film, I was a better horseback rider than either Billy or Bruno. And when I say better, I mean worse. My horseback riding was so bad that I was getting huge laughs. Billy and Bruno were riding like the semi-professionals that they had become—low in the saddle, reins loose in the hands, and commanding their horses. But I looked like a real city slicker, hanging on to the horn, sliding around the saddle, unbalanced, and bouncing up and down, investing my real ineptitude and fear into my character's comic lines and actions. I looked ridiculously out of my element, and TJ had made me feel safe enough to find the comedy and the character. Billy was sitting up front, and when the reel ended, he had an epiphany. "Fucking Stern is getting all the laughs. We are supposed to *not* know how to ride, just like him. Bruno and I need to ride a lot worse because we look like we know what we're doing." The next day of shooting, the two of them tried to ride as badly as I did, but they couldn't even come close. They bounced around and tried to look unbalanced, but they had gotten too good. It took them a few days of shooting to finally be able to be as convincingly bad at riding as I was. Next time you watch the film, see if you can spot it.

The second thing that happened at those first dailies was not as trivial. Bruno was playing a city slicker who was a wanna-be tough guy, complete with a Burt Reynolds-style mustache, and thought it would be good for his character to have a big wad of chewing tobacco in his cheek. But while we were watching the dailies, it became apparent that he had so much tobacco in his mouth that it was difficult to understand his lines. Also, that much tobacco produces an enormous amount of tobacco juice and that juice needs spitting. He couldn't complete any of his lines without interrupting himself with a cowboy spit-take, and it was distracting. When the lights came up, Billy and Ron pulled Bruno aside to talk to him about how he should cut way back on the chew, or maybe not use it at all, because it was really messing with the comedic rhythms of the scenes. Bruno got very defensive, saying they didn't know what they were talking about, and that it was his character to create, not theirs. But they wanted to address it early, after we had all just seen what a distraction it was. Bruno really got his back up, voices were raised, and he ended up storming out of the room. And that was it. He decided that he and Billy were no longer friends, breaking a twenty-year-old best-friendship on the spot. As far as I know, he did not speak to Billy ever again. Not during the entire filming of the movie or in all the years afterward. It crushed Billy. I don't think it affected the film at all, because they are both such professionals, but it was a wound on the psyche of the set and so unnecessary.

The upside for me was that it drew me and Billy close. We started going to dinner together after work. I could see how hurt and confused he was about this small comment taking down their entire friendship. We would have a lot of laughs and talk about the movie, but the conversation always went back to Bruno. He struggled between feeling guilty for having said anything, and feeling angry that Bruno would take it this far, especially after Billy wrote the role for him and went to bat to get him the part. I wanted to be the go-between, but I really didn't know either of them very well yet. Bruno was nice to me, but I could see he didn't want to fix his problem with Billy, so I stayed out of it, focusing instead on the marvelous part I was playing and the phenomenally talented people I was playing with. Billy crushed his part in every scene, Bruno was great and funny, the rest of the gang of city slickers were all perfect for their parts, and the scenes flowed so easily because the script was so well written. When Jack Palance came on the set, everyone had to up their game just a little bit more. His character dies halfway through the movie, so he was only on set for a few weeks, but it was so fun to act with a real live Western Movie Star, especially playing the sad and meek character I was portraying.

Every day was a new challenge and another great scene. Phil was a great role. He goes through an enormous change, with very emotional moments always punctuated by world-class jokes. My wife leaves me, I have a breakdown, I save Billy's character from drowning, fight the bad guy, and get the girl in the end. The locations were where they had shot many old westerns and were stunning and peaceful. TJ was an awesome horse and I ended up doing things I never would have dreamed I could do. When Billy's character gets swept down the river, I chased him on horseback along the riverbank, jumped off the horse, ran out into the river on a slippery log, and reached out and grabbed him heroically just before he went over a waterfall. In another scene, I rode TJ as we slid down a long muddy embankment, then crossed a rushing river with all the cows swimming around us in the deep and fast water. It was thrilling to do this scene, especially knowing there were safety people everywhere and trusting TJ completely. The horseback riding culminates with the three of us galloping across the open plains while singing the theme from *Bonanza*. These were amazing, eight-year-old Danny's fantasy moments coming to life, moments I still cherish to this day.

Meanwhile, while I was having the adventure of a lifetime, Laure was in a living hell. All by herself, she had packed up our house, moved the three kids to Moss Beach, enrolled them in their new schools, unpacked all our stuff, and everything else that goes into a life-changing move to a brand-new town. I finally got three days off together, and I flew back to see everyone and our new house. When I arrived at the house, before I even got to give everyone a hug and a kiss, a very low-flying airplane buzzed right over my head. What the fuck? Now the kids were jumping on me, and Laure and I were hugging and kissing hello, and another plane came buzzing right overhead. What the double fuck? When I said to Laure, "Wow, does that happen often?" she looked very upset, and we decided to ignore it for the time being. There were so many planes buzzing our house that weekend that we had to ignore it, because the problem was so big that it would have overwhelmed the weekend. But the turd in the punchbowl was definitely there. We had only seen the house twice, both days so magical and beautifully misty. But that mist meant those were not good days to fly, so there were no planes taking off from the AIRPORT AT THE BOTTOM OF THE HILL THAT GAVE FLYING LESSONS ALL DAY LONG, WITH ITS TAKEOFF PATTERN RIGHT OVER OUR HOUSE, THAT NO ONE TOLD US ABOUT!!! The dream of moving the family to a quiet place in a small town was immediately shattered, and I was crushed. Every plane overhead was a reminder that I was an idiot to have bought this house so impulsively, that I was a terrible husband for leaving Laure to deal with it, and that when *City Slickers* was over, I would either have to try to sell this piece-of-shit house and move the family again, or I would have to have my ears removed and a possible lobotomy. We did decide that we were definitely not selling the house on Highridge Drive, because we might be moving back into it. I was so discombobulated that I could hardly focus on reconnecting with the kids and Laure. When it was time to go back to work, I was sad to say goodbye to everyone, but truthfully, it was also a relief.

It was right about this time that my little movie, *Home Alone*, hit the theaters. Until this point in my career, I had never given one thought to the Box Office Numbers. Never. The only thing I ever paid attention to was critical response and if it was running in the theaters. *Breaking Away* and *Diner* were critics' darlings and they played for a couple of months in a few theaters in each city. *Milagro Beanfield War* was loved by the critics but stopped playing in the theaters pretty quickly. *Blue Thunder* had a good run and others had been ignored. But there was a whole other Hollywood game going on that I knew nothing about called, "Who Is Number One at the Box Office This Week?" I have since learned that this is the *only* Hollywood game that matters, because it means that your movie is making the most money of everyone's movies. That's the reason the studios make movies: to make money. Billy of course knew how important it was when he came into the makeup trailer one day with his *Hollywood Reporter* trade paper and told me that *Home Alone* had opened at Number One. I had no idea of the significance, but it was certainly good news. The next week we were Number One again, and Billy was impressed that such a little movie could stay at Number One for two weeks in a row. This went on every week for the rest of filming, because *Home Alone* went on to be the longest running Number One movie in history, staying in that slot for twelve straight weeks. Each week, Billy was more and more incredulous, trying to make me understand that this was a very big deal, but I had no idea of any way to take advantage of it as an opportunity for advancement. I was just proud of the movie, and the thought of audiences laughing at all of the silly stuff I had done made me smile. All I knew was that I was working on a great film and hoping I could get another good job after this one ended, and maybe *Home Alone* would help.

We finished the shooting in LA, where I had some great scenes to do. There was a comically humiliating scene of my wife and I losing our shit and getting divorced in a big party scene, ending with me spending the night in a child's bed at Billy's house, sharing the room with his son, played by a sweet and funny kid named Jake Gyllenhaal in his first movie ever. (I like to think I made a huge impression on him and kind of taught him everything he knows about acting in that one little scene. You're welcome, Jake.) But the craziest scene we did was recreating the traditional Running of the Bulls in Pamplona on the back lot of Universal Studios, the opening scene of the movie. We had been talking to Ron Underwood for weeks about how he was planning on shooting this sequence. He had been such a stickler for realistic action with everything else so far, so we were a bit concerned about how he would give it that same realistic feeling without us having to actually run down the street with real bulls chasing us. He assured us it would be done safely. They were building a series of low fences along the authentic-looking Pamplona street. The bulls would be running on one side of the fence, and we would be running on the other, but with the right camera angles and lenses, it would look like we were running right with them. The day we got to the set for that scene, the first thing we noticed was that there were no fences.

"Where are the fences?" we asked Ron.

"Oh, yeah. We tried some camera tests with them, but it didn't work, so we took them down."

"Oh, well what is the new plan?"

"The new plan is that you guys are really going to run with the bulls. But we are going to have a couple of stunt guys running right behind you so that if any of the bulls go crazy, they can try to stop them before they get to you."

"The stunt guys are going to stop the bulls? How will they do that?"

"You know, like rodeo clowns. They distract them or something. Now, let's get out there and give it a try."

I can see why they saved this scene to shoot last, because it was one of the most dangerous and crazy things I have ever done. When they said, "Action," Billy, Bruno, and I took off running with all of the extras and stuntmen. Then the wranglers released about fifty or a hundred wild bulls, who chased us down the street! When the shot ended, we ducked into a doorway or found someplace "safe" to hide until the bulls ran past us. Then the cowboys would herd the bulls back to the starting place so we could do it again. After several takes, the bulls were onto the game and stopped running so hard. You would think that would make it safer, but no. Instead, the wranglers started firing off shotguns to spook the bulls and get them to run even harder. Absolutely crazy. On one take, Billy got tripped up and fell down on the sidewalk. I was able to scoop him up and drag us both into a doorway. We were both kind of shaken up, and it was the only time I felt they were pushing us into unsafe territory. But having survived it, I am so glad it happened that way. I mean, I actually got to run with the bulls in Pamplona!

The movie wrapped, and I finally got to go home to Moss Beach. It would be good to have time to get to know my new house, my new town, and finally get to focus on my beautiful wife and magnificent children. And those fucking planes.

SEQUEL TIME

Moss Beach was beautiful. We committed to staying there at least through the school year, and we actually loved it. The planes still made me crazy, and I felt stupid for having not done enough homework on the property before we bought it, but we made the most of it. I signed up to coach Henry's Little League team. The school seemed nice, and the teachers were good. There was a sweet little tavern just down the hill and Laure and I would go there for drinks on occasion. The neighbors were good people, and it was what we had hoped for living in a small town. Except for one thing—*Home Alone*. The movie was a worldwide sensation, and I had suddenly become more famous than I ever could have imagined. In the eyes of our neighbors, and especially the kids in school, Marv had moved to Moss Beach. It was a layer of weirdness that made us all feel a little out of place. I could hide as much as I wanted to, but my kids had to deal with it every day. Being the new kids without any old friends, they suddenly had to navigate these uncharted waters, trying to figure out who actually wanted to be their friend and who was just trying to get invited over so they could meet Marv. I still feel bad that they had to go through that confusion. It was weird enough being an adult and dealing with it.

Home Alone was so big that my agent got a call saying they were going to make a sequel to the movie, *Home Alone 2: Lost in New York*, and would I be interested in being in it. My answer was simple and to the point—Hell, yes!!! A sequel, are you kidding me? I had never even thought about being in something that would be worthy of a sequel, but this would be fun. And lucrative! Sequel money! It was announced in the *Hollywood Reporter* that Macaulay Culkin had signed up for the film and was being paid five million dollars and 5 percent of the gross box office. Not bad for a ten-year-old kid. I started fantasizing about what my salary might be, doing the calculus to try to figure out my relative worth. I knew Mac was the star of the show, but Joe and I seemed securely in second place. So I told my agent to just get me whatever Pesci was getting and that would be fair, and he said he would get back to me.

The movie wouldn't start until the fall, so I tried to take my foot off the gas pedal, career-wise, and keep it simple for a while. I would drive up the coast into San Francisco once a week to record *The Wonder Years* and fly down to LA to direct a couple of episodes too, crashing at our Highridge Drive house. I was getting good at directing, freer with the camera, the actors and producers trusting me. And I had enough credentials to start making the leap into directing a movie. I interviewed for a couple of films, but my agents didn't seem to have much of an interest in my directing career because I could make a lot more money as an actor.

But the negotiations for *Home Alone 2* were going nowhere. It took months for them to even make me an offer, and when they did, it was for six hundred thousand dollars, double my original salary, but not quite the pot of gold I was hoping for. I asked if that was the same as Joe was getting, and they said it was not. They didn't know what Joe was getting, but the studio wouldn't tie my salary to his. It was every man for himself. I asked if I could see the script, and they told me it wasn't ready yet. I thought it was crazy to ask me to sign up for a film that I hadn't even read the script for. But I also felt that old feeling—"You almost fucked it up the first time, backing out of *Home Alone* because of a small amount of money and time. And you also almost walked away from *City Slickers* because of your pride. So don't be greedy and fuck this up too! That is more money than you have ever made in your life!" But I did need to see the script to know what they were asking me to do, so I used that to delay closing the deal, which just added to the stress. I was on edge anyway, because by now, Laure and I had come to the decision that we had to get out of that house. Every time a plane flew over my head, my PTSD kicked in, which in turn made Laure feel horrible and helpless to help me.

So when the school year ended, we sold the Moss Beach house to a commercial pilot, who loved the sounds of airplanes taking off and landing. Go figure. We all moved back into the Highridge Drive house, but it still had all the same issues that made us leave in the first place. We spent that summer escaping up to Malibu to visit Cheech and to hang out at Westward Beach—a beautiful, wide, empty beach where the kids would play until the sun went down and we would eat peanut butter and lettuce sandwiches. And one day it dawned on us, "Why don't we live out here? Instead of commuting out here to be at the beach, why don't we live at the beach, and I will commute into the city?" We found a house to rent and moved in just before the school year started. Malibu was everything Moss Beach was supposed to be—a small town, a surf town, nature all around, great neighbors. The school was small but smart, and I could drive into town whenever I needed to. And I wasn't the only famous person in the town. There weren't that many celebrities out there at the time, but Johnny Carson, Lou Gossett Jr., and Barbra Streisand certainly outshone me by a mile, which was weirdly comforting and let me function like a normal person again. We would live in Malibu for the next twenty-five years.

I finally got the *Home Alone 2* script, and it was so good! John Hughes is a genius. He had written another brilliant comedy and given my character a ton of funny and silly stuff to do. In the first movie, Harry and Marv start off feeling threatening, especially Harry, but by the end, you know what idiots they really are. In the sequel, John wrote them as live-action cartoons from page one. So that meant even more physical comedy challenges. I knew I had to do this movie, no matter what, but I also wanted to get a fair deal. Knowing Mac's salary was five million plus percentages made my offer look pretty unfair, especially because the sequel would showcase my character just as much as anyone's. I knew they couldn't do the movie without me, but I was also insecure, since I almost blew it the first time. I didn't want to be too greedy when I loved the movie and the part so much, which was why I was an actor to begin with. The studio upped their offer to eight hundred thousand dollars, but I also found out that Joe was getting somewhere between two and three million plus gross percentage of the profits. My agent told me this was the best he could do, that I should take the offer, and we would get a better payday somewhere in the future. So I did what any rational person would do. I fired my agent. It was a prideful thing to do, but I also knew that if this was the best he could do, then he wasn't very good at his job.

The movie was supposed to start shooting in the winter, so I stayed home, took the kids to their new schools, and tried to deal with the game of chicken the producers were playing. With no agent, I now had to negotiate my own deal. I accepted that Mac was the star attraction. And I accepted that Pesci was a bigger star than me, so he could probably get more money than me. My position was that I wanted one point five million and 2 percent of the same kind of percentage that Joe and Mac were getting, whatever that was. They would not budge, and I would not budge. (I guess they hadn't heard about my epic battle with the Washington Shakespeare Festival, where I held out for the hundred dollars I was owed.) The film was shooting in New York, and I wouldn't go until I had a contract. By this point, it was days away from shooting and they were painting themselves into a corner. There was no way they could rewrite the whole script without me, and I wasn't getting on a plane until it was squared away. I finally got a call from the head of the studio, my old friend Joe Roth. I explained my position and why I felt justified, especially compared to what my fellow actors were getting and the contribution I made to the success of the first one—and the one we were about to do. He was empathetic and said he would personally explain the situation to business affairs people. He said it would take time to resolve it and asked me to start shooting, even though I didn't have a contract. I trusted Joe completely and agreed to go. Confident it would get resolved somehow, I finally felt the thrill of knowing that I was about to start filming a ridiculously funny film, with a great part, tons of old friends to work with, and making a boatload of money at the same time.

I got to New York and reunited with Chris Columbus, Joe Pesci, and John Hughes. My dearest old friend John Heard was back playing the dad and our insane stunt men, Leon Delaney and

Troy Brown, were back too. I hadn't worked in New York since we moved away, and it was exhilarating to shoot a big movie there. My dad had a meeting in New York and came to the set, one of the only times any of my family have been on one of my movie sets. I was dressed as Marv, with an iron-shaped scar on my head, hiding behind a tree or whatever stupid thing I was doing that particular day, and my dad was there to try to find solutions to homelessness and social justice. But I have a picture of us on that day, and I do see a hint of pride beaming through. He knew this was something extraordinary and was tickled to see his kid being good at what he does.

One of my favorite New York scenes was the one where the bird lady throws bird seed on us and we get attacked by a flock of pigeons. The pigeon wrangler told us the plan—Joe and I would lie down, he would throw food on us, and the flock of pigeons would land and cover us up. And he wasn't kidding. There were so many fucking pigeons! It felt weird lying under them, having them walk around on us and peck food off us. Joe decided he wasn't going to do it, so Troy laid down with me instead. I had the idea that when we were attacked, I would rise up out of the pigeons and recreate the scream I used in the first *Home Alone* when the tarantula crawled on my face. We got in position, the wrangler covered us in bird food, and an enormous flock of pigeons practically drowned us. My eyes were squeezed tight because I didn't want to get shit or piss in my eyes, or get my eyes scratched out by pigeon claws as I waited for the director to yell "Action." It seemed to take a very long time for him to give the command, but he finally did. I took a deep breath and opened my mouth to emit my trademark howl, only to have my tongue meet the raw belly of a live pigeon! It was a taste and a sensation I will never be able to forget—salty, slimy, warm, goose-fleshed, alive—and instead of a scream, I could only leap to my feet and try to spit that shit out of my mouth, and mind, as fast as I could. We did take after take, 50 percent of which included having more live pigeons in my mouth, but we got the scene the way we wanted it, so I guess it was worth the recurring nightmares I experience.

One of the bit players in the movie was Donald Trump. He was a crass and ridiculous New York character at that point, and he had just taken another bite out of the Big Apple when he bought the famed Plaza Hotel which, at the time, was the opposite of crass and ridiculous. Donald ended up doing a cameo, but his real contribution was letting us film there, lending the luster of the Plaza to the movie. The day he was filming, he asked to meet me. He was a "huge" fan of mine and the producers wanted me to chat him up, so I did. He was not a great conversationalist and kind of a nothing personality, but the meeting paid off brilliantly. The Oak Room is the bar inside the Plaza Hotel. One night Leon, Troy, and I were hanging out there drinking, when who should walk through the bar but Donald and Ivana, his wife at the time, waving to the guests and wanting to have his picture taken. (I now recognize that behavior when he crashes people's weddings at Mar-a-Lago.) Donald spotted us and proclaimed so everyone could hear that he would be picking up the tab at our table. We all raised a glass to him in thanks and he left the bar, feeling like the host-with-the-most. We drank until there was no more booze left in that bar. We stayed until four in the morning, closing time in New York, and bought round after round of drinks for the entire bar. To this day, Leon and I dispute how much the final tab was, but it was at least seven thousand dollars. We still feel really good about that.

The bulk of the movie was shot in Chicago. I had a breathtaking two-bedroom suite at the Four Seasons Hotel, so Laure and the kids could come visit. I was recording *The Wonder Years* every week at a great recording studio, and I felt incredibly lucky to be doing those wonderful scripts and picking up that paycheck at the same time. Downtown Chicago has great music, and I went to the Blue Note jazz club as many nights as I could, blown away by the level of talent and creativity. (Side note—speaking of *Home Alone* and jazz music, you need to listen to Joe Pesci's music. Joe is an extraordinary jazz singer, and it is not an overstatement to say that his talent is on par with the greats like Sinatra, Tony Bennett, and Ella Fitzgerald. He records under the name Joe Doggs, and his voice will blow your mind! He sings in a high tenor and his interpretations of classics like "All or Nothing at All" and "Love for Sale" are so full of insight and love that you will never look at Joe Pesci the same again.) It was great to hang out with my old friends from the first movie—Pesci and Heard and Leon and Troy—and make new friends on this one, notably Mr. John Hughes himself.

John hadn't been around too much on the first *Home Alone*. As I would learn, John was a bit of a recluse who devoted himself to his writing. He lived on a stunningly beautiful three-hundred-acre farm outside Chicago, with his family and his office and natural beauty, so I can understand why. But for whatever reason, once we got to Chicago, John visited the set on a regular basis. He was deferential and supportive of Chris Columbus as the director, and he was mostly just there to have some laughs and see his creation come to life. He had written so many funny things for my character to do and I wanted nothing more than to make John and Chris laugh in every scene. One of the greatest moments of my acting life was when we shot the scene where Marv comes into the basement, goes over to the sink, which the kid has rigged with electricity, and proceeds to electrocute himself. The first shot of the sequence was a wide master shot, with the camera and crew backed up against the wall so the whole basement and all the action could be seen. I asked Chris if he had any direction or notes before we shot the first take, and he said that I should just try one and see what happens. I had some idea what I was going to do but, having never been electrocuted like this before, it was going to be a new experience, and I was kind of curious as to what I was going to do myself. When Chris called, "Action," I came into the room, went over to the sink, grabbed the spigots, and just went for it, instinctively channeling the Saturday morning cartoons I loved as a kid, or maybe the Chaplin movies or Jerry Lewis movies that made me laugh so hard. I started shaking and yelling and acting as electrocuted as I could, for as long as I could. I was very into the physicality of the moment, but the moment wouldn't seem to end. I don't know a lot about acting, but I do know that it starts when the director says "Action," and it ends when the director says "Cut." The electrocution went on a very long time and there was still no call to cut the scene. Having taken more electricity than is healthy for one man, I finally let go of the spigots and reacted to the aftermath of that trauma, dancing around like electricity was still coursing through my system. I thought maybe this would be a fun ending and Chris might be satisfied with the first take and call "Cut!" But there was not a peep. By this point, I was starting to run out of gas, so I incorporated my exhaustion into the scene, the electricity wearing off both for the actor and the character. I dropped to my knees and then to the floor, final spasms jerking my body until I became still, a heap of ash. I had nothing more I could do, and still I didn't hear "Cut." What the fuck? As I lay on the floor, I finally broke character and refocused my eyes to reality. I saw the crew and equipment at the end of the room and right next to the camera, rolling on the floor in laughter, I saw Chris Columbus. It turned out he was laughing so hard that he couldn't say "Cut." That is still one of the greatest compliments

I have ever received as an actor. Such a confidence booster, and a validation that I was on the right track.

Knowing that I was free to be as much of a classic-style physical comedian as I was capable of being opened the door to the silliest side of me and let me pay tribute to all of the physical comedians I had always loved dearly. There is the scene when I pull an entire wall of paint cans onto myself, covering myself in paint and making the floor very slippery. I had a blast doing as much slippery silliness as I could, trying to look as out of control as possible. But if you notice, I do take one beat in the middle of it to do a rather graceful little cha-cha move, trying to feel as much like Dick Van Dyke as I could channel. Doing the scene of getting hit in the face with bricks is about as classic a cartoon moment as one could ever hope to get. What kid wouldn't want the chance to hop inside a cartoon and do the silly stuff I got to do? I took full advantage of the opportunity, with such realistic-looking props and sets. I remember Chris standing just off camera, laughing his ass off and throwing foam bricks at my head, with me doing a stupider and stupider reaction with each new brick. I think the crew might have taken turns throwing them at me too because it was such a fantasy from all of our cartoon childhoods.

Because the physical comedy in this film was even more exaggerated than in the first film, the danger of the stunts that Leon and Troy had to do was even greater. There is a scene where Marv comes into the house, falls through a hole in the floor, and lands face down and spread eagle on the concrete basement floor. My part of that sequence was to step into the close-up shot and then fall out of frame. Leon's job was to do the fall itself, and then I popped back in, post-fall, for the reaction shots. It was quite scary to watch Leon do this stunt. He really did fall from the first floor to the basement floor, face-down and spread eagle. The only concession was that instead of an actual concrete floor, he landed on a bunch of cardboard boxes they had covered with a tarp to look like a concrete floor. I was worried and asked Leon if there wasn't anything better to fall into than cardboard boxes, perhaps foam or an airbag. He said that this is what the generals had decided and he was just a soldier. And he fucking did it! Wile E. Coyote could not have done a better face-plant than Leon did!

Troy had to do a stunt where Harry falls flat on his back onto the top of a car. Again, terrifying to watch. They had a real car and had "scored" it, meaning they had made cuts in the roof structure so that it was barely staying together and would break away when Troy landed on it. Troy was lifted by a crane, lying flat on his back, ten or fifteen feet above the roof of the car, and when Chris yelled "Action," dropped onto the car. Evidently the roof was not "scored" quite as much as it should have been and therefore did not give way completely upon impact. It looked right out of a Bugs Bunny cartoon—until the shot cut and Troy didn't move. He was knocked unconscious, but he was a rodeo rider and shook it off pretty quickly. I got a little banged up (strangely, the worst was climbing out of the basement on a tower of tables, TV sets, and other junk, all of which had very sharp edges. My legs were black and blue for a month!), but Leon and Troy took the physicality to a genius level that contributed to the success of those movies as much as anything.

Laure and the kids came to visit, and we had a blast in Chicago, eating at restaurants and going to see Michael Jordan play. Macaulay was staying in a different hotel, but we picked him up and took him to the park with us to play. He was a sweet kid but had lived a very different life than my kids. He didn't know how to play tag or throw the ball around. He was more of an indoor kid and had a lot of adult pressure on him from show business and parents and such. We realized he had formed a friendship with Michael Jackson, because when we picked him up, his hotel room was stacked, literally from wall to wall and ceiling to floor, with toys. Every conceivable toy, as if someone went through Toys "R" Us, took one of each, and dropped them in his room. All a gift from Michael Jackson. It made all of us feel really bad for Mac. My kids had experienced a taste of the distortions that fame can bring, but seeing what Mac's life was like put things in a different perspective.

John Hughes and I started spending time together, mostly giggling. He was so smart and experienced, and I loved hearing his thoughts on moviemaking. He gave me some of his unproduced scripts to read, one of which was called *The Bee*—a pure physical comedy movie about a man who is trying to get his work done in his home office, but becomes completely distracted by his determination to kill a bee that has gotten into the house, eventually destroying his entire home. John had been having problems with the structure of the story, how to keep the tension up and not be repetitive. I loved the script and came up with a couple of solutions, and before I knew it, John asked me to come on board as the director to help develop the script and star in it. (We worked on it for the next couple of years, and I even got to spend time at his farm with him, and it is one of my biggest regrets that we never got to make that film.)

The more film they shot of me, the more I had them over a barrel in terms of my contract, especially because they liked my footage so much. With no agent and no lawyer, I negotiated the contract directly with the head of the studio, my friend, Joe Roth. Joe was truthful, respectful, and fair, and although Mac and Pesci got a lot more than me, I did get more money than I had ever made in my life: one point five million and 1 percent gross point of the film. Of course, I still had to pay my former agent 10 percent, and lawyer 5 percent, and accountant 5 percent, and 35 percent for taxes, so I probably came away with five hundred dollars in fresh cash, which was awesome! Having Joe Roth's confidence and friendship meant the world to me. Our families loved each other, and we had so many laughs together. I respected him so much as my director in *Coupe de Ville* and now as my studio boss. But his influence on my life as storyteller was just getting started.

ROOKIE DIRECTOR—
MIRACLES ON WRIGLEY FIELD

L ife was very good. The house we rented in Malibu had fruit trees and a swimming pool and the kids were so happy living there. There was so much activity at the house with the three kids' schedules, so we hired an incredible young woman named Robin Landon to be our nanny and help Laure manage our life. We started looking for a house to buy and soon found a place we loved—it was at the end of a dead-end road, on an acre and a half, and best of all, it had a path from the backyard directly to a private beach called Little Dume, a surf mecca and the most perfect little family beach you could imagine. The house was kind of shitty, but we didn't care about that. If "location, location, location" is the ultimate guiding principle in real estate, this was a one-in-a-million opportunity. We were ready to meet the price of one point three million, because I had now saved enough to pay in cash. I still had *The Wonder Years* paycheck coming in every week, and once we had sold the house on Highridge Drive, we would be in great shape. There was only one problem. Before we could buy it, the house was confiscated by federal marshals, who had arrested the owner for some kind of embezzlement or something. They told us that once the trial was over, the government would probably put it back on the market, but they had no idea how long that would take. We were very disappointed and went back to house hunting but were happy in the rental house and in no rush to move again.

One day I got a call from Joe Roth. He had a movie for me to direct called *King of the Hill*, about a twelve-year-old kid named Henry who loves baseball and ends up pitching in the major leagues for the Chicago Cubs. He thought the script needed work, but he wanted to make it in the summer and felt I could make a really good movie out of it. "Do you want to read the script?" My mind was blown. I had been trying to get a movie made as a director for a long time. By this point, I had been hired as a director to develop a script at Imagine Entertainment called *Clipped*, about a man who gets a paper clip stuck deep inside his ear and suddenly possesses magical powers. I was the original director of *Ace Ventura: Pet Detective*. I worked on that movie for a year, trying to make sense of the story and the script. The jokes were lame and the plot was obvious and hokey, and I finally left the project because I couldn't see how to pull it off. Well, Jim Carrey was hired after that, and it turned out the script didn't have to make sense and the jokes could be whatever they were, because a force of nature was unleashed in that movie, and that was the magic element I did not see coming. I had probably developed four or five movies by this point, but none of them felt close to actually getting made. *King of the Hill* was already a green light. Joe sent me the script and we set up a meeting for the following week to talk about it.

The script did need work, and I dug in. This was another story about Kid Empowerment, one of my favorite genres of film-making. Between the two *Home Alone* movies and all of the great *Wonder Years* episodes, I had read enough top-notch scripts now to understand structure, character arcs, defining stakes, building comedy moments, and how to get the audience fully invested in a film. When it came time for our meeting, I was fully prepared. I told Joe about all the work I wanted to do on the script—developing the characters, new storylines, and expanding the fun of the kid's journey into the world of major league baseball. I had page notes, dialogue fixes, and new characters to share, but Joe stopped me.

"This all sounds great, but I really don't need to know about all of this. You would be the director, and you can make any movie you want to. All I really need are just five trailer moments."

"Five trailer moments? What do you mean?"

"I need to sell this movie to make money on it, and I need five big moments in the film that we can put in the movie trailer and commercials to make people want to come to see it. That's how this works."

Coupe de Ville was an intimate comedy about family and small moments, and I don't remember him as a director trying to make any big moments that would play well in the trailer. (Maybe that's why it didn't do so well at the box office.) But as the president of 20th Century Fox, Joe had his eye on the prize, and it was a great lesson. It turns out that not only are those Five Big Trailer Moments great selling tools, they are also really fun and big moments in the film, helping to make the rollercoaster ride of the movie constantly entertaining. What a gift he was offering! We shook hands on the spot.

I had my first meeting with the writer, Sam Harper, and the producer, Bob Harper, in a conference room at Fox. I told them how much I liked the idea of the film, and how I had some thoughts on how to make it better, and we opened our scripts to page one. Since the film is about an extraordinary season of baseball, I had the idea of the movie starting out on Opening Day at Wrigley and then, through a fly ball, transition to our hero, Henry, and his friends playing baseball in his backyard. This was a very different opening than was written in the script, and my proposal was met with a resounding silence. Another peripheral producer who was in the meeting was the first to speak. "Well, I think the opening in the script works just fine. Are you planning on making changes on every page? Because we will be here forever."

I said something to the effect of "Yes. Yes, I am. This is what I talked to Joe Roth about. I am going to make the changes that I think the script needs to make it great. I am going to lay out my ideas, and I want honest feedback on what you think. So yes, this is going to take a long time and a lot of work. So let's keep going." Bob and Sam were great. This was the first film for both of them, and they trusted my experience. My ideas were strong, well-thought through, and necessary. And once they saw that I was open to their ideas too, the floodgates opened. Sam and I dove into the script, stripped it down, and rebuilt it together.

Movies are successful when the casting is right. I first offered the role of Henry to Jake Gyllenhaal, who was such a sweet kid on *City Slickers* and was perfect for it, but his parents had different plans for his career. I think we were turned down by the kid from *Free Willy* too, but mostly we put our energy into a nationwide search for The Kid. The kid who would have the innocence, cockiness, humor, and awkwardness that the role demanded. We watched videotapes of kids from all over the country, and even flew some in for screen tests, but were having trouble finding the right kid to play Henry. My son Henry, who had absolutely no interest in show business, saw me struggling to find the right kid and said that if I needed him to play the part, he would try to do his best. He was so adorable in wanting to help out his desperate dad. Luckily, one day Thomas Ian Nicholas walked in the door. He was so perfect for the role I could barely contain myself. He read all of the scenes with heart and humor and could make acting adjustments when I asked him to. Once we locked him in, the movie came into focus. We just needed to cast our leading man to play Chet Steadman (named after my childhood best friend from Bethesda, David Stedman), the old, washed-up baseball pitcher whose life will be turned upside down by this twelve-year-old boy. We rewrote the character with Sam Elliott in mind, but he turned us down. One day Gary Busey came in to meet about playing the part. I had loved him in *The Buddy Holly Story* and *Point Break* but didn't know too much else about him or his reputation as a bit of a madman. But I found out quick. Gary burst into the room with an energy that only Gary possesses. "Good morning, Mr. Stern! I am Gary Busey, and I am here to bring you the NEWS! Are you ready for the NEWS!? Are you ready for me to bring you the NEWS?"

I guess I was a little dumbstruck by the question and didn't quite know what to say, so he continued. "Do you want the NEWS?! Do you even know what the NEWS is!??!"

I was a little taken aback and getting slightly annoyed, so I said something like, "The news is reporting on when new things happen. Right?"

"Wrong!! The NEWS stands for North, East, West, and South! Every direction! And that is how I am going to play this character, from every direction. I am going to bring it from the North, the East, the West, and the South! I will make you laugh and make you cry and everything in between. Now, feel my head."

"I'm sorry, what?"

"Feel my head!" He grabbed my hand and placed it on the

side of his skull. I didn't want to be rude and resist too much but he did have to use a little extra force to keep my hand there to complete the examination of his skull. "That is a steel plate you are feeling. I had a pretty bad motorcycle accident a couple of years ago and they had to put this plate in my head. And ever since they did, I have had such a new connection to the world. I am so blessed to be here, and I want to be a part of your movie!" There was more bizarre conversation, and he did some sort of theatrical exit, leaving us all in shock and hysterics at the nonsensical behavior. He looked perfect for the part, was certainly charismatic, and had been great in other movies but, no way, he was too crazy. We made an offer to Nick Nolte, who turned us down, and maybe one other person, but we were getting close to the start of shooting and had to have someone who had some kind of box office track record for the studio to be comfortable. Joe Roth said that if I could handle Patrick Dempsey's nuttiness, I could handle Gary. And so we cast him.

I had a good cry when it was time to leave the family, upset to have to leave these wonderful people and the complicated and beautiful life we had made in Malibu. I moved back into the Four Seasons in Chicago, into the same two-bedroom suite I had on *Home Alone 2*. I knew the staff at this point, the jazz clubs, and restaurants, and felt weirdly at home there. The job was intense. I only had a few weeks to get everything ready to start shooting: writing the script with Sam, auditioning local actors, scouting locations, setting the shooting schedule, and hiring the local crew. The talent pool in Chicago is deep, and we put together an incredible cast with actors from Steppenwolf and Second City. The crew was outstanding, bringing their creativity to every aspect of the film, from costumes and props to set building and camera operating. But the most amazing part of the experience was the baseball itself. I loved to play baseball, coached Henry's Little League team, and went to major league games whenever I could, but I had never seen the game played at the highest level up close and personal. Wrigley Field is the oldest baseball stadium in the world, the Vatican of Baseball, and it was one of the most powerful experiences of my life to get to know every square inch of it as we searched for the best places to shoot our scenes, put our cameras, build our sets, and store our equipment. We hired Tim Stoddard, a former major league pitcher, as our technical advisor. Tim was in charge of training the actors to look like baseball players, as well as helping choreograph the baseball action in the movie. We spent weeks on the field planning the shots, although I did not pass up the opportunity to goof off a little and take batting practice, infield practice, and catch fly balls in the outfield, crashing into the famous Ivy Wall. It was my deepest childhood dream come true. Unbelievable. The baseball players were astonishing. Their skill level, accuracy, strength, fearlessness, and discipline are beyond belief. We had Barry Bonds, Pedro Guerrero, and Bobby Bonilla do cameos, and the way they hit the baseball sounded like gunfire.

Our cast was terrific, but we didn't have any major movie stars in it, and the studio asked me if I could play a part in the movie. They thought my connection with the target family audience from *Home Alone* might help get some butts in the seats. I told them I really had my hands full trying to direct this very complicated movie. Besides, there wasn't really a part for me. But when they told me they were willing to pay me seven hundred thousand dollars to be in it, I was suddenly inspired to write one, and that is how the baseball coach Phil Brickma came to be born. Since the movie was an homage to baseball, I thought it would be fun to have an old-timey character like Brickma, who has maybe taken one-too-many fastballs to the head in the pre-helmet era of the game. (There is a scene in the movie when Brickma is taking batting practice, fouling balls off the top of the batting cage and having them ricochet back and hit him in the head. I had gotten pretty good bat control from taking batting practice, and it took a few takes, but I finally got a couple of them to actually come back and hit me in the head. It was such a tiny moment, but one of the most satisfying I have ever filmed, combining my love of athletics and physical comedy, with the pressure of the whole film crew watching.)

The other thing I wanted to accomplish with the character was to have him not be in too much of the film. I wanted to be behind the camera when we were filming, and not have to be in front of the camera focused on my acting. So I came up with the idea of having Brickma get himself trapped in various places, so that he would miss all the big games in the movie. It was so fun to come up with new ideas and have the crew carry them out so perfectly. I was in my hotel suite when the idea of getting trapped in the tiny space between the two doors of the adjoining rooms hit me and made me laugh. I told the set designer the next day, and in three days, they had built the set and we filmed it. The production designer and crew were so good and flexible.

It dawned on me that a great model for the film was *The Wizard of Oz*. Henry Rowengartner slipping on the baseball, breaking his arm, and then being able to throw the ball so hard that he winds up playing for the Cubs is the tornado that takes Dorothy to Oz, and they both enter worlds beyond their imaginations. So I asked the set designers to make the doors to the Wrigley clubhouse look like the doors to Oz. Sure enough, when we came to the set to shoot the scene of Henry entering his Oz, they had built doors just like the originals. We played the scene as an homage to that film, including the gatekeeper saying the famous line, "Well, why didn't you say so? Now that's a horse of a different color!" I saw the Ray Charles Pepsi television commercial one night after shooting and thought it would be great to have Henry Rowengartner become so famous that he does the same ad. Before I knew it, Pepsi had given us permission, the crew had built the set, found backup singers, made the kid's tuxedo, and we filmed the scene, which turned out to be another big "trailer moment" in the film. What a gift directing is, leading a collaboration of so many brilliant people in a coherent direction to tell a story to an audience. It was everything I hoped it would be and so much more.

But you do have to be the leader. The very first shot of the very first day of shooting, I looked to Jack N. Green, the Academy Award-winning cinematographer.

"So where do you think we should put the camera?"

"Where do *you* think we should put the camera?"

"I'm not sure. I thought you were the cinematographer."

"You've been working on this script for months and seeing each scene in your mind. So you know the story better than anyone. I just got here a week ago and I'll be gone when we're done shooting. This is your story. So when you have been imagining this scene, where was the camera?"

It was such the perfect thing to say, empowering me in a way that has informed the rest of my work and my life, and it made me take the reins of the film in just the right way.

I loved the actors. I embarrassed myself more than once on the set as I cried watching their performances. Directing Gary Busey was a bit challenging, but he gave a great performance and I grew to like him a lot. But one day I lost my shit on him. The Cubs had a doubleheader and had granted us twenty minutes between games to film on the field, with a real sellout crowd in the background. It was an amazing opportunity for a Big Trailer Moment for our little film, but twenty minutes is not a lot of time. We rehearsed a lot and knew we had to execute our plan perfectly. Our movie crew and cast stood in the runway to the field as the first game reached the bottom of the ninth. The only one missing was Gary Busey.

"What the fuck is going on? Where's Gary?" I asked the assistant director.

"Gary is having a problem and doesn't want to come out of his trailer."

"Well, tell him to get out here now! We're about to start!"

The game ended and we jumped into our first shot, a huge Steadicam shot of Henry taking the mound for the first time, the camera circling him and taking in the visual power of the sold-out stadium. The crowd got into it and started chanting his name, and it sealed the deal for the authenticity of the film. The next shot was going to be when Busey's character comes out of the dugout to talk to Henry on the mound and calm his nerves. But Busey was still not coming out of his dressing room. I got on the walkie talkie, had the poor assistant director hold his walkie up to the window of Gary's trailer, and proceed to rip him a new asshole. "Get your fucking ass out here in thirty seconds or I am going to fire you and then beat the shit out of you. You are so lucky to be in this fucking movie, and if you fuck this up for me, I will fuck you up forever!" Or something like that. Thirty seconds later, a golf cart carrying Gary pulled onto the field next to me, and Gary got out and started apologizing. I didn't give a shit about his apology, I just wanted to shoot the scene. But he had removed the fake mustache we had him wearing. (I still had Sam Elliott's image in my mind and wanted him to look like that. But Gary couldn't grow a mustache, so he wore a fake one.) I was under so much pressure and so pissed that I grabbed the mustache out of his hand, smushed it onto his upper lip as hard as I could, and told him to just do the fucking scene. Of course, the scene ended up being great. We got amazing footage that day that made our little film look so much bigger than the budget should have allowed. I have run into Gary many times since then, and he always tells me that that was one of the great moments of his life, and that he loves me for having been totally real with him and forcing him to be a professional when he was lost in his own head. Go figure.

We finally finished shooting the movie. I said goodbye to the beloved Chicago friends I had made and headed back to LA to edit the film. This was when we were still editing actual film, with a splicer and tape, on little Moviola editing machines. The editor cut the film on one editing machine and I would be on the other machine, going through all of the footage and different takes and marking which ones to use. We had shot so much baseball footage that they let me hire a second editor, the genius Raja Gosnell, who I knew from when he edited the two *Home Alone* movies. Raja cut all the baseball sequences brilliantly, cutting between action shots, emotional moments, and crowd reactions to build tension and tell the story, showing me a movie that I hadn't even realized I'd shot. Suddenly we had a great movie on our hands. The studio decided to invest a little bit more money, and we hired John Candy to come in and play the sports announcer in the booth. We built a beautiful press room set on the soundstage, three stories high with a huge backdrop to make it look like he was really at Wrigley Field. We wrote out a whole new script for John, adding in new jokes and narrating the action on the field, and spent three days filming him. I had met him when he did his scene in *Home Alone*, but getting to direct him was a chance to see his greatness up close. He was so funny, kind, creative, and fully committed, and he added so much to the movie that it is hard to believe that his entire role was an afterthought.

The test screenings went well and helped make the film better. We make the movies for audiences, so it was fun to be in a give-and-take creative partnership with all of these unknown people— something I didn't expect to enjoy, but did immensely. When we locked the film, it was time to hire a composer to write the score, and when Bill Conti said he was interested, I jumped at the chance. Who better to write the score to my heartwarming, underdog, sports-themed movie than the guy who composed the score to *Rocky*? Bill and I went through the film together a few times, deciding where there should be music and what the feeling of that music should be. I waited anxiously for about three weeks until finally Bill invited me over to his house to hear the score. I was nervous and excited to see how the film played with the new music he had written, but when I got to his house, I realized there was no film to watch and no music recorded. I asked him what he had been working on all this time and he said, "The themes."

"The themes? Not the score?"

"You can't have the score without the themes." Bill sat down at the piano and said, "Here is Henry's Theme," and proceeded to play about five or six single notes. Bum, ba-bum, ba-bum, ba-bum. "What do you think?"

What I thought was, "What the fuck? I have been waiting for a month for you to write the score to the film, which opens in six weeks, and all you have is Bum, ba-bum, ba-bum, ba-bum?! I'm fucked!" I didn't say that, but I registered my surprise that it was in such a rudimentary state.

He said, "How about this one?" and played me another six-note sequence, which he informed me was the Theme of Baseball. "And this last one is for his mother, Mary's Theme."

"Great," I thought, "now we've got fifteen notes! Only fifty million more to go before we have a score for the film!" And that is when he pulled the rabbit out of his hat. He explained, through words and his piano playing, what magic these tiny themes held. He played me Henry's Theme in so many different ways—Henry triumphant, Henry carefree, Henry afraid, Henry heartbroken—all with those same six notes at their center but with completely different emotions and orchestrations. He did the same with Mary's Theme and Baseball's Theme, expanding them with great flourishes and then bringing them back to their simplest truth. And then he intertwined them, showing me how the moment of Henry's first time on the mound would play musically, with Henry's Theme playing on top of Baseball's Theme to create an enormously emotional moment. Bill Conti is a fucking genius, and it is my honor to have scored two films with him. I left his house thrilled beyond belief, and Bill went to work. Once he had the themes, the writing was easy for him, and the score was soon ready to be recorded. We had an eighty-piece orchestra record his score while the movie played on a screen, and it was thrilling to feel the movie come alive in a whole new way. Bill conducted the orchestra and kept checking in with me to make sure I was loving it, which I was. There was one patch where I told him I thought the energy wasn't exactly right, and he rewrote that portion on the spot . . . for an eighty-piece orchestra! "Horns, you play measures 180–255 while the strings play measures 95–133," or something crazy like that. All the musicians made notes on their sheet music and in five minutes Bill had made that passage of music perfect. It was truly amazing to be a part of that creative process, and the score still makes me cry in parts. We mixed in the music and the film was done. It opened to very good reviews and ended up making sixty million dollars in the United States and more in Japan and other foreign markets. The studio was very happy, and Joe Roth asked me to set up a production office on the lot to find my next film to make. I could not have asked for a better experience than directing *Rookie of the Year.*

NO-BRAINERS

In the meantime, the Malibu money-laundering case got resolved and we got a call from the federal marshals asking if we were still interested in buying the house with the path to the beach. We met them the next day, signed a contract for a price of one point one million dollars, gave them a deposit check, and suddenly the house was ours. At the same time, we had noticed the abandoned old house next door and had the realtor find out whose it was and if they wanted to sell it. We got the answer that they would take six hundred thousand dollars for this little beach bungalow, and we said, "We'll take it." We paid for them both in cash, since I had just socked away a couple of incredible paydays, and Laure and I suddenly owned two houses on three acres of prime real estate, with a swimming pool and a path to the premiere surfing beach in all of Malibu. I had the most beautiful wife in the world, my kids loved their lives, and since our house had access to Little Dume, we became the hangout place for all of our kids' friends, which brought so much wonderful energy into the home. It really was the greatest and happiest time of my life.

When it came time to sign on to do the sequel to *City Slickers*, it was a no-brainer, for better and worse. I had loved making the first one so much that there was no way I would not want to join in the fun again. And this time, I had the all-powerful Creative Artists Agency as my representatives, so I would not have to handle the negotiations myself. Like I said, a no-brainer. But there was a fly in the ointment—the script. The original *City Slickers* was a film about friendship, about risking your life to honor your obligations, even if that obligation is just bringing a herd of cattle to safety, and it was one of the funniest and most heartfelt scripts I have ever read. *City Slickers 2—The Legend of Curly's Gold* had funny things in the script, but its message was about greed and searching for gold to get rich, which was the opposite of the moral of the original story. Bruno Kirby told Billy he wouldn't work with him again, so they had no choice but to leave his character out, which left a big hole in the heart of the film. In his place, they added a very annoying and unsympathetic character, played accordingly by Jon Lovitz. And even though he had died in the first movie, they brought back Jack Palance to play his long-lost identical brother, an obvious and flimsy movie device which undermined the reality of the world we were trying to create. Billy probably should have directed the film himself, but instead hired a very weak director who was expected to kowtow to Billy's vision for the film, but who was very bad at kowtowing and wore his resentment on his sleeve. My part was okay, a few funny scenes and jokes but nowhere near the character arc and complexity of the first film. By the time I finished reading the script, I was having real doubts about whether I should do it. I was starting to get a reputation as a good comic actor and needed to have material I believed in. Then my agent called and said they would pay me two point one million dollars. I immediately shut off my brain and said yes. What am I, stupid? It was a no-brainer.

Sadly, the movie ended up kind of lame, but I had a wonderful time doing it. We shot it in Moab, Utah, which is an otherworldly, beautiful place. We worked at incredible locations where many classic John Ford Westerns were shot. I rented a little house on top of a mountain, with views forever, and a hot tub too. At the bottom of the mountain was a golf club, with membership included in the rental. I had tried golf a few times and liked it, but never took it seriously. But I played every day I wasn't working and got pretty good. One of the set decorators on the film happened to be an ex-pro golfer, and he gave me lessons on the set, which I would take directly onto the golf course. In a scene directly out of *Caddyshack*, on my last day on the course it was pouring rain. I was the only person out there and I played the game of my life, powering through some lightning scares to finish one over par. One of the great accomplishments of my lifelong sporting activities. I have played only a few times after that and sucked as bad as ever. None of it stuck, but man, was I in a golf groove there for a couple of months!

It was great to spend time with Billy, but he had a very full plate—starring in the film, producing it, and overseeing the direction as well. Lovitz was nice but always had a bit of an act going on, so I didn't really get to know him much. The real gift of friendship on this film was getting to know Jack Palance a bit more. We had a lot more time together than on the first film, and this time I could see that his passion for his work outside of show business— his painting, family, poetry, ranching—was hugely important and necessary to his sanity. Living "the life of an artist" brought him deep satisfaction, with his acting career being just a small part of it. I started to conceive a plan. What if I made enough money that I never had to work again and could spend all my time at home, being a dad and a husband, with my work consisting of making art of all kinds and volunteering for causes I believed in? How much money would I need to save, invested in only the safest possible treasury bills and bonds, to be able to use the interest to pay for all of the needs of my family? The idea of "living the life of an artist," having the freedom to pick and choose how I spend my precious time here on this Earth, seemed like not just a beautiful vision but a true possibility. And even more, an obligation. If I actually had the opportunity to buy my own freedom for the rest of my life, and didn't take it, it would be an insult to every man and woman working their asses off just to get a few weeks' vacation with their families and who would leap at the chance to be able to afford this kind of unheard-of independence. I wasn't there yet, but I could see the path forward.

My production deal at 20th Century Fox was great. I hired a development team and assistants, all looking for books and stories to develop for me to act in, direct, and produce. We bought the rights to a few and dove into trying to develop them into scripts that the studio would want to make. We came across a film called *Tenderfoots*, a family, kid-empowering movie about a group of Cub Scouts who get kidnapped by a thief on the run. The script was not very good, but the idea was strong and the studio was happy to have me direct and star in a film that would appeal to the same audiences as the *Home Alone* movies and *Rookie of the Year*. We hired new writers, Goldberg and Swerdlow, who had written *Cool Runnings*, and who were really funny and great with structure and character development. We developed the script into an epic comedy, complete with climbing a mountain, fighting a bear, and riding the rapids of a raging river, and the studio greenlit the film. Having already directed *Rookie of the Year*, I felt comfortable and confident at the helm of the film and started hiring some of the great people I had worked with on other films. I was running on all cylinders, storyboarding the action sequences, scouting locations in Lake Tahoe, auditioning actors, working on the script, etc. Over the Fourth of July weekend, I had some time off. I was so exhausted I thought I must be coming down with something. But on Sunday, my lips were looking kind of blue, and my doctor met me at his office, just to be sure. He took one look at me and put me in the hospital immediately. It turned out I had a bleeding ulcer and had lost 50 percent of my blood supply. They cauterized it, and I spent a couple of days in the hospital recuperating before I was released. Now I just needed to rest, have my body build back up my blood supply, and avoid stress as much as I could—which is hard to do when you are directing, producing, and starring in a twenty-million-dollar comedy. We decided that I would still produce and star in the film but would hand over the directing reins to someone else so that my day-to-day workload would be that much less. We hired a very nice guy, Greg Beeman, who understood the situation. I had just watched Billy Crystal unofficially codirect *City Slickers 2* and wanted to avoid confusing the cast and crew as to who was in charge, but since I had been directing the film up until my ulcer, Greg understood that the crew was my crew, I had cast the actors, scouted locations, etc., and we got along very well, personally and creatively.

He made it easy to focus on playing the role of Max Grabelski, the petty thief who ends up being a reluctant hero and father figure to a group of ten-year-old Cub Scouts. We had written some crazy set pieces, and now I actually had to shoot them. I got the fearsome pleasure of shooting a scene with the legendary Bart the Bear, playing dead as he was pawing me (which was so much more terrifying than having that fucking tarantula crawl on my face). There was a scene in which my character is climbing a sheer cliff and, sure enough, one day I found myself being lifted thirty feet into the air on a crane. A mountain climber, attached to the sheer cliff on ropes from above, met me, attached my harness into some rings that had been drilled into the mountain, and left me dangling in the air. I am terrified of heights, but somehow sucked it up and did the scene. Probably not the stress-free activity my doctor wanted for me but an experience I will never forget.

One of my favorite show business moments happened while we were shooting the sequence where the kids and I get swept into a river and free-fall down the rapids, heading for a waterfall . . .

(Side note—you need to know that the most important element on any film set is the catering. The flow of food on a movie set is mind-boggling. The major fuel source for the entire Entertainment Industrial Complex is Fritos. It has become Pavlovian, our need to be fed on set on a regular basis. I am not talking about three meals a day. Of course, we need those provided for us. Full breakfast, anything you want—from pancakes to burritos, BLTs, oatmeal, seventeen kinds of cereals, coffee, coffee, and more coffee. Keep the crew fueled! Craft Services keeps it popping with tables filled with peanuts, candy, donuts, peanut butter, and jelly. You name it, it is there. But that is not enough to keep the crew going. No! We need snacks as well! Pigs in blankets, sandwiches, dips! Who the fuck knows how they do it, but they bring new stuff all day, every day. God forbid they bring ham sandwiches two days in a row! Grumble, grumble, the crew must be fed something surprising! This all takes place before eleven, and then we finally make it to lunch, the big meal of the day! This can be anything and sometimes everything. Meat, meatless, salads, desserts, beverages, ice cream. Sometimes a sushi chef might show up and the crew goes crazy. Then it's back to work, another few rounds of snacks, both served and self-serve, and then, if you go late enough, they might bring in fifty pizzas, or Chinese food from local restaurants, which is called the Second Meal, a misnomer if ever there was one.)

Anyway, I had to jump into an actual raging river and be taken along by the current through some rapids. It was really fun and physically challenging. There were so many safety people around that I knew I wouldn't get hurt, so I let myself really go for it, even though it felt dangerous each time. I went pretty far down the rapids each take, and there was no easy way to get me back to the starting place for the next take because the riverbank was such tough terrain. So we hired some Olympic kayakers—amazing athletes who had the strength and ability to paddle their kayaks back up the river and the rapids. I would jump in the river and float downstream, doing the scene while trying to stay on the route I had practiced, and when they yelled, "Cut," my kayaker would come get me. I held onto a rope attached to the back, and he paddled me back up the river to the starting place. In one of my great "Only in Hollywood Moments," on one of my trips back up the river, I saw another kayak coming up beside us and passing us by. His strength was impressive, but even more impressive, he was balancing an entire tray of cappuccinos on the fucking kayak! Balancing a fucking tray of cappuccinos while paddling upriver, through rapids going the wrong way, and not spilling a fucking drop. All to get a caffeine fix for the crew upstream. It had to be the World Record Time for such a challenge, which I hear will be an Olympic event in 2032. I nearly drowned laughing as he passed me by.

I had a great time filming the movie with my friends and crewmates, rewriting as we went and using everyone's creative input to make a really funny movie. I loved working with the kids on the film, and had gotten Freddie Hice, the stunt coordinator from *Home Alone*, to do the stunts. We had a blast doing the physical comedy. Once we finished filming, the director announced he had taken another film and left, leaving the editing, scoring, and other post-production activities to me. Since I had been codirecting the film all along, that made it much easier to do my job, which was to make the film as good as it could be, and then help market and sell it as best as I could. The movie came together well, and the test screenings went great, with lots of wild laughs from the family audiences. But we got caught in a pickle. The film went before the Ratings Board, and they gave the film a PG-13 rating instead of the PG rating we were hoping for. There were two scenes in particular they deemed too risqué for a family audience and that they wanted us to cut, and they happened to be two of the biggest laughs in the whole movie. One was a scene where the Cub Scouts piss off the side of a mountain while singing a song, and the other was a scene where my character is teaching them about the birds and the bees while demonstrating with Barbie and Ken dolls. We tried recutting the scenes but nothing we did, short of cutting the scenes altogether, would satisfy the Ratings Board. I really wanted to keep the scenes and thought it wouldn't matter that much between PG and PG-13, and the studio backed me up. We finished the movie and, once again, I got to score the film with Bill Conti, who brought his magic to it. I was very proud of what we had done, but when the movie opened, I learned a very hard lesson. That PG-13 rating really did matter. This was a movie about ten-year-old Cub Scouts doing heroic things. The people who look up to ten-year-old heroes are six-year-olds or eight-year-olds. But if the youngest audience member can only be thirteen years old, then, to them, the heroes of this movie are a bunch of little babies. A thirteen-year-old doesn't look up to ten-year-olds; they want to be like sixteen- or eighteen-year-olds. Parents didn't want to bring their impressionable little kids to it, and slightly older kids didn't want to watch a movie about kids younger than them. So the movie did not open well. I am still very proud of the film and all of my work on it, and I loved the experience of making it. But I still like to win and be successful, and having it not be a hit hurt.

Now, I don't usually do extravagant things or waste money, and I don't like to leave home either, but the legendary Boston Garden, home of the Celtics, was closing and I went crazy and bought myself a trip back to see the final game. I had loved the Celtics at times, and also hated them passionately sometimes too, and the history of that building and all of the amazing moments that had happened there inspired me enough to get off my ass and make the trip to see it before it closed. Unfortunately, the final game was sold out and I could only get a ticket to the next-to-the-final game, but I took it anyway. The building was everything I had imagined it would be—the parquet floor, the steel rafters, the intimacy of the place, and the crazy, die-hard fans. I had a good seat, and at one point a young man came over to me and asked if I was Daniel Stern (which I was). He was a producer for the radio broadcast for the game and asked me if I would come on the show at halftime and do an interview with Tommy Heinsohn, the great ex-Celtic player. I said "absolutely" and did a really fun interview. After the show, the young producer, Mike Casey, who also happened to be the son of one of Boston's bench coaches, asked me if I wanted a ticket to the final game. Are you kidding me? Fuck yeah! The gods were with me! Being at that last game at the Garden was maybe the greatest sporting event I have ever been to. They had the all-time great Celtic players take the floor and take a bow. The fans went nuts, kissing the floor, never wanting to leave. I stayed until the end, then went with Mike to the bar where the players go to drink, and we drank with everyone. One of the great nights of my life. Who could have ever predicted that just a few months later I would be back in the Boston Garden, on the parquet, playing hoops, making a film, and getting paid millions of dollars to do it? You are looking at the luckiest man in the world.

ON THE PARQUET
WITH LARRY BIRD

Playing sports has been a huge part of my life. I was so bad at academics, but good at sports, which gave me a feeling of success—although I was the slowest fucking kid in the class, which was always so embarrassing. I could punt, pass, kick, shoot, and throw better than anyone, but anytime we had to run fast and jump high, I literally came in last, beaten not only by all of the girls (humiliating!) but also by Fat Petey (as we horribly called him) and Charlie Aquista, who I believe had braces on his legs. In kickball, I could kick the shit out of the ball, over the outfielders' heads (even though they played deep when Stern came up), but I was lucky if I could make it to second base by the time they retrieved the ball from where the girls were playing Four Square and get it back to our game. I am talking *slow*.

In junior high and high school, I started to love basketball.

We mostly played half-court, so running was not a big part of the game. My jumping abilities were pathetic, but I was already taller than almost everyone so I could rebound well, my passing skills were excellent, and I could hit from outside with uncanny accuracy. When I got to New York, I played in some tough games on the playgrounds and in a league at the YMCA, and in LA played almost every day in very intense games at the gym in Cheviot Hills Park, across the street from 20th Century Fox. Anyway, *I love playing basketball!*

So I was over the moon when I got the job for *Celtic Pride*, a movie about two crazy fans, played by me and the legendary Dan Aykroyd, who are diehard Celtic fans and who kidnap the opposing team's best player, played by also-legendary Damon Wayans, to help the team win the championship. The best part was that the movie was going to be shooting the basketball scenes at the Boston Garden. My experience of being at the last game there sealed my love for that building and the history of that team, and the stars aligning so that I was going to go back and shoot a movie there, with Dan Fucking Ackroyd, playing a character that lives and dies for the Celtics, was mind-blowing. Not only that, to get Damon to look like the best basketball player in the NBA, the producers held a month of professional basketball training camp, first in LA and then in Boston. Even though I had no basketball-playing scenes, I talked my way into being part of the practices with the professional basketball players, which was humbling, to say the least. Damon had all the pressure on him to get into tip-top shape, and he did, but I could come and go as I wanted. I was playing an out-of-shape gym teacher and had the perfect excuse to skip the tough parts of the workout and go have a hoagie or two.

Truthfully, I don't remember too much about the actual movie, and to this day I have never seen it. It was Judd Apatow's first script, and it was really funny, but life off-screen was so incredible that making the movie was the least interesting part of the experience.

I had a huge, two-bedroom suite with an enormous living room on the thirtieth floor of a fancy downtown Boston hotel. Laure and the kids came to visit, and even my parents stayed with me for a couple of days. I got Mike Casey, the coach's kid who got me a ticket to the final game, a job as a production assistant on the set. Mike became a great friend and, boy, did he know how to have fun in Boston. We went to bars, sporting events, and great restaurants. One of his friends owned a pizza parlor and we would go there after getting really drunk and make pizzas. So fun! But getting to run around with Dan Aykroyd was like being in the presence of a High Priest of Partying. Dan arrived in Boston from LA by train. Not a regular train; Dan had been loaned a private train car by someone rich and famous (maybe the owner of *Rolling Stone* magazine?) and had it attached to Amtrak trains that took him across the country. When he arrived in Boston, he had the train parked at the rail depot behind Massachusetts Institute of Technology, and he lived there while we shot the movie. The first time I met him was on his beautiful, old-fashioned-feeling train car—carpeted walls, wood paneling, a bar, private bedrooms, and a porch off the back to watch America go past you, backwards. We drank and smoked cigars and got really fucking high. I loved him from the first minute I met him. Dan owned part of a nightclub in Boston, the China Club, and put me on the list where I could go in any time and have a table and free drinks. Crazy disco blasting, beautiful people all around me dancing their asses off, and unlimited drink and food. But Dan never went. The only time I was there with him was when he invited a bunch of the cast and crew to all go together. But instead of joining his guests, Dan had a walkie-talkie and acted as security for all of us. He didn't have a drink or dance, just kept on his walkie, taking us through the secret back channels of the club and into crazy, private rooms. Goddamn, that was wild!

Laure came to visit for our anniversary, and Dan found out what restaurant we were going to and set it up so that Laure and I had a private room there, with a twenty-course meal, matching wines, and romantic music. We stayed there for four hours having dinner and, of course, Dan picked up the bill. Crazy generous man. We got a break in the filming to go home for Christmas, and Dan and I had to try to make it from the set to the Boston airport, known for its horrible traffic, at rush hour on the busiest travel day of the year. Dan had his motorcycle brought to the set, a motorcycle, he was proud to tell me, that was an officially decommissioned police motorcycle, the kind with the windshield. I hopped on the back of the bike and Dan whipped through traffic like a fucking stunt driver, weaving in and out of tight spaces and tilting it at extreme angles until we arrived at the tunnel at Boston Harbor, where traffic was just too clogged for even Dan to penetrate. Time was running out for us to make the plane, but have no fear, Dan had it handled. You see, he had arranged for a boat to meet us wherever the hell we were on the side of the highway. One person got out of the boat and took the motorcycle from Dan, we got into the boat, zoomed across the harbor and right to the airport, where a car met us and took us right to the terminal. *Planes, Trains, and Automobiles (and Motorcycles and Boats)* in real life!! Dan is a one-of-a-kind person, a friend and a hero.

Unfortunately for the film, the director was the wrong man for the job. Not only was he inexperienced and a bit intimidated, but he had absolutely no understanding of basketball. (And the whole movie is about basketball!) I knew we were in trouble when I saw him on the court one day at rehearsal trying to take a shot. He looked like Jim Carrey attempting to make the worst basketball shot ever. Steven Hawking had a better chance of hitting the backboard. He didn't even know the rules of the game, let alone the rules of how to film the game. Having just directed a sports movie, I knew how many individual shots you need to make a sports sequence feel real and exciting—hand on ball, following the passes, geography, defenders' POV, clock ticking, etc. But the director only spent a few days filming the basketball sequences, which was a waste of the talent and effort that had gone into staging the games to look authentic. Instead, he spent weeks filming Dan and me in the crowd, being super fans, as well as other crowd stuff. I had a blast improvising with Dan and acting like insane fans, so I hope there is funny stuff in the movie (like I said, I haven't seen the film). But I am pretty sure the basketball sequences are underwhelming.

The film had a lot of cameo appearances by the legends of the Celtics. The same giants I had watched take their curtain call at that Final Game at The Garden just few months ago—John Havlicek, Bob Cousy, Kevin McHale, and Red Auerbach—I was now standing next to, doing scenes with, and listening to their stories and jokes. These were incredible athletes I had looked up to my whole life. But the legend of legends was Larry Bird. He was a competitor like no other, an athlete who used every ounce of talent he had and knew how to win. People have called me Bird throughout my life—some because I looked a little bit like him, some because I played basketball a little bit like him, and some because they thought I looked like Big Bird. I had narrated a documentary about him, learning a lot about what a hard, hard life he led, which only made me admire him more. So the day Larry Bird came to the set to act in a scene with me and Dan, I was as star-struck as I have ever been. He was a reserved person, but I used every ounce of charm and humor I could muster, and he warmed up. I have a photo of us laughing together that I cherish not only because I revere him but also because I got him to laugh, which isn't easy. When the crew broke for lunch, I watched as Larry got his tray of food and went back to his camper. I made the bold move of knocking on his door and asking him if he wanted to have company for lunch and, to my utter disbelief, he said yes. So Larry Bird and I sat at the little table in that Winnebago having lunch together, just the two of us. I literally cannot remember anything we talked about because it was such a near-holy experience, being that close to a true legend. I just hope I wasn't drooling.

When the parquet was not being used for filming, I went down on the floor and played basketball during the breaks. So many great players were just standing around, and I got to shoot around with them for hours. And because I was playing all of the time, I started to really feel at home on that court and impress some of the players with my long-range shooting abilities. This led to what is truly one of the greatest days of my life, right up there with becoming a father and my wedding day. One of the technical advisors on the film was an incredible player named Gus Williams, an All-Star during his twelve-year career as point guard, who I loved when he played for my hometown team, the Washington Bullets. Gus was a great guy and an amazing shooter, and we had had fun hanging out on the court while the director was off making whatever movie he was making. On this magical day, I challenged Gus to a game of H-O-R-S-E (maybe there was a small bet on it, but I don't remember). We were both really in a groove that day, and we played a fierce game with the whole crew watching. We hit half-court shots and behind-the-backboard shots, and then the other guy matched that incredible shot with another. But in the end, I beat him. I couldn't believe it—and he couldn't either. He said, "Let's play again," and we went right back at it. Again, magical shot followed by identical magical shot—and the game lasted a long time. We stopped to shoot a scene and then came back during breaks. This time, Gus won. We had to go back to filming at some point, but we met on the court for one last game to determine the real winner. The crew was heavily invested, cheering us both on. I wanted to win really badly, but Gus had much more pressure on him—an NBA great being beaten by an actor is not something he wanted to have happen on the floor of the Boston Garden. But it did. I beat him in that final game. Truly the greatest sporting achievement of my life. Gus was a little pissed, but his begrudging acceptance of how good my shot had gotten is one of the greatest compliments a man could ever receive. *Celtic Pride* was an experience of a lifetime, if not the movie of a lifetime. It is still hard to believe it all really happened.

The movie finally finished, and I went home. I had been away for three months—three months of my marriage and my kid's lives that I couldn't get back, and once again I had to catch up with everyone and everything that was going on. Life went on without me. Even though I was having these amazing experiences, I was the one missing out on the good stuff, not them. No matter how much fun I had on the film, it didn't compare with living the messy, joyous life Laure and I had built at home. My paycheck from *Celtic Pride* put me over my goal of saving enough money that we could live off the interest. If I played my cards right and was smart, I would never have to take another job for money again. So it was time to put my money where my mouth was. It was time to stop working for a while and just be home.

BARBRA STREISAND
IS GETTING MARRIED
AND I'M NOT INVITED

I had been working for a paycheck since I was eight years old and pretty much said yes to any opportunity to bring home cash. I have been driven to make money my whole life to take care of myself and I do everything in my power to give my family security and provide for them what they need and want. So I never imagined making enough money to say, "I have made enough money." Now that reality was staring me right in the face. I had to face the fact that I also *liked* making money, because psychologically, it made me feel worthy, worthwhile, valuable, validated, hardworking, smart, and all the other feelings work gives us. To turn down work was hard to do, but also liberating. My whole life I had wanted to be a hippie, live close to the land, get married, find a community, and raise a family. I now had the chance to do just that, in the most amazing, financially free way possible, and I would be a fool to pass it up.

Besides, I had done three movies in a row that did not have great success at the box office, and that meant my turn at the trough was going to come to an end soon. When I started as an actor, the movie's commercial success or failure had nothing to do with me. My only responsibility was to give a good performance. But when your name is above the title and the studio banks on your personal popularity, the box office numbers are a direct reflection of how the studio thinks their investment in you worked out. I never made the huge bucks—the five-million-, ten-million-, and twenty-million-dollar paydays that actors can make on a film—but even at my pay level, it is a very different kind of pressure and expectation that has nothing to do with how well you acted. Frankly, I was kind of tired of acting anyway. Directing films was the right job for me. So as I settled into my family life in Malibu, professionally, I decided to invest the next few years of my time into finding a great film to direct, and to only take acting jobs in Los Angeles.

In hindsight, the least interesting thing I did during this time was develop movies. I wasted so much time working on scripts that never turned into films. They were all great, and I believe all of them would have made great films, but the sad truth is that a script is only a blueprint for a film, so if the film doesn't get made, the script is as worthless as the paper it is written on. The accompanying heartbreak that comes with realizing that the film is not going to get made, and that you have wasted all of that time and creativity, is hard to recover from. *Guam Goes to the Moon*, a wonderful script I developed for Paramount about a ragtag group of ex-astronauts flying old rocket equipment to the moon, actually paid for actors and set building, and pulled the plug just weeks before we were supposed to start the film. And I had turned down a great movie called *Varsity Blues* to do it, so I felt like I lost two scripts I loved. I worked for years on a wonderful film called *Winterdance*, adapting Gary Paulsen's non-fiction book about being a novice dogsledder and running his first Iditarod. I wrote that script with Goldberg and Serdlow, going to Alaska to research and getting to run with the dogs through the Alaskan wilderness, but Fox wouldn't greenlight it. Years later, they sold it to Disney, who turned it into *Snowdogs* with Cuba Gooding Jr., and it was heartbreaking to see the story contorted into a lame Disney comedy. I worked on a script about professional bass fishing for a year and a half, called *Don Wayne Wyoming*, only to be asked by the head of the studio, "Does it have to be about bass fishing?" What a waste of my fucking time. The most painful one was not getting *The Bee* made with John Hughes. John had so many projects going on and by the time I could focus on it, he was too busy to work on it. Working on so many scripts did get me more confident in my writing abilities, so that had value. But when I think about the man-hours that I and thousands of other screenwriters have wasted on unproduced movie scripts in Holly-wood, it is almost too much pain to comprehend.

Those years I stopped working turned out to be the most productive of my life. I got really good at living a life of freedom and didn't waste a day. We had a gardener named Vitalino, who was a genius at his job. He carved pathways to connect our two houses, repurposing all kinds of stones and wood he found on the property. He planted an enormous vegetable garden, and over the years, turned our three acres into a beautiful, natural wonder-land. Laure speaks fluent Spanish, having spent her high school years in Madrid, and so she can communicate with everyone in California. But Vitalino didn't speak English and I am a dummy and still can't learn Spanish, so our verbal communications were always a comic event, a combination of physical gesturing, pointing, attempts at a foreign language, and always ending in one last non sequitur that would make us question what we had just decided or discussed. But we both knew who was boss. It was him. He taught me what "getting back to the land" really meant—the hard work, the inventiveness, using the right tool, understanding physics, weather, waterflow, and all kinds of land management that go into every agricultural endeavor. He inspired me to get my hands dirty, and I worked with him many afternoons. He would assign me menial tasks he thought I could handle—digging a hole or carrying rocks for the wall he was building. Eventually I broke out on my own and claimed the land around the little house as my area to work. I carved out the White Trash Sculpture Garden, where I made an installation of discarded washing machines, toilets, and other junk I had acquired and painted, including a dismantled Coke machine that the previous owners had left behind. My biggest accomplishment was building a chicken coop on the back of the garage. I hadn't built anything since I was a carpenter's apprentice for a time back in New York between auditions, and it felt good to see it completed, filled with chickens, and producing a dozen fresh eggs every day. I adapted immediately to the laid-back, surfer lifestyle of Old Malibu. Our neighbors were a firefighter, an electrician, an architect, a retired couple, and Clark Gable's grandson, all in modest houses like ours. I never wore shoes, and on more than one occasion left the house without them on my way to somewhere that definitely required shoes, like the doctor or something. I made the little house next door my office/man cave. I had never in my life had my own place before, always sharing a space with family, roommates, wife, and children. It was very freeing to be able to completely focus on whatever I wanted to without distraction. And when I was done, I just walked up the path, back home.

But the most satisfying part of controlling my own schedule was being able to spend so much time with my kids. The biggest miracles in my life are my children, and I reveled in taking advantage of the unprecedented opportunity of not working and just being there for the kids. Malibu was still a small town, having just opened their own high school a year before we got there, and it gave space for all the kids to find themselves. With our path to the Little Dume surfing beach, our house was where all our kids' friends came after school, to do homework and then go to the beach, and Laure and I were in heaven getting to witness all of these amazing kids growing before our eyes. Henry was a star athlete and student and had a wonderful group of friends. We loved to play intense games of basketball in the driveway or Risk in the living room. He was in so many advanced classes, and I was astounded by the seriousness with which he took his studies. We had a blast working on his bar mitzvah together, after which all my friends were sure that he would be the future president of the United States. He started clubs in school to bring kids of different cultures together. He organized a weeklong Holocaust Survivor celebration, where a dozen or so survivors and liberating American soldiers came to the school and spoke directly with the kids about their experiences. He was an amazing kid, and obviously on his way to great things. We had a big, old Chevy Suburban, and that is what I was teaching him to drive, taking him on the small streets of Point Dume.

Sophie was coming up right behind him. Very different kid than Henry, much more like I was as a kid. She was not a good reader and wasn't particularly interested in school. But she was great at music and dance and was funny as shit. Watching her journey as a girl growing up taught me more about life than just about anything I have experienced. I only knew how boys grow up in a society, with Henry following basically the same path as me, and I guess I assumed that a girl's journey was similar. And it was, for a while. But around fourth grade, Sophie's friends all started forming subgroups, gossiping about each other and doing "mean girl" things to each other. I knew and loved all these kids, so I was shocked to see them hurt each other like that. I said to Laure that I felt bad that Sophie's friends turned out to be this way, and she explained to me that this was just how girls are and that this behavior was perfectly normal.

"Normal? Playing head games with friends and gossiping about them is normal for girls?" It turned out she was right. I did not know that while boys were torturing each other in physical ways, girls were learning to play three-dimensional chess in the emotional and psychological Game of Life. It was an eye-opener. Sophie also had to deal with having such a brilliant and accomplished brother, much as I had to deal with my sister's academic success. So when we worked on her bat mitzvah speech, I told her that I wanted her speech to kick Henry's speech in the ass. And she did just that—talking about women's representation in the Torah, her role models, her dreams, her vision of how the world should be, as well as so many great jokes and laugh lines. She blew us all away.

Ella was still a little kid through these years. She always had the odd mix of a total academic nerd and terrific and fearless athlete. She rode her bike to Point Dume Marine Science Elementary School and excelled in reading and science. They took kids to the beach and did experiments and studies; Ella loved doing all of it. She also loved dance classes and soccer, but it got a little scary when she started taking horse-riding lessons where they learned to do rodeo tricks like standing on the horse and sliding around the saddle while the horse gallops. I hated watching that shit, but she loved it. She was so innocent, and we could still play pretend games and roll around on the floor, but I knew it wouldn't be long until I would lose a big part of her to the mean girl games, where dads are sidelined for a lot of the time. Laure and I loved taking them all to the local diner, Coogie's, for dinner and then getting frozen yogurt and window shopping at the surf shop. Just hanging out together as much possible, listening to them, guiding them, helping them become who they wanted to be. We were making it up as we went along, like every parent does, and we were committed to trying our best.

I also realized that my celebrity from being in movies about empowering kids could be used to help empower real kids, in real life. I had already coached my kids' sports teams, as well as being a classroom dad to help tutor math and reading and playground supervision, but there was more I could do. My fame from *Home Alone* gave me an immediate connection with kids and parents. I noticed that the most common question they wanted to know was if it hurt when I got hit with the paint cans and the bricks. The parents were as naive as the kids in terms of the editing, stunts, music, and photography tricks that go into making any kind of media, and I found that concerning. It is great to enjoy television and movies, but you must be wise to the manipulation that the media-maker is using to tell the story they want to tell, otherwise you will be ripe to be manipulated in ways that can be dangerous. The need to be literate in understanding media is just as important as the need to be a literate reader. I met a terrific woman who ran The Center for Media Literacy, an organization that trains teachers and develops textbooks and lesson plans for teaching Media Literacy to kids of all ages. I took the training and bought the materials and signed up to teach a three-week course at Malibu Middle School and High School. It was so much fun, teaching five classes a day for three weeks, and the kids loved having a class that talked about movies, television, current events, and marketing. I saw how well the course worked and wanted to see if I could help get it into schools throughout

California. Laure was already serving on the PTA and connected me with the director of the statewide California PTA. I gave a talk at their monthly meeting, going through some of the highlights of the class I was teaching, and they totally got how important it was. They arranged for me to meet with other PTAs throughout the state. The next year they named me Honorary Chairman of the California PTA, which enabled me to spread the message and get into meetings with boards of education and nonprofit education committees. I taught the course for three years at Malibu High and up and down the state of California. (I believe in my core that this should be a mandatory course in every school, in every state, in every grade, and should now include the critical thinking skills to analyze social media and disinformation, as well as mainstream media and entertainment. We need to be literate in all of it to navigate this clever world we live in.)

I gave my time to environmental groups, media literacy groups, and NORML, which wanted to reform discriminatory marijuana laws that sent people to jail for ridiculously long terms. Owning and using my celebrity for these causes made the distortion it caused in my life feel worth it. *Home Alone* opened so many doors and gave me people's attention for a minute. My message about educating and empowering young people aligned perfectly with the message of the movies people knew me from. It was different than the social justice work my dad did, and different than the hard work my mother did as an elementary school teacher, but giving back to the community was in my blood, and it felt good to be getting those muscles back in shape, using my unique toolbox to get stuff done. By this point, Laure had become very involved in the schools, moving up the ladder in the PTA and making a name for herself as an incredible community helper. She had befriended Robyn Gibson, another powerhouse woman who had children in the same public schools that we did, who wanted to support our fledgling school system. Laure and Robyn launched a plan for a big party called Celebration for Education to raise funds for the school system. The famous record producer David Foster agreed to host it on his twenty-acre Malibu estate and to organize a celebrity show that would attract high-end donors and raise a boatload of money. And they wanted me to be the master of ceremonies, along with Robyn's husband. Did I mention her husband is Mel Gibson?

Mel is a serious filmmaker, actor, and producer, but underneath that sexy exterior is a silly man who loves to laugh and tell jokes and puns. We all started hanging out together, planning the big show. Mel was the biggest movie star in the world at the time, and he could get anyone to do anything. We had the biggest studio executives buying tables, and Jay Leno agreed to do stand-up. David Foster got Lionel Richie and Natalie Cole to perform with a huge band and erected an enormous tent to do the show in. Laure and Robyn sold hundreds of thousands of dollars in tickets and set aside tables for kids and teachers and school officials. They got auction items donated for trips on private planes and vacations in Australia. Mel and I were lucky enough to get an incredibly funny *Simpsons* writer, Mike Scully, to write us some jokes and schtick. We played really well together and egged each other on, daring each other to do something sillier. The show was a fucking home run, one of the greatest pieces of crowd-pleasing theater I have ever been a part of. The audience went nuts for the music and the jokes. We had kids perform that night, including Sophie, who crushed it playing in front of all those people. And when it came time for the auction, Mel and I raised hundreds of thousands of dollars. Not only did we auction off the high-end items Laure and Robyn had secured, but we made money auctioning weird shit too. We got bidding up to three thousand dollars to be the first one to get their car from the valet after the show. I got five thousand dollars from a woman to come on stage and pour a bottle of champagne down Mel's pants. I will never forget the deliciously sinful look that woman had in her eye. We stayed up late that night in the tent at David's, counting the money, imagining the improvements to the schools this was going to pay for, and feeling the buzz of the electric night of performances. The money went to the school district and paid for so many things, from programs to teacher's aides to building a theater at the high school, which I got to help design and open. But the long-term win from Celebration for Education was the unleashing of Robyn and Laure and David and Mel and me as a fundraising team.

Life was fully engaging with the family, our house, and my volunteer work, but I was also a creature of show business and had been my whole life. I was forty years old and felt like I still had some stories to tell, that I might have something to say, but developing movies was not the way for me to say it. One evening Henry was doing his homework, and he had a book from his English class called *Bird by Bird*, by Anne Lamott, which is a book about how to write. I looked through the table of contents to see what it was about, and a chapter heading caught my eye—"Shitty First Drafts." Of course, juvenile as I am, it made me giggle that they had the word "shitty" in a schoolbook. But I was intrigued enough to open the book and read the chapter. The point of it was that every single thing ever written, from Shakespeare to the Declaration of Independence, started with a Shitty First Draft. A new writer can't be afraid of writing a shitty first draft, because that is mostly the only kind of first draft there is, and without it you have nothing. Nothing to work on, to shape, to throw out. Resign yourself to the fact that it will be shitty. The "Shitty First Draft" theory has become a guiding principle in my life as an artist and has freed me to give myself a break when trying to create a new sculpture or a new character (or a new book!). It's going to be shitty to start with, but have faith that it can only get better. Something opened up in me that night and before I knew it, I was sitting at a typewriter (yes, a typewriter) writing a scene.

They say you should write about what you know. Laure and I were twenty-something years into our relationship at that point. At forty, I had already lived more than half my life with her. She is the most fascinating, brilliant, loving, sexy, frustrating, selfless, selfish, nurturing person in the world to me. So I spent a day or two writing dialogue between a husband and wife. I can't remember what exactly, but I can guarantee you it was shitty. And then, that next day, July 1, 1998, a strange idea hit me from above. I was in the little house trying to write again when a helicopter started hovering very low in the sky and just sat there. Then another one joined it. The sound was unbelievably loud and disruptive, and they just stayed there. I couldn't focus on writing, so I gave up for the day, went back to the big house, and asked Laure what the fuck was going on with the helicopters. She said, "Barbra Streisand and James Brolin are getting married today. Those are news crews and paparazzi. She lives on Point Dume and there are a whole bunch of celebrities there."

"So how come we weren't invited? I'm not famous enough?" I asked, which made us both laugh.

When I sat down the next day, I realized who the husband and wife were and what they were talking about, and I started writing a play called *Barbra's Wedding*. It was about Jerry, an unemployed actor, and Molly, his wife, who happen to live next door to Barbra Streisand. It takes place on the day of her wedding, to which they have not been invited. I was giving myself a chance to vent all of my frustrations at being an actor. The neuroses, fears, shame, and ego that I felt about show business could come through Jerry in a comic way. And all of Laure's frustrations, compromises, and sacrifices she has made by being married to me, as well as our deep-seated love for each other, could come out through Molly. I didn't know where it was all going, but I wrote this dialogue that day and made myself laugh out loud. It was enough to inspire me to pound out a shitty first draft. Then a little less shitty, but still very shitty, second draft. An equally shitty third draft. A much-improved fourth draft, and on and on . . .

Jerry is looking out the window at the wedding next door.
Molly is on the couch with a migraine from the helicopters.

JERRY
What do these people have in common with Barbra Streisand?

MOLLY
What does anybody have in common with Barbra Streisand?

JERRY
What does James Brolin have in common with Barbra Streisand?

MOLLY
They have something in common, evidently.

JERRY
How could they? I mean she's music and movies and he's like . . . Love Boat and AAMCO commercials.

MOLLY
They're in love.

JERRY
I know. I meant—

MOLLY
That's why people get married.

JERRY
It's just a strange combination.

MOLLY
I'm sure they are very much in love.

JERRY
I know. But how do those two people find each other?

MOLLY
They're lucky.

JERRY
He sure is lucky.

MOLLY
They found each other.

JERRY
He is one lucky son of a bitch.

MOLLY
They love each other! They need each other!

JERRY
Why? Why do those people need each other? How do they get so lucky?

MOLLY

Because people . . . people who need people . . . are the luckiest people in the world!!! . . . I don't know. What are you asking me for!?

DEEP DIVING INTO MALIBU

I n the wake of the success of Celebration for Education, Laure and I formed a nonprofit organization called Malibu Foundation for Youth and Families, whose mission is to improve the lives of the kids and families in Malibu. Robyn Gibson joined the board, as did a core group of dedicated parents, school administrators, teachers, and other involved citizens. We held town meetings to hear what the needs and concerns of the people were. Number one on the list was that in Malibu, there was nothing for kids to do after school except hang out and surf. Kids were getting into drugs and trouble with too much time on their hands while their parents were still at work. We set our sights on starting a teen center of some kind. It was daunting to think about how to set up the infrastructure for something like this, with teachers and aides and activities and insurance, and so many unknowns. As a social worker, my dad had worked a lot with Boys & Girls Clubs of America and suggested we talk to them. Laure and I met with Allan Young, who ran the Boys & Girls Club in Santa Monica, and we were blown away! The club served five hundred kids a day with food, homework help, a gym, sports leagues, and dance classes. The place was buzzing with young people energy. Laure and I saw what our dream of a teen center actually looked like. Allan dedicated his life to the Boys & Girls Club mission, serving on the national committee as well as running his club. He knew the trouble kids can get into in every kind of community if they are not given constructive options like going to the club, and he offered to help us get one up and running in Malibu. He told us we needed three things to get started—a piece of land, a building (and the money to build it), and three years of operating expenses in the bank. The last thing you want to do is build a club, have the kids love it, and then have to shut it down. The principal of the high school and middle school agreed to let us have a small corner of the blacktop on the school campus, a perfect spot that kids could just walk to after school. The dad of a kid on our baseball team was a major real estate developer and said he would give us two of the construction trailers he was using at the building site for the landmark Cathedral of Our Lady of the Angels. I drove downtown to see them. They seemed pretty small, but good enough to get us started. Now we just needed the money. Laure and Robyn went into overdrive on their fundraising and were very successful. With the star power of Mel behind us, and an incredibly important mission that was easy to understand and support, we met with the wealthiest people in Malibu to give our pitch. We continued to have town hall meetings to raise awareness and get smaller donations as well. It was impossible to do fundraising outside of Malibu. It is a very tough sell to ask people to give to the "poor children of Malibu." But the people who lived in our hometown knew that this club was vital to the youth and families of Malibu and were generous. It was important to have everyone in the community invested in this, both emotionally and economically, so every donation, from five dollars to five thousand dollars, was equally significant.

Mel and I became good friends through all of it, spending a lot of time together with our families. He was very idiosyncratic. He had a shaman of some sort, Dr. Hung, who had him drinking all kinds of weird concoctions, including a daily shot of liquid which came out of a jug filled with dead snakes and vines, which was supposed to promote long life and strong boners. He took me to his country club to play golf and we had a lot of laughs. Robyn and Mel gave us their estate in Connecticut to celebrate our anniversary. It was an amazing English castle on a hundred acres of rolling countryside, complete with sheep, sheepherders, gardens, stone walls, creepy statues, giant fireplaces, and ancient stone stairs that led to an actual dungeon, which they had remodeled into a state-of-the-art screening room. We loved every minute of it. Our families were committed to serving our community and we had good times together making things happen.

In the meantime, I did a few acting jobs in LA, including *Very Bad Things*, the first movie Peter Berg directed and wrote. It was a crazy, dark comedy about a group of friends who accidentally kill a prostitute in Vegas at a bachelor party. Christian Slater, Cameron Diaz, and Jon Favreau starred—great actors, great script, and a great role for me, getting an opportunity to be funny in a whole different way than I had before. But the thing that is burnt into my memory is a prank I played when we were shooting on Halloween in the middle of the desert. It was a night shoot from five in the afternoon to seven in the morning, a horrible scene where we dug a shallow grave and buried body parts that we had chopped up and wrapped in plastic. I love Halloween and I have a very special mask

I like to wear on occasion, which looks kind of like a demented version of Alfred E. Neuman from *Mad Magazine*. It fits tightly so it looks realistic, especially because your eyes are very clearly seen. Although it has decent hair, I like to wear it with a hoodie and sometimes stuff a pillow in my belly to make the body language even weirder. But the key to the character is silence. My six-foot-four body wearing this creepy mask with an odd smile is scary enough, but when you add in the incredible uncomfortableness of the silence, people start squirming. Anyway, I brought the mask that night and when I had a break, I went into my dressing room, changed into the mask and my hoodie, and started silently roaming the set. Everyone stared at me uncomfortably, but no one said a thing. I snuck back into my room, changed back into my costume, and returned to the set. My next break, I did the same thing. This time I got a few comments like, "Who the fuck are you?" and "Are you part of the crew?" I came back to set and heard people talking about who it could be. Somebody asked me if it was me, and I said no, I hadn't even seen it. To get them off my scent, I let my stand-in in on my mischief. He put on the mask and hoodie and paraded around for a minute while I was on set, so people could see it couldn't possibly be me. I thought I was home free.

I made two more visits to the set, both of which became much more dangerous than I had anticipated. The next-to-last lap I took around the set was cut short as I ran into Peter, the director. He yelled, "Who the fuck are you? This is not cool! Not cool at all! You know some people have issues with clowns, okay! We don't need any fucking clowns here! Now get the fuck out of here!" (Evidently Peter has major issues with clowns, which was something I did not know about him.) I headed back to my camper to change but was met by Jeremy Piven, who played my little brother in the movie. Jeremy grabbed me and pushed me into the side of one of the Winnebagos, telling me I was a pussy and too scared to show my face. I did notice he was too big a pussy to take the mask off my face, but I really thought he was going to punch me. I made it back to my room and changed. Things were getting tense on the set. It was Halloween night, in the pitch-black desert, we were burying body parts in a shallow grave lit only by car headlights, and there was a creep in a mask stalking the crew. I probably should have quit then, but I pushed it. My last foray came at lunch time, which was probably midnight. The crew were eating at picnic tables in the desert when I came sauntering around the edges of the lunch area, only to realize they definitely did not think this was funny anymore. The Teamsters, the grips, and the electricians all got up from their tables and came toward me. I was completely shitting myself, but they were afraid of me too. I was terrified they would rip the mask off and find out it was me this whole time. But they didn't know if I had a weapon or rabies, so they just kept circling me. We worked our way far enough from the lunch area that we were on the edge of the dark desert. They retreated a bit, and I kept silently smiling and nodding as I drifted out into the night. I circled back the long way, got back to my room, changed clothes, and went to lunch. We finished the second half of the day at dawn, when they called "Wrap." The crew knew my car was a white, 1992 Cadillac DeVille (I loved that car!), and I did a lap around everyone before I drove away, wearing my mask and hoodie, and being cursed by each and every one of them.

(Crazy follow up to the story—years later, it was Halloween again. By now I had bought three more identical masks because I loved them so much, and I convinced Laure to go out with me, both of us wearing the masks. The street next to ours was the best Halloween street in Malibu, and we had just finished scaring people and getting dirty looks from our friends and neighbors, who had no idea who these two creepy characters were. We were heading back down our very dark, dead-end street when a car came down the road toward us. Laure and I decided to give one more scare before we went home. We stood in the middle of the street, forcing the car to stop, with the two of us just standing silently in the headlights. The driver got out of the car, and it was Peter Fucking Berg! Hardly anyone ever drove down our dead-end street, and for some reason, right now, Peter Berg was on my street? What the fuck?! It turned out he was friends with our next-door neighbor and was going to say happy Halloween to their kids. It also turned out that he still had an issue with clowns, because as I took my mask off and introduced him to Laure and laughed at the amazing coincidence of it all, he was not laughing. He was kind of upset and freaked out. And he never hired me for another movie either.)

I finally got a not-shitty-at-all draft of *Barbra's Wedding* finished, and I wanted to see how it would play in front of an audience. Dan Lauria, the actor who played the dad on *The Wonder Years*, also ran a very cool theater in Hollywood called the Coronet. Dan loved the play and offered to let me do a reading there. Through my Steppenwolf Theatre connections, I reached out to Laurie Metcalf, one of the greatest actresses ever. She agreed to do the reading with me, and I went over to her house to rehearse. I had worked on every single line of dialogue for months, and I thought I knew just how it should play, but holy shit, was I wrong. I thought it was a play about Jerry losing his shit and melting down as he realizes what a failure he has been, with Molly being the stable one, trying to calm Jerry and getting frustrated at him. But from the very first beat, Laurie played Molly just as fucked up as Jerry, suppressing her rage at the wedding next door by cooking the most elaborate lunch she can think of. Laurie said the dialogue completely differently than I expected to hear it, finding jokes I didn't even know I had written, emotions that I had not anticipated. And her fresh take made me perform Jerry in a way that surprised me and brought the show to life as only the best actors in the world can.

We performed it to a sold-out audience at the Coronet and brought the house down. There were producers and a director from Steppenwolf at the show, and they were all interested in getting the play done. They thought it needed work but wanted to help me develop it. I couldn't have been happier, and I was inspired to get back to work on the next draft. The director had directed a great play by Steve Martin, and one day I got a call from Steve, who had read my play. I was shocked to be on the phone with him, and even more surprised when he told me how much he liked it. He said, "But it isn't finished." I agreed it still needed work, but he said, "That's not what I mean. You're ending the play too soon. The play is about this marriage, and you haven't resolved that part of the play yet. You end the play with a cry for help from Jerry, which is funny, but is not the correct ending for the play. You need to write more and finish the story of Jerry and Molly." It was such a brilliant note, and such a confidence-builder to be taken seriously as a writer by one of my comic heroes. I had rewritten a lot of movie scripts, but *Barbra's Wedding* was 100 percent my own voice, and that it was connecting with people was so creatively satisfying. I got back to work on the next draft, but I also wanted to try writing something else, to see if I could do it again.

I had been pursued by Les Moonves, the head of CBS, about starring in a TV series. At this time, there was a strict line between working in television and the movies, and my whole career had just been in the movies. There was something tempting about doing a steady show in LA, but I hadn't read anything good. So I began to write a TV series for myself called *Community Center*. Keeping it simple, it was about a guy named Danny who runs a Boys & Girls Club, has two kids, Henry and Sophie, a father named Lenny (my dad's name) and an administrator at the club named Chicki (my mom's nickname). I made Danny in a happy divorce so there could be funny dating stories as the show progressed, so no Laure character. The focus of the show was on Danny raising his teenage kids, as well as stories about the wonderful things that go on in community centers all over the country. The story and script just flowed out of me, and I was really proud of it. I sent it to Les Moonves and told him this was the show I wanted to do. Les was very complimentary about the show but said he was going to pass for now because he had already decided on the TV pilots he was going to make that season. He said he had one new pilot he wanted to make that he really loved and asked me if I would read it. Since he was kind enough to read my script, I decided to read his. It was called *Partners*, a word that still triggers PTSD in me.

TELEVISION—
SUCCESS, WRAPPED IN DISASTER

Partners was a comedy about a cop with a wife, teenage kids, and an annoying and wild partner. It was well-written, and when CBS turned down my show and immediately offered me this one, I was open to it. They offered me a boatload of money, made me an executive producer, promised casting approval, and agreed to shoot the series in LA, although the pilot would be shot in Vancouver. They had a big-name director, Brett Ratner, and big producers like Barry Sonnenfeld attached as well, and it was being produced by Columbia Television, and so I said yes. We cast great actors, including Jeremy Piven, who I had just worked with on *Very Bad Things*. He brought a lot of passion and was funny and wild, and I thought we would have a great chemistry. But when we got to Vancouver and began shooting, trouble began as well. Brett and Jeremy behaved very erratically on set, showing up hours late, yelling at people, and seeming unnaturally jacked-up on something. But the worst part was that some of the women on the set confided in me that Brett and Jeremy were sexually harassing them, and they were afraid. I was an executive producer on the show as well as the star, and I took all of this unprofessional behavior very seriously. I didn't want to confront Brett or Jeremy directly because I had to work with them both up close and personal, and I wanted the show to be good, so I passed on the information to the other executive producers. They told me to just keep quiet about it and they would handle it. The misbehavior continued throughout, but we finally finished the show and came back to LA. I was called into a meeting with the other executive producers, as well as the head of Columbia Television, to discuss the show and the issues I had with Brett and Jeremy's behavior on and off the set. They were angry with me for bringing it up because they thought the show had a good chance of getting picked up and they didn't want any controversy to hurt our chances. I said I didn't want that either, but if we did get picked up, we needed to make some changes to our team because I didn't want to do a show with people who disrespect other people that way. A top-level executive at Columbia yelled at me, "Don't you say a word about this!"

I said I wasn't going to say anything.

"Don't you say a fucking word to anyone, or we'll sue you, do you understand?!" Sue me? Where the fuck did that come from? The threat sent a chill down my spine.

"I'm not going to say anything."

"You better fucking not, or we will sue you!"

"I'm not going to say anything! And stop saying you're going to sue me."

"Don't you tell your agent, Les Moonves, or anybody else because we have a lot of money riding on this and I will sue you if you fuck this up!" I left that meeting very shaken and surprised at how it went down. The number of times he brought up suing me was crazy, no matter how many times I told him I was not going to say anything to anyone. This was obviously way before the MeToo movement started helping people call out sexual harassment on the set, so I just curled up in a ball and shut my mouth. (Interestingly, both Brett and Jeremy have been caught up in MeToo revelations, both publicly accused of sexual harassment in the last few years, as has Les Moonves, the head of CBS.) A few days before CBS was going to announce whether our show had been picked up, I got a phone call from one of the executive producers. I picked up the phone and he immediately started yelling.

"Did you call Les Moonves? Did you call Les Moonves and tell him you didn't want to do the show?"

"What the fuck are you talking about?"

"Did you call Les Moonves and tell him you didn't want to do the show? Why would you do that?"

"I didn't do that. I have no idea what you are talking about."

"Les Moonves said you called him and told him you don't want to do the show!"

"I didn't call Les Moonves. Why would he say that?"

"He said you called him in New York."

"How the fuck would I call him in New York? I have no idea how to call Les Moonves and never would call him anyway. So Les Moonves is lying."

This stopped the producer's ranting at me.

"Well then what the fuck is going on?"

"I have no idea."

"I'll call you back."

I hung up in shock, blindsided and with no idea what was happening. The producer called back.

"Les said he didn't speak to you, but you left him a message at his hotel that said you don't want to do the show."

"A message? I left him a message at his hotel? In my voice?"

"No. A message with the operator."

"What the fuck are you talking about? I didn't leave him a message. Why the fuck would I do that?"

"Because you don't want to do the show."

"Yes, I do. Look, I have no idea what's going on here or who left a message at Les Moonves's hotel, but it was not me. Have Les call me and I will tell him that I didn't leave any message and somebody is fucking around here, and I do want to do the show."

A little while later, Les Moonves called and I explained to him that I did not call him or leave him a message.

"I didn't think it was you. It was weird to get this message in my box."

"Very weird. I don't know what is going on, but I hope you pick up our show."

"We'll see. I like the show but, honestly, right now it is on the bubble."

We said a very nice goodbye and I called the producer back and told him that the conversation went well, we cleared up that bizarre incident, and that the show was in the running. But my level of paranoia kicked into overdrive. Who the fuck left a message for Les Moonves with my name on it?

The day came for the announcement and *Partners* did not get picked up. I was disappointed because I thought it was a good show and good part, and I was hoping the Brett and Jeremy situation would get cleared up once we got a commitment for the series and went into production. But those feelings of disappointment quickly changed into terror when I got a call from my agent saying that Columbia Television was suing me for twenty-five million dollars for sabotaging the show. The next day there was an article in the *LA Times* with my fucking picture next to it saying the same thing, along with the accusation that I had called

Les Moonves and told him not to pick up the show. Twenty-five million?! If you added everything I had in the world, it would come to about six million, so I didn't know where I was going to come up with the extra nineteen million! They were going to wipe me out, everything. Our house and our savings were at risk, along with my reputation. I had no idea what to do. My new agent at ICM was absolutely no help, afraid and wanting to stay on the good side of Columbia Television— fucking wimp. All of a sudden, I had to find a lawyer, which I knew nothing about. I hooked up with a tough and smart litigator who thought the whole thing was ridiculous, and he was not only going to fight them tooth and nail but countersue them as well. He put together a case, getting phone records to prove there was no phone call or message from me, getting Les Moonves to give a deposition to testify about his phone call with me, and developing his countersuit against Columbia, claiming they were defaming my character and trying to blame me for the financial loss they suffered when the show didn't get picked up. It was good to have someone fighting for me, but Jesus, it was so expensive! I had to pay for his time at hundreds of dollars an hour, his assistant's time, photocopying, parking, and who knows what else. It felt like I was going to end up owing the lawyer twenty-five million dollars before it was over. I started to experience anxiety like I have never felt, bad enough that I got a prescription for Xanax (which didn't do much of anything). Plus, they wanted me to hire a publicist so I could get my story out in the press and defend myself and my reputation. But that would be another huge expense, and I didn't want to talk about it anyway. I just wanted it to go away. So I called my old friend Joe Roth and asked him how to make it stop. He said, "You need a rabbi."

"A rabbi?"

"Someone to talk to both sides and help come to a solution.

They are pissed at you, and you are pissed at them. You need a rabbi to help you find an ending."

Joe engaged his personal lawyer, a powerful man with connections to Columbia Television, and came back with a solution. If I gave them back the money they paid me for the show, they would drop the lawsuit. My lawyer advised me not to take it, that we would definitely win, and they knew that and that is why they were offering this. If it was just about right and wrong and there hadn't been so much money at stake, I would have loved to have seen justice in the matter, have the Los Angeles Times print a retraction and rewind the clock. But I couldn't afford that risk, financially or emotionally, and I was relieved to get out of the situation with the same money I started with. But the damage was done, and that bullshit would follow me around for years. I still have no idea what happened or why, and I was stung that no one stood up for me when the accusations were so clearly false. I wish I had been braver about standing up for the people who were sexually harassed on the show and had asked for my help. I should have made a bigger stink about that part of the story, which got washed away in all of the other controversy, but I had no idea how to fight that fight by myself. Thank God for the MeToo movement. And Fuck Brett Rather, Fuck Jeremy Piven, Fuck Les Moonves, and Fuck that top-level executive at Columbia!

Luckily, I had an incredible life to fall back into. We had finally raised enough money to launch Boys & Girls Club of Malibu. Allan Young helped us find a great executive director who knew the programs Boys & Girls Clubs had and had experience in hiring staff. Soon the double-wide trailers were loaded onto huge tractor trailers and driven to the Malibu school campus blacktop, where they were met by a hundred of our fellow community members, there to use their skills to help build this community center for their children. Carpenters built a deck around the buildings, electricians and plumbers hooked up their systems, carpet was laid, walls were painted—it makes me cry with joy to remember that building being put together by all of us. Mel was there hammering nails, Laure and Robyn overseeing everything and feeding people. The school administrators helped to put the fencing in, giving up a piece of their territory because they knew our club would provide things for the kids that the school alone couldn't. And when the doors finally opened, the kids flocked in—getting homework help, playing sports, learning leadership skills, organizing trips, meeting kids from other clubs, and all the incredible experiences Boys & Girls Clubs around the world offer. I was and still am so proud to be a part of the Boys & Girls Club family.

I was forty-two when Henry got into Harvard and flew away and out of our lives. Our nest was emptying, and we could see how quickly it would go by with Sophie and Ella too. But it was good to have him living his dream, and it gave us more time to focus on the girls. Driver's licenses and jobs, sports, and more homework than I could even comprehend. Sophie tried her best at school, but her focus was on her friends and her music. Ella was now dealing with the trials and tribulations that young girls put each other through, but she never lost her positivity and love of learning. And Laure was running the show—getting the kids off to school and activities, running the house, taking care of our money, working full time as president of Malibu Foundation for Youth and Families, and then ending the day by making dinner for all of us. A force of nature.

My work in Media Literacy, Arts in Education, and Boys & Girls Club brought me into contact with politicians (you know, the people who actually control the purse strings). I found myself in a private meeting with John McCain, pitching the importance of Media Literacy. David Foster had a fundraiser for Al Gore, who we spent some personal time with. He was a brilliant man one-on-one, but he was a fucking lox as a public speaker. I joined Maria Shriver's committee, fundraising for Arts in Education, while I continued teaching my class at the high school. I was still coaching Ella's basketball team and loving the community, but Malibu had begun to change. The retired neighbors next door moved, and the new people tore down the little house and built a little mansion in its place. The hardware store at Point Dume closed and was replaced by something far less necessary. Laure and I spent more time in rich people's houses, wooing them to donate to the Malibu Foundation or join the board, but I felt myself losing touch with the very community I was dedicating my service to.

Careerwise, I was laying low. *Partners* took it out of me, and I was happy to ignore show business and get back on the plan of living a life of creative and financial freedom. But then I got a call that Les Moonves wanted to meet with me. At his office at CBS, he told me how sorry he was about how things happened with *Partners* and reiterated that I didn't have anything to do with the show not getting picked up. He apologized for not being able to speak out in my defense, but that Columbia Television executive was determined to sue me, and CBS did a lot of business with them, and that was just the way things worked. He also said that he still believed in me and thought I could be a big star on television, and that he wanted to make *Community Center.* He was going to introduce me to some great TV producers who could help me develop the show, and then we would make the pilot. My jaw was on the floor. I was so thankful, relieved, elated, dumbfounded, and humbled. And creatively, I had just had a rocket lit under my ass. I was going to do my show! Un-Fuck Les Moonves! (And then Re-Fuck Les Moonves for his horrible sexual attacks on the women he tried to grope in that very office!)

My (new) agent made an incredible deal—more money than

I made on *Partners*, and I was the executive producer/writer/creator/star, so it was my ship to steer. My first brilliant move was to connect with Mindy Schultheis and Michael Hanel, two novice producers. They knew what made good television right off the bat and have been producing great shows ever since. They were so funny, supportive, and smart. We hired great actors to play Henry, Sophie, Lenny, and Chicki, and shot the pilot on locations all around LA. It was an amazing feeling seeing it all come to life, these words that I had written, a story I had made up, now being acted out and filmed. The editing went great, the music clicked, and we turned it in to CBS. Within a couple of weeks, I got the call to fly to New York because they were going to announce that the show, now called *Danny*, had been picked up for a twelve-episode series commitment! I was on top of the world that I was going to get to run my own television show. This show was an artistic and personal expression of where I was in my life, with my community center and my kids, and now I was going to get a chance to tell the stories I wanted to. We hired a writing staff, pitching and shaping stories, and eventually writing scripts. We built huge sets on a soundstage. I hired a great crew and great directors. When we finally started shooting, the machine went into overdrive and my responsibilities were mind-boggling. Writing future shows, casting upcoming shows, shooting current shows, editing the shows we'd shot, and scoring the shows we'd edited, all while acting in every scene. I have never been so fully engaged in an artistic endeavor as the four months we spent making those episodes. They were stories taken right out of my life—teaching Henry to drive, Sophie managing the mean girls, struggling with government bureaucracy at the community center, dealing with my dad getting older—so I lived and breathed every frame of film on every episode. Our premiere on CBS was scheduled for September 18, 2001, and I was set to go on every talk show they could book to get the word out about the show. We were in the middle of shooting our eighth episode on September 11th. We had a late call that day, so I was sleeping when Laure woke me up and turned on the TV in time to see the second plane hit the second tower at the World Trade Center. We watched and cried and were terrified. But I had to leave for work. When the crew got there, we were all in a daze and just gathered around the TV and radio to follow what the fuck was going on. One of the crew had a relative who worked in the towers, and he couldn't get in touch with them. We tried to focus to shoot some scenes, but it was impossible. I cried my eyes out in my dressing room. Even though the studio wanted us to keep shooting, we decided to call it a day. We came back the next day to keep shooting the shows, but the air had definitely gone out of the balloon. The network preempted all television shows with wall-to-wall coverage of 9/11 for weeks. They rescheduled our premiere a week or two later but no one, including me, felt like watching a new TV comedy, and the show tanked. We were still shooting when we got the call that they were pulling the plug on the show after only airing one episode. The cast and crew had an incredible party that night, all of us drunk out of our minds. As I left, I got pulled over by a cop. Three cars, filled with my crew members, pulled up and surrounded us, pleading with the officer to let me go. And he did.

I was exhausted and relieved in some way that the show was over. I had had the greatest artistic experience I could ever imagine, spending millions of other people's dollars on my vision of my story, employing hundreds of people and making dear friends for life. The fact that it didn't have a long run on television doesn't change any of that.

TOO MUCH OF
A GOOD THING

The writing bug bit me hard. Creating *Danny* and seeing it come to life made me want to get *Barbra's Wedding* produced. I wanted Steppenwolf Theatre to do it. Everything they do is so well-done and smart. But Steppenwolf produces very challenging theater, and I think my play was a little too Neil Simon-y for them, so they decided not to do it. But in a lucky twist, the head dramaturge at Steppenwolf, who was a fan of my play, got a new job at the Philadelphia Theatre Company. She showed the play to the artistic director, and they decided to produce it in May 2002. I was in shock, having just been given another incredible gift from the Gods of Show Business. A first-class production at a first-class theater of the play I wrote sitting in my underwear in Malibu. Unbelievable. We hired a terrific New York director, got John Pankow and Julie White, two brilliant Broadway regulars, to play Jerry and Molly, and got to work designing the set and getting ready for rehearsals.

But before we got into rehearsals, I was offered a TV show for ABC called *Regular Joe*. The script was really funny, written by the creator of *King of Queens*, and even though I didn't need the money, the deal was even crazier than the other shows, one hundred and thirty-five thousand dollars per episode. With that kind of bread on the table, it was a great chance to pad the old bank account before my luck ran out, and I would have to have been a fool to say no. *Regular Joe* was a traditional sitcom in front of a live audience, and I played Joe, a regular guy with a wife and teenagers and a job running a hardware store. Doing a sitcom is kind of like acting in a play or a film, and it was a learning curve as an actor to figure out who I was performing for—the audience or the camera (the answer is the camera). The people were great, the actors were terrific. We rehearsed for a week and then performed in front of a live studio audience. The filming went well, although it felt strange when we did a second or third take that the audience laughed at the same jokes over and over again, even though they just heard them five minutes ago. They knew they were also performers in the sitcom, playing the role of the laugh-track audience perfectly. It was a very easy gig, especially since I was just acting and not involved in the writing or producing, and when it was done, I went off to Philadelphia to begin my new job—playwright.

I loved the process of rehearsals. My job was to sit in the theater, watching the actors and director create each moment of the play. Blocking the action, learning the lines, practicing their props, and the millions of details it takes to put on a play. If a moment wasn't working, I was there to explain the intention of it, to listen to what the problem was, and make adjustments. They challenged me to make the play as great as it could be, transforming it from ideas on a page into a living, breathing, dynamic piece of theater. I rewrote sections of the play every night. I have always loved being the actor who helps the playwright find his play, but I did not understand the importance of the actor's contribution until I was the playwright. Goddamn, that was a hell of an artistic experience for me. Laure and the girls came and loved it. Henry came down from Harvard, and my parents came up from Chevy Chase. The play opened to rave reviews. New York producers came down to see it, and before I knew it, I had a deal to bring the play to the prestigious off-Broadway theater, The Westside Theater. Broadway producers called The Dodgers would be producing the play, with the renowned Manhattan Theatre Club coproducing and adding it to their season. Might be the proudest I have ever been—the dyslexic high school dropout was now a fucking New York playwright.

At the same time, ABC picked up *Regular Joe* as a mid-season replacement, which was fantastic. Six more episodes at that salary was a lot of extra cake, and the writing and part were really good. And there was satisfaction in getting a show on network television again. It meant I still had value in that marketplace. Since it was a mid-season show, it wouldn't start shooting until January 2003. That gave me six months of no pressure from my agents to look for acting work because I was unavailable, and I could focus on *Barbra's Wedding*. I learned a lot about the play by watching the audience reaction in Philly and made more adjustments before it opened in New York. I was excited for the work and the free time to be at home. The only hiccup was I was starting to lose my mind.

Part of it was politics. By this point, George W. Bush and Dick Cheney were beating the drums of war, questioning people's patriotism, keeping the country on edge with color-coded "terror alerts," and trying to divert attention away from their massive failure to protect the country from the horrific attack on September 11th. The obvious lies they were fabricating about the weapons of mass destruction (WMD) were printed on the front page of the *New York Times*, the Democrats shook in fear of being called "unpatriotic" if they voted against the war, and I was consumed by the ugly turn our country was taking. (Please watch Stephen Colbert's legendary speech at The White House Correspondent's Dinner, in which he scathingly ridiculed both the White House and the correspondents for being so dangerously bad at their jobs. It was a brave act of speaking truth to power, an act of patriotic heroism, and a ray of hope in that moment of crisis. I salute you, sir!) There were still many questions about the Bush family letting the Bin Laden family leave the country, as well as the physics and science that contradicted the official storyline of 9/11. But it wasn't just politics. Malibu itself was making me crazier by the day. Our peaceful little oasis being destroyed one McMansion at a time, their owners more entitled by the minute. My heart broke with every jackhammer blast. Our whole family had devoted itself to making Malibu the best community it could be, giving our time and energy to help keep the small-town integrity that we loved. But I could see the writing on the wall. Malibu was being bought up by a bunch of fucking assholes that I didn't want to live near or be associated with.

For our whole marriage, Laure and I dreamed about getting a farm in the country. We rented cabins in Woodstock as soon as we had a couple of extra bucks and almost bought the house there. We bought the house in Moss Beach. We looked at property every time I went on location in Lake Tahoe, Colorado, Utah, or Montana—always doing the equation of how much the farm would cost, how much land we could get, how much time it would take to get there, and how often we would use it, and always coming up with no good answer. We wanted a big piece of land with water on it, but the only thing like that near LA was in Santa Barbara or Ojai, and we couldn't afford more than a few acres of land there. Besides, they seemed like they had already been taken over by the same privileged class of people that were currently taking over Malibu. The places we could afford were all so far away that we would have to take a plane or drive for twelve hours to get there. There were places out in the desert, but that was not the kind of living that appealed to us. The dream of the farm in the country was getting further away just when it was turning from a dream into a necessity. I felt more and more like I needed to escape, but I had nowhere to go. By now I had a computer, and one day I was looking at Ojai real estate online, and a house with four hundred acres was for sale for one point eight million. I did a double take because in Ojai (a) there was never a piece of land that big for sale and (b) if there was, it would cost about ten million or more. I looked at the ad more closely, and it was for a ranch in Tulare County, not Ojai. I had never heard of Tulare County and was astonished to see that it was about a three-hour drive from Malibu, in the foothills of the Sierra Mountains. I called the owner, made an appointment, and Laure, the girls, and I drove up there. It was an easy drive up through Bakersfield up to the Sierra Mountains. The owners had us for lunch and the place was amazing, jaw-droppingly beautiful, drenched in fall colors. It had a grape vineyard, a part of the Tule River running through it, an historic battlefield on the property, huge trees, and steep mountain trails. I had no idea how big four hundred acres was. It's big! The house was tiny, both in size and in scale. I barely fit through the doorways. It must have been an old hotel of some kind, because there was a row of motel rooms on the property, down a little gravel road, which was absolutely charming. The girls fell asleep on the ride home and Laure and I drove back that night, living the dream we had envisioned on our honeymoon, when we saw a farm in Pennsylvania and said one day we would have some kids asleep in the back seat and a farm of our own.

That house was too expensive for us because we didn't want to go into debt or take money out of the nest egg we were living off of. But within a couple of months, I came upon an ad for a nearby ranch, 350 acres for six hundred thirty-five thousand dollars. How could this be? It was a third of the price of the other place for almost the same amount of land. Between the money I made on *Danny* and the money I was going to make on *Regular Joe*, if this place was decent, I could afford it. I drove up and met the realtor. He took me around the property in his truck. I had absolutely no sense of direction and didn't know where on the property we were, but it was the most beautiful ranch I had ever seen. It was a beef cattle ranch, with mountains and meadows and barns and dirt roads, tucked down a long driveway off a small road. The house was a thousand-square-foot cabin with a porch and a fenced-in backyard, to keep the cows out and the dogs in. The realtor was an old cowboy who said he loved this ranch and that "it had a lot of character." He took me into the house to meet the owner, a heavyset cowboy in overalls, sitting at a typewriter at the table in the tiny living room/kitchen area. He told me his wife was sick and they needed to sell. The ranch had been in their family for generations (the creek that ran through it was named after their family), and it hurt like hell for them to give it up. He told me about his cattle operation, the water rights, and the neighbors. He had already broken off 145 acres and the original house and sold it to the family that lived there now, and he couldn't break up the original ranch anymore. I asked him if it got hot in the summer. He said, "Oh, about seventy-eight degrees." I thought I'd found paradise until he added, "That's what I keep the air conditioning at in the summer. Outside it gets up to about 105."

He gave me the paper he had typed up, which was his calculations for the price—what the average acre cost, how much it had cost him to put up the cabin, etc.—and the total was six hundred and thirty-five thousand dollars. He said, "I won't take one penny more and I won't take one penny less." I told him I understood. He said, "If you want this ranch, I'll need to meet your wife first. And I will need you to both promise that you will take your responsibility to this land seriously, keep its character and respect its history." I can still remember that moment so clearly, and I have taken my oath to him seriously ever since. I called Laure on the way home and told her excitedly, "I found it! At long last, we are going to have our own ranch. A 350-acre cattle ranch!" Laure drove up the next week and, of course, impressed the owner to no end. A forgotten part of Laure was about to emerge and change the course of our lives once again. Laure's family history is of California farmers, going all the way back to the late 1800s. Laure's grandparents owned a walnut farm in Northern California, so she knew in her bones how to talk about water, weather, markets, and everything else that goes into ranching and farming. She is so sophisticated and yet it turns out she was completely at home in the middle of California ranch country. The owner and his wife both shed a tear that day, sad to be saying goodbye to their family ranch, but knowing they were passing the torch to very capable hands.

The Westside Theatre had a show close and became available, so *Barbra's Wedding* was now starting rehearsal for its New York debut on January 13th. That also happened to be the first day of rehearsal for the first episode of *Regular Joe*. I couldn't believe it. Two hugely important pieces of work that needed my full attention, both happening at the exact same time. It was frustrating to have it all happening at once, but both shows had strict opening dates and lots of money riding on them, so I just had to suck it up for a couple of months. The producers of the play rented the community theater in Malibu for two weeks and bent the rehearsal schedule around my TV schedule. I had done a lot of work on *Barbra's Wedding* and loved watching the actors and director bring it to life again, investing it with pain, laughs, and a physicality that took it to a whole other level. In the meantime, *Regular Joe* had been entirely revamped. The actor who played my father had been replaced by the sublime Judd Hirsch and, after many attempts to find someone to replace the actress who played my wife, they gave up and made my character a widower. The scripts were funny, and the shows went great. I got two weeks off from the show and went to back to New York to attend the technical and final rehearsals and the first week of previews.

I don't think I have ever felt so overloaded in my life as I was those weeks in New York. As if it weren't enough having my NY playwriting debut and my ABC TV sitcom happening at the exact same time, we also took possession of our brand-new cattle ranch that week. A twenty-year dream come true, and I was too busy with these other amazing experiences to be there. If ever there was a case of an embarrassment of riches, this was it. And yet, there was a dark cloud hanging over the whole thing, and my memories always include that sickening feeling. Bush and Cheney pulled out all the stops for military action at the United Nations, trying to get other countries to support their proposed war. The weeks I was in New York for those final rehearsals were the same weeks that Colin Powell held up his phony anthrax vial, that the UN inspectors testified that they had done exhaustive searches and found absolutely no WMDs, and that people all over the world took to the streets to protest the needless conflict the Bush administration was forcing on the world. Henry came down from Harvard to stay with me for a few days and we went to the huge rally outside the UN. Such a helpless feeling, knowing our country's corrupt and inept leaders were willfully ignoring the facts and the truth and tarnishing America's reputation.

I went back home, finished shooting the last episodes of

Regular Joe, and then hightailed it back to New York for final previews and opening night of *Barbra's Wedding*. I did a bunch of press for both but was also competing with coverage of the run-up to the Iraq War. The play opened on March 5th to great audience reaction and great reviews. The play ran for six months, which was a very solid run, and was published by Samuel French, the flagship publisher of plays. The Iraq War began on March 20th. It got terrible reviews and ran for over twenty years. *Regular Joe* premiered on March 28th and was canceled within a month, because who the fuck would want to watch a new sitcom about a regular Joe at his hardware store when the networks filled the airwaves with the sensational wartime footage the Bush administration provided. It made much better television. George Bush had now fucked the country over in ways that would change history. He was too arrogant to take security warnings seriously before 9/11, letting his guard down for the worst attack ever on our country. He lied his way into an illegal war, destroying our credibility, our morals, and our economy. And because of the chaos these events created in the media, he destroyed the chances of both *Danny* and *Regular Joe* becoming successful TV shows, thereby depriving the world of all of those sweet stories-that-could-have-been. I far as I was concerned, this was war!

PAPIER-MÂCHÉ
SAVES THE DAY

T he life I had been living and loving was coming to an end. I was always going be their dad, but the kids were flapping their wings and leaving the nest and didn't need me in the same way anymore. I had a turn being a movie star and television star and had prepared financially for the time when the parts and the money no longer came easily. So now I needed to figure out satisfying things to do with the leftover time, although I guess I had already decided what this new Daniel Stern's life was going to look like. He was going to be an artist, a public servant, and a rancher.

I had only seen our new ranch just that one time, when the realtor took me around and I met the cattle rancher who owned it. Laure had gone up, met everyone, and took care of all the real estate closing stuff while I was consumed with *Barbra's Wedding* and *Regular Joe.* She had made a deal with a local cowboy, Will, to lease the pastureland and run his cows on our property, not only giving us a little income but also having someone there every day to keep an eye on the place. Our lifelong fantasy of owning a farm in the country had come true on paper, but now we had to figure out what the reality of that actually was. When we finally got our first chance to go up there, it was like a movie. Specifically, *City Slickers.* We drove up with a bed, a table and chairs, and some food packed into our Chevy Suburban. (That's another plug for a GMC car, and I want it known that I am wide open for an endorsement deal.) The drive was gorgeous and easy, and the land was just as beautiful as I remembered, maybe more so. We drove by the barn and the pump house and on up to the wood cabin, cruising by the cows and their adorable babies behind the fences. We unloaded the furniture, set up the kitchen and bedroom, and got the wood-burning stove going. It was simple and romantic and just as we had dreamed. We ventured out to see our land, heading up one of the dirt roads in the Suburban into the pastureland. I drove along the rutted road in four-wheel drive for half a mile or so when we got out to marvel at the feeling of being in such a perfectly natural setting, in the middle of nowhere, green hills surrounding this beautiful little valley. Laure hiked up one side while I strolled in the open pasture.

The sight of her on that mountainside is something I will never forget, but not because of how beautiful she was. It is the memory of those fifteen or twenty cows that suddenly appeared on the edge of the mountain above her. It didn't make a lot of sense, because cows are nervous around people and aren't really that curious. I didn't start to feel uneasy until I looked up at the ridge of the opposite hill and saw another large group of cows congregating. What the fuck was going on? I had been around enough cows on those *City Slickers* films to know they are afraid of everything, completely non-aggressive animals. That's how you herd them, by chasing them in the direction you want them to go. These cows looked different. They looked like they wanted to come after us. When another herd of fifteen or so came up the road and blocked our way back, I started to get a very, very bad feeling. Laure was about a hundred yards up the hill when I yelled to her to get back to the truck. At first, she poo-pooed me, saying I was being ridiculous. But she started to run once she noticed the cows moving in on us, slowly surrounding us like a pack of wolves. I hopped into the truck, which was facing the wrong way on the tiny dirt road, and performed a brilliant nine-point U-turn. But moving the truck only served to rev up the cows, and they went from walking toward us to running toward us. Laure was still ten yards from the truck and the cows were about to catch up with us, so I started driving, slowly, trying to get the cows blocking the road to back the fuck up. Laure still swears I was leaving her there, which I wasn't, but she did have to jump into the truck while it was moving pretty quickly. Once I busted through the cows on the road, I drove a little faster, which only spurred them on, and suddenly Laure and I were in a fucking cattle stampede, our first time on the land! Does it get any more *City Slickers* than that? It was as surreal a moment as I have ever experienced. The cows were running close to the truck. One's huge head was parallel with my driver's window and another with Laure's window, then dropped off as the terrain forced them away, only to be replaced by another stampeding cow. When we got to the gate in the fence, I got out and waved and yelled at them while Laure opened the gate and drove the truck through, then I scurried through and locked it behind us. We could not understand what the fuck happened until a few days later when we saw Will drive into the pasture in his Chevy Suburban, same color as ours, and unload bales of hay for the cows and their babies. We still laugh about that perfect beginning to our ranch life. We learned that we had so much to learn, and how fun it was going to be.

I loved doing chores up there and man, does it get hot in the summer. But I loved that too. I painted the whole house and worked with Will and his family when he branded the cows and gave them shots. He was an amazing rancher—fixing fences, birthing cows. Sometimes he rode his horse and sometimes he rode his Quad all-terrain vehicle. I bought a Quad and started shadowing him but also exploring the property on my own. I was probably the only Jew, the only Democrat, and the only actor within a hundred miles of the place, and I had never felt so at home. Ranching is about fixing problems with the tools that you have at hand, and I loved the practical creativity I discovered in myself. I learned how to take care of the plumbing, irrigation, fencing, retaining walls, landscaping, and pest control. I bought my first shotgun, pistol, and rifle and learned how to use them. There was no cell phone reception. Sometimes I had to climb the pole and jiggle the phone wires to make the landline work, which was just like the guy in the *Green Acres* TV show I watched as a kid. We bought a couple of recliners and looked out the window for hours at hawks flying, the pond glistening, the sun setting. Our neighbors were great and helpful and respectful of our privacy too. We had always hoped to have a place like this, but we never knew if the reality of it would match the fantasy. Now Laure and I began to discover that farm life was even more fulfilling than we could have ever dreamed.

I think getting my hands dirty at the ranch made me want to get my hands dirty back in Malibu too, because I had a dream one night that would change my life forever. I was in my kindergarten class and my teacher, Miss Burton, was showing me how to do papier-mâché—taking strips of paper, sinking them into the mixture of flour and warm water, sliding the paper through your fingers to get off the excess liquid, and then laying the paper onto a bowl to make a mask. It was such a sweet dream. I loved that teacher, and the art felt so fun, warm, and creative. The next morning, I got some flour, a bucket of water, and the *Los Angeles Times* and went out to the garage. I got some chicken wire and made a big ball and started laying papier-mâché on it, and by the end of the day, I had a huge, funny-looking head. The next day I painted it. Then, I made a body out of irrigation pipe, covered it in my old clothes and shoes, and stuffed it with newspaper. When I attached the huge papier-mâché head to it, it was bigger than me and made me laugh. And it made Laure laugh too. So I made another one, and then another one after that. I loved creating art when I was a kid, but I had forgotten about it in the chaos of my life, marriage, family, and career. I had been putting all my creative energy into acting, directing, and writing, but all of those projects need funding and other people. This papier-mâché dream had awakened me to a whole new direction to channel my creativity, which I could control completely and would always give me work to do, because I am a man who needs to work.

Although there was plenty of work to do for the Boys & Girls Club. We were expanding by the day and our foundation needed as much attention as Laure and I could give it—fundraising, overseeing the board and the staff, and trying to lay the groundwork for a strong future that didn't require us to run or manage it. Mel Gibson and I did another gala fundraising show for the celebrities in Malibu. It was incredibly successful, but kind of obscene in the amount of ego and money that filled up the banquet tent. Where else could you have Kenny G performing an annoying breathing trick of playing a single note indefinitely on his sax, and then get a bidding war going among the audience to get him to stop? We made ten thousand dollars on that alone. But I was getting a little tired of being the pitch man for the Malibu Foundation. I believed in building and sustaining something so vital to the community, but the begging for money by throwing parties and golf tournaments was starting to wear me down.

Even though I was living in a wonderful bubble, I was still very aware of how ugly the real world had gotten. Bush and Cheney had led us into an unnecessary war, and their Mission Accomplished theatrics disgusted me. Henry got a job on John Kerry's campaign and of course, being Henry, became friends with Senator Kerry's daughter. He introduced me to the family, and I ended up not only campaigning for Kerry, but shooting a great little film that his daughter directed. Senator Kerry would have been an incredible president, but he was not a great public speaker. He and I met on two occasions, for me to give him "acting advice" on how to loosen up and be more emotional in front of the camera to fight back against the Swift boat lies that Bush was encouraging. The poor man had so many bigger things on his mind than to listen to my advice, but he was very kind and receptive. He was such a humble and funny person, and how America picked Bush again is beyond my comprehension. I thought there wasn't much I could do about any of it except stay informed, work for change, give money, and raise my voice. But there was one thing I hadn't thought of.

I got a fan letter one day from Captain Sandra Chavez, stationed in Baghdad, Iraq, asking if I could send her an autographed picture for her celebrity wall. She also mentioned in passing if I would ever consider coming over on a USO tour. The USO, I thought—is that still around? The last I heard of it, Bob Hope was doing shows for the troops in Vietnam. Anyway, how the hell would an anti-war activist go to the war zone and talk to soldiers without the subject of how fucking stupid and reckless the war is coming up? That didn't seem like a real morale booster. But I certainly couldn't pretend like I believed in this "holy war" Bush was forcing on the world. Also, I didn't have "an act" or anything I could fit into a USO show, so what would I do there? I wrote back to Captain Chavez, asking her a lot of questions, along with an autographed picture. I was also trying to get some on-the-ground reconnaissance about security there because the General in Charge of the T.N.T.D. Branch of my brain (Try Not To Die) was demanding a lot of information about entering an active war zone. Captain Chavez replied, excited I was considering it. She made a compelling case on what it would mean to her and the troops for me to make the trip. She said I would not be expected to perform and told me about the USO Handshake Tour, where I could go to different bases, say hello to the soldiers, take pictures, and sign autographs. Yes, it was a dangerous place but there would be tight security around me and their record of protecting USO folks was perfect so far. She said she understood my anti-war stance but this had nothing to do with that—there were people of all political opinions fighting the war. This was about assuring the people serving in Iraq that Americans back home remembered them and respected their sacrifice, especially around the holidays. She told me how much they loved my movies, especially *Home Alone*, and if I were to make the effort to go there and say "Merry Christmas" to them, it would mean more than I could imagine. I talked it over with Laure, and she was as moved as I was. For all those reasons, as well as my need to see what was going on with my own eyes, I said yes.

The USO is an amazing organization, devoted to keeping alive the human connection of our warriors and our citizens, a way for both the soldier and the person from "back home" to say a love-filled "thank you" to each other and give a ray of understanding to the madness of war. My Handshake Tour was set for December 18–26, 2003. I would fly to Baghdad and then to various bases throughout Iraq, depending on the security situation at the time. I was allowed to bring another person with me and asked Henry if he wanted to be my assistant, and he jumped at the chance. This seemed like an incredible teaching opportunity to take him to see the reality of war. "You want to be in politics? Well, let's see what war is really like."

I had to wait a couple of months to ship out, and at first, it felt great. Saying "I'm going to Iraq" held a power I hadn't felt before, a certain street-cred that comes with actually putting your ass on the line. I even started getting calls to appear on cable news shows but declined. As departure day got closer, my knees started to turn to Jell-O and the reality of what I had agreed to became terrifying. George Bush had predicted we would be met with parades and flowers for "freeing" Iraq but had no real plan for how to occupy an entire country after chasing away Saddam Hussein. Reading the paper every day about improvised explosive device explosions killing our soldiers, bombings throughout the country, helicopters being shot down, and all of the other horrors of war brought a real personal panic now, not just a political one. I was mad at myself, questioning my motives for going into this chaos, and guilt-ridden that I would be risking my son's life as well. I got the smallest taste of what it is like for a family to have a member "go off to war," and it is traumatizing. To be brave is not only to face your fears but to stare them down, and force optimism to overwhelm your pessimism, if for no other reason than to help your family stay strong.

My mission was to be a bridge between our soldiers and citizens, and I would be there at Christmastime, so it seemed appropriate to bring the gifts of love and laughter along with me. I reached out to the schools in Malibu, and they had the kids write letters and holiday cards to the soldiers for me to give out. And I reached out to my funny friends—Crystal, Cheech, Gibson, and Reiser—for some jokes to tell in case I needed to be entertaining at some point. I was still wrestling with my courage and feared my comedy act would be less Bob Hope and more Bob Hopeless.

"Hey everybody, I don't know what the fuck we are doing here, there's no way we can win, and we are all going to die. Good night!" Here are a couple of the best of the jokes my friends gave me:

"What's so special about the stealth bomber? They say it flies in undetected, bombs, and then flies away. Hell, I've been doing that my whole life."

"I was really nervous about coming to a war zone, but the captain was very supportive. He promised to keep a supply of my blood type on hand, even if he had to kill the chicken himself."

"How do you know when it's bedtime at the Neverland Ranch? When the big hand is on the little hand."

Five days before we were supposed to leave, Saddam Hussein was captured in a "spider hole" on a farm somewhere near Tikrit, Iraq. The still-terrified part of me wondered, "Does this mean I don't have to go? I mean we got him, what do they need me for? I'm just going to be in the way of them packing their bags to get the fuck home." But there was no turning back, and so I embraced my role of ambassador. When I picked up letters from schools, I realized how much people were investing me with their messages of love and thanks, and that felt great. Laure and Ella and I read the letters and cried at the kids sending letters of love, thanks, hope, news, humility, commitment, and honor. I read a letter from a high schooler that started with, "What is bravery?" and it made me tremble. The day came to leave. The letters took up a whole duffle bag and a half, and the football I thought was necessary ate up some prime suitcase real estate too, so I did not have room for too many clothes, but that was okay. I was cautiously optimistic that we were going to survive. They would never let anything happen to a celeb, not even Bob Hopeless. Real soldiers and their loved ones have been saying goodbye since the beginning of the time, and I got a small taste of those countless heartbreaks. The lead-up to leaving is a slow-motion goodbye, but the goodbye itself is so short. You have to make your body walk away. Legs moving feet, one in front of the other, taking you toward chaos and the unknown.

I flew to London and then to Kuwait, in first-class filled with drunken men in robes. I was met by Tracy, who was my USO escort for the trip. The airport access road was lined with soldiers posted every twenty yards on both sides, and when we got to the Marriott Hotel where we were staying, it was surrounded by tanks and barbed wire. It turned out that the Marriott was the home of the International Arab Conference. The presidents and sheiks of at least twelve large Arab countries were staying in the same building as us. The king of Jordan was there. All roads within two hundred yards of the hotel were blocked off to any car that didn't have a particular piece of paper that we didn't have. I was carrying two enormous duffel bags, my backpack, winter coat, and camera bag. Dragging the hopes and underwear of Malibu, Tracy and I made our way through the guns, dogs, ID checks, baggage screening, personal screening, and intrusive wand screening, into the lobby, which was another world completely. The lobby was filled with more robes. Damn, that is a good look! And so comfortable! Tracy took me to the twelfth floor to meet the butler.

"Butler?" I said.

"The twelfth floor has a butler. He will run your bath, unpack your clothes, whatever you need."

My room was nice, with a view of a vast desert of dirt and sand that came right up to the hotel, with a random tent every few hundred yards in the distance. Ding-dong. Guess who was there? Henry! Who flew in from Boston. I hadn't seen him in a while, and Jesus Christ, was he big and beautiful. We called home to say that we were okay and stuffed our faces on potatoes, salmon, eggs, croissants, and coffee that the butler kept bringing. Just crazy to think where we were and where we were going.

IRAQ AND BACK

The military staged the invasion of Iraq from Kuwait, the central hub for the supply line of goods and services needed for the huge undertaking of invading a country. Soldiers leaving the battlefield came to Kuwait to decompress and be physically and mentally assessed before being either sent home or back to another deployment. We spent our first day there, driving to the different camps where our soldiers were deployed. I met hundreds and hundreds of people that first day and felt an immediate connection, drawn to each other by a common curiosity. Soldiers came toward me taking off their sunglasses and gloves, and I took off my sunglasses too so we could really see each other, all of us thinking the same thoughts about each other—"What the fuck are you doing here? I've seen your picture on TV, I've read about you in the newspaper. You look just like I imagined, but who are you really?" I chatted

with each new person for a few minutes, shook hands, signed autographs, and posed for pictures. Henry turned out to be the perfect
person to bring. He was the same age as the soldiers, so when I
had to move onto the next person, he continued the conversation
with people who wanted to talk a little longer. The troops were
happy to see me and were the politest Americans you would ever
hope to meet, but mostly, they were tired and burnt-out from their
twelve-month rotations. They were exhausted from the anxiety of
the mortar attacks and Humvee explosions. One kid came up to
me and caught me off guard. His dialogue was so hokey it felt like
he was reading a script, but he wasn't. "We've been catching a lot
of terrorists and it's true what they say. 'It's really scary to see your
first dead guy but after that, you kind of get used to it.'"

The next morning, we went to the airport to fly into Baghdad,
and while we waited to be issued our sleeping bags, helmets,
and bulletproof vests, we played basketball with the Air Force
soldiers in an airplane hangar with a huge hole blown in the roof
by a missile. Our ride into Baghdad was on a Lockheed C-130
Hercules—a huge, cavernous warplane, the kind you see in old war
movies, that can carry tanks and Jeeps and hundreds of soldiers.
The flight crew invited Henry and me to fly in the cockpit, and the
two of us collapsed ourselves into the tiny bucket seats in back,
trying to stay out of the way. They gave us headphones so we
could talk and listen to each other as well as hear the tower. The
tower was operated by Kuwaitis, which is only as it should be, but
the communication was not confidence-instilling.

"This is Air Force 346920. Tower, could you please repeat
that? Did you say Saleed?"

"Saleesh."

"Saleesh?"

"Saleech."

"Saleech?"

"Saleed."

"So is that, Simon-Alpha-Largo-Edgar-Edgar-Dollar?"

"Could you repeat?"

There is such a thing as too much information, and I was definitely hearing things I didn't need to know. The copilot then informed the captain there was black smoke coming out of the "left sidebar," but they decided it was probably some minor oil burn-off and we were on our way to Baghdad. "You can't over-think these things. Sometimes you just have take your best shot," said Captain Hale after taking off, a great philosophy for anyone. He was a reservist who flew in the first Gulf War, as well as for Trans World Airlines, and was called up unexpectedly. I spent the flight standing over his shoulder chatting, a lot of it commiserating about how hard it is for a dad to find a way into his fifteen-year-old daughter's life. When we started to descend into Baghdad he told us, "We are going to be doing a tactical approach and landing. I am going to descend very rapidly and in a slightly unconventional manner. I am going to be coming in right over Saddam's Water Palace. We are going to be really low, so you are going to have a great view of it. The tile on the roof is amazing. We have to go in as fast as we possibly can. The speed gives us options in case we need to take emergency evasive action." Henry and I started to head back to our seats to get out of the way, but the captain stopped us. "Actually, it would be better if you could stay up here with us. We can use the extra sets of eyes. Keep looking out the window. If you see anything like a trail of smoke, or something that looks like a fence post flying at us, let me know."

"Oh . . . Okay." The radio man and navigator left their stations in back to scrunch up in the front with the rest of us to get a better vantage point—seven of us with our noses pressed to the window of the cockpit, watching for flying fence posts. Henry and I were, in the tiniest way, in the battle.

Dive-bombing into Baghdad was an E-Ticket ride. This C-130 is a big old machine. They have been using the same model since the 1930s, with some technical upgrades, so it really felt like being in a Jimmy Stewart movie—the headphones crackled, seven large faces pressed to the windshield, the plane rumbling and creaking, as Old Reliable Captain Hale tried to create an impossible-to-hit moving target. The mechanized voice from the computer blared the message over and over, "You are too close to the ground! You are too close to the ground! You are too close to the ground!" He skimmed just above the ground in this flying eighteen-wheeler, approaching the airport. He pointed out the Water Palace and he was right, the tiles were magnificent, especially at a 180-degree angle. Right above the runway, he pulled into a straight-up climb. I mean, straight up! He circled back to the airport to land on the second pass and, just like that, we were safely in a war zone.

The Air Force had set up a huge camp at the airport and Henry, Tracy, and I dumped our stuff in a tent which was going to be our home for the next few days. We felt relatively safe, but it was a dangerous and fluid situation, with bombs going off in the distance, helicopters landing, fighting equipment parked everywhere, and ammunition being loaded and unloaded. The USO and the military handled me like the entertainment cargo that I was, expertly shipping me from place to place according to an itinerary I had no control over. It was an emotional rollercoaster, laughing and joking with one group of warriors, tearing up with others who shared their fears and losses with me, and in stunned silence looking at a refrigerated tractor-trailer, filled with dead Iraqis who had yet to be identified. I steeled myself in a way I never had before and learned things about this side of the Human Experiment that I had very little understanding of. The Bush military brain trust had no real plan on how to best engage in urban warfare, and it was left to these soldiers to figure out how to deal

with the local populations, to tell good guys from bad guys, all
while trying to gain the trust of a city they were invading. The
soldiers we met were incredibly smart and well-trained, but what
was even more impressive was their understanding of the importance of the human interactions that would be needed to really
win this war.

That first day we went from station to station across the entire
base, seeing the cogs and gears of the war machinery and saying
"Merry Christmas" to the warriors who make it all happen. I
had seen pictures of war on TV, of soldiers patrolling, fighting,
wounded, and dead. But I had failed to realize the city of people
behind those pictures, like the unsung movie crews I worked with.
You never see pictures of our brave young women and men doing
laundry or sanitation work or serving food. But their asses are on
the line too, and nothing is going to happen if the troops don't
get fed. Each unit was so proud of their contribution, gave us
a tour of their place, and had us try out their equipment. The
fire department let me drive a "war fire engine," a monster-sized,
bullet-proof truck with huge water tanks and remote-control
hoses that can send water a hundred yards. I was hosing down
one of Saddam's old Boeing 747s when Henry got out of the truck
to take my picture, so I aimed the hoses at him and chased him
around the runway. He hid behind the fire captain's Jeep and I
ended up soaking them both pretty good, which got a huge round
of applause from the troops.

We met the soldiers who went on the streets of Baghdad to find
and buy back weapons and bombs. The captain told me that a lot
of the weapons they recovered were turned in by kids, and they
could buy a mortar from a ten-year-old kid for a Tootsie Roll. He
showed us a shed where they kept the confiscated weapons before
they destroyed them, pulling out guns, bombs, a bucket of grenades,
and a suicide vest. In a ridiculously dangerous slapstick moment,

another soldier hurrying by accidentally kicked over the bucket of hand grenades, sending them flying around the shed, clanging off the cache of unstable weapons. The world stood still for a good five seconds, which is five years in "you're a dead dog" time, but those guys thought it was the funniest thing they had ever seen. Later in the day, we met the guys at EOD, Explosive Ordinance Destruction, whose job was to destroy the confiscated weapons. Henry and I took turns blowing up the bombs and mortars, remotely triggering explosions. I've been on movie sets with big stunts and big explosions, and this was a very different sound. It came through the ground as much as it came through the air. The sound waves had a real physical presence. You could almost see the sound waves pushing through the ground and the air.

We met Major Sugiyama, who led SFS, the Security Force Squadron responsible for the safety of the airport, who let me drive a gun-turreted Humvee that they used to chase down the people who were lobbing bombs into the base. I tried on the fifty pounds of equipment that each of them wore when they patrolled the vast perimeter. The soldiers got a good laugh at how awkward I was in it, and I made a mental note to get in touch with my chiropractor when I got home. When I asked if they were keeping Saddam captive on the base, he gave me a sly smile and said that was information that was above his pay-class. But I thought I smelled the rat.

We saw corruption as well, though we didn't know we were seeing it. In the flight tower, we met an Australian pilot and his mate who had just flown in. They pointed out their plane, maybe a Boeing 727, and told me it was filled with money. They were flying in all the new money without the picture of Saddam on it from wherever it was printed. They didn't know how much there was in value, only in weight. Two tons of fresh dinar, which we later found out disappeared. We only saw Abu Ghraib from the outside, later to discover that torture and war crimes were being committed inside while we were there. We saw private companies with political connections like Raytheon, Halliburton, and Bechtel setting up permanent shop on the bases, taking over energy fields and palaces, paying their American workers much more than the average soldier was making, and using cheap Bangladeshi workers for the physical labor. And everywhere we went, the food was shit. Fast food, junk food, corn dogs, and bad cafeteria food was all there was to eat for these poor people. How the fuck are you supposed to function at the level necessary in this life-and-death world when all they give you for fuel is fast-food crap?!

We saw glimpses of the horror of war as well. Rescue Ops' job was to helicopter into a "situation," get the wounded and dead onto the helicopter, and bring them back to the hospital. They had to be able to parachute, scuba-dive, fly helicopters, shoot guns from a helicopter, and, oh yeah, be doctors! They had just gotten back from a mission. A Humvee with two soldiers had rolled into a river. Another soldier driving by jumped in and saved them both but drowned. Rescue Ops soldiers jumped out of their helicopter into the water, rescued the two soldiers and recovered the body of the other, and their exhaustion and sadness were palpable. Lt. Col. DeLorenzo oversaw the large grouping of tents housing triage centers at CASF, the medical facility housing x-ray machines, recovery areas, administration desks, and operating rooms. He carried the weight of the world on his shoulders, getting twenty-five injured soldiers flown in every few hours, stabilizing them, operating if they had to, and getting them on a transport plane to Germany as fast as they could. "We are the best because we have to be. We owe our best to our warriors," he said. The kids who worked at the morgue did their work under a huge American flag, which was so moving to see. I visited the hospital and had to hide my shock at how gruesome the injuries were to these young men, chatting about my movies and signing autographs while my heart broke for them. And frankly, it must have been slightly surreal for them, dealing with their own fears and sadness and pain only to have Marv from *Home Alone* standing by their bedside.

I hosted Bingo Night, with three to four hundred men and women who took the game seriously. The final game of the night got crazy with the whole place cheering and chanting. But most fun for me was a chance to give out the letters I had brought from the schools in Malibu. For an hour after the game, hundreds of soldiers hung out and read letters, and we laughed and felt a connection between us and home. One letter from a second grader said simply, "Dear Soldier, I hope you don't die. I like carrots." We laughed for five minutes about that one. Beat that, Bob Hope.

I thought sleeping would be tough, but it wasn't. The war does not stop at night; it actually accelerates, because the enemy likes to attack at night. Outgoing mortar fire was muffled by the sounds of planes and helicopters taking off and landing, transporting more guns, more wounded women and men to the hospital in Germany, and more corn dogs to keep the troops fed. I slept differently than I had ever slept before, restful but aware. I had to pee in the middle of the night, walking the two hundred yards to the latrine through a very different kind of "City That Never Sleeps." When I got back on the cot, I felt good—alive even while sleeping. Weirdly peaceful.

The third day we were supposed to fly out in the morning to Kirkuk, then into Tallil, where we would spend the night. But for security reasons, they wanted us to stay in Baghdad for the moment. I was relieved to not have to take as many dangerous flights, and there were enough soldiers to meet in Baghdad to keep me busy for a year. We visited the other side of the airport, now escorted by a new military officer, a rather flamboyant man who we will call Major Fun. He asked us if we would like to go into downtown Baghdad to the Haji Market and "maybe buy some jewelry for your wife." We loaded into an armed convoy of Humvees and Jeeps and drove into the city. A husband and wife owned the jewelry store. Evidently Major Fun spent a lot of money there, and they were very glad to see him. He assured them that we were okay and said that I was a movie actor. The woman let out a little squeak and said, "Home Alone?" She got out her camera. They hugged me and Henry and showed us all the jewelry and paintings and boxes. By the time we finished shopping and headed for a restaurant across the plaza, word had gotten out that the *Home Alone* actor was in town. I will never forget the group of kids who had been playing soccer in the road, surrounding me, chanting, "Marv! Marv! Marv!" The power of the movies crosses all boundaries and cultures, and the Power of Marv to bring these kids, who were living their childhood in a war zone, a smile humbled me to my core. But Major Fun had a lot more tricks up his sleeve.

On our way back to the airport base camp, he took us to Saddam Hussein's Water Palace, the one we had caught a glimpse of as we rocketed into town. He spent the entire thirty-minute drive telling us of all the "fabulous" marble that Saddam had used to build the palace and a critique of what he would have done with the place if it was his. Saddam's palaces were actually a series of palaces inside enormous compounds, and one of the palaces at the Water Palace was his son Udai's, of the famed boy band Udai and Qusay. (Udai was a horrible person. At a party for Mrs. Mubarak, the First Lady of Egypt, he beat a man to death in front of everyone. No charges, no arrest.) The palace had been bombed, the "fabulous" marble turned to rubble. Major Fun said, "You should take some home. Everyone takes some. You can ship it. If you send it from the base, it goes straight through and no one checks it. I've sent all kinds of stuff home. My mom is keeping it at the ranch. Here, take something like this." He picked up an hourglass piece of gray-and-white speckled smooth stone, about two feet high and eight inches around, which had been part of the marble railing at Udai's bachelor pad. It weighed, I found out when I shipped it home, fifty-five pounds. It was beautiful, and I was overcome with greed. "How fucking cool would it be to have a big-ass piece of Udai's palace at my house? And free shipping!" Henry wasn't sure it was cool, but it was a once-in-a-lifetime opportunity and I took it. I put it in the back of the Jeep, and we rode away with it. I was officially a looter.

We drove further down the Water Palace road until we arrived at the big man's house, Saddam's Palace. Henry and I were blown away by the grandest ballroom imaginable, 150 yards long, fifty yards across and fifty feet high, like an arena football stadium. It had marble floors and columns, and grand balconies at either end, overlooking the lake and orchards and gardens. Except it was all smashed. It turns out bombs have real consequences. They are not just numbers and maps, they are concrete and rebar. They are life and limb. Piles of lumber and metal—and marble. Major Fun came up the staircase carrying a pristine piece of white marble, engraved in Arabic and with beautiful faces sculpted in relief. This thing must have weighed at least a hundred pounds and he was all aflutter with his home decorating find. His physical training paid off as he summoned his inner Arnold Schwarzenegger (and his inner Martha Stewart) to make it back to the Jeep with his ultimate living room accessory. He said he probably shouldn't be doing it but "what the hell," as he wrapped it gently in a blanket and laid it next to my ill-gotten gains.

Our last night in Iraq, we were invited to join the Special Forces Unit for dinner at their camp, which was in a different palace, Saddam Hussein's Personal Palace. This one had not been bombed and had been taken over by our troops because it was so secure. When we arrived, our jaws dropped at the ornate rooms we walked through to get to the cavernous dining room, complete with the biggest marble table imaginable. (Major Fun was probably trying to figure out how to sneak it back home.) We mingled with fifty or sixty soldiers, athletic Young Turks, all Special Forces elite. We sat down for a dinner of boxes and boxes of Whoppers and Quarter Pounders and Hot Apple Pies, with Red Bull to wash it down. It was the perfect metaphor for the war, eating off the table of our enemy to prove we have won, but serving an American Shit Sandwich to our warriors, and with no seat at the table for the Iraqis who suffered under Saddam.

The commanders sent word from upstairs, asking if we would like to go say hello to them. The Young Turks selected to escort us were thrilled, as most of them had never been to the Command Center. They lived up the road in another palace, so we were all excited as we ascended the spectacular staircase into the inner sanctuary. Major Fun was overcome by the design of the staircase and started sashaying up the stairs like a glamorous movie actress saying, "If I had a staircase like this, I would glide up and down it every day," which caused the macho Young Turks' jaws to drop about a foot. So funny.

The Command Center was where they planned all of the raids, killings, capturings, and reconnaissance missions, which the Young Turks then carried out. The first commander I met was Mario, a handsome, incredibly strong-looking Latin man in his forties with an easy smile. Mario was discipline personified. While Mario showed me around, Henry and the Turks took off to explore, like kids at a haunted house. Mario was as surprised as anyone to be living in one of Saddam's bedrooms and sleeping in his bed. The servants who worked there told him that Saddam used to have young girls, twelve or thirteen years old, one in this bedroom and one in another across the hall, and go back and forth between them, and Mario couldn't get that out of his mind. He told me that before he was stationed here, he was in Afghanistan living in a cave for six months, and he seemed like he would be just as comfortable in either place. Talk about stories to tell.

Mario introduced me to John, the other commander, standing by a detailed set of maps on the wall with pins stuck in them. Also in his forties, he seemed like he might have gone to an Ivy League school or something: smart, doing something good but somewhat secretive. He gave me a tour which included the other bedroom in Mario's nightmare Saddam story. John had a mattress on the floor and Saddam's armoire up against the window as a shield against incoming shrapnel. He had rigged a clothesline running from the armoire to a nail on the wall, on which he was currently drying his socks. Henry and the Young Turks ran in excitedly, saying, "You got to come do this! It's so cool." Mario, John, and I followed them into the bathroom where they were taking turns having their picture taken sitting on Saddam's gold toilet holding his gold AK-47. I knew it was a picture I would regret even before I took it. Talk about shitting on the guy.

John and Mario opened up a little about the war. They guessed we would be in Iraq for at least ten years. They confessed that the mission was vague now that the original mission of finding weapons of mass destruction had been abandoned. They asked why I came, and I said I wanted the troops to know that *all* Americans supported them. "I am a Democrat who thinks very little of the Bush administration. I come from Malibu, one of the more liberal communities in the country. And every man, woman, and child I told that I was coming here invested in me their love and thanks to deliver to you. We are for you, we are with you, and we are worried about you. People are against the war because of the politics of it, not the warriors. And Malibu sends all their love and gratitude." I think I told them something that they didn't know, and that they were pleased to hear.

John presented Henry and me with a Special Forces Challenge Coin, a gold coin with the Special Forces insignia on it, making us honorary members of the unit. He said, "The thing about the coin is that you have to have it with you at all times. If you are ever in a bar and one of your Special Forces brothers slaps down their coin, and you don't have your coin with you, then you have to buy the drinks. But if you do have your coin, then the guy who slapped down has to buy." We all shook hands and said goodbye. I don't know what came over me, but as we were climbing down the stairway, I noticed a room on the second floor where a meeting was going on and, for some inexplicable reason, I decided I should "entertain" these guys. There were about fifteen men sitting around a big table with maps in the middle, an overhead projector, and video screen, obviously in the middle of a very important meeting. And I thought, "Wouldn't it be funny if I took the Special Forces Challenge Coin that I just got and slammed down on these guys? When am I ever going to get a chance to do that?"

I strode right up to the big table and without a word, slammed my coin hard, startling the men, men who are very dangerous when they are startled. The room froze for a good thirty seconds. No one said a word. Henry and the Young Turks had followed me into the room, but were now silently slithering away, trying to act like they didn't know me. This was supposed to be funny but no one, and I mean no one, was laughing. The smart thing might have been to pick up my coin and run but, like or not, I was a freshly minted honorary brother in the Special Forces, and I was determined to use the power of my coin to make them laugh. They definitely wanted me to get the fuck out of there, but I stared them down, one by one. I wasn't moving until they slammed down their coins. Lives hung in the balance. The sooner they gave up, the sooner they could get back to their planning session, which you can bet involved lives hanging in the balance. One by one, I broke them. They went around the table, digging into their pockets. Most had their coins with them. Some slapped down an empty hand. One guy slapped down a condom, sending a clear message as to what he thought of this comic bit. When we'd gone around the room, I pointed to all the ones who had failed to produce and who now owed me a beer. I picked up my coin, wished them a Merry Christmas, and strode back out of the room. That group of guys either had the driest sense of humor I have ever witnessed, or they really were on the verge of killing me. The Young Turks greeted me as though I had just scored the winning touchdown. "Do you know who those guys are? Do you have any idea of what you just did?"

"I thought it would be funny. What was going on in there?"

"We have no idea. Those guys are totally top secret. Those guys don't even have names! . . . Damn, you're crazy!" (No, just an idiot who forgot there was an actual war going on that these people were fighting!)

Next thing I knew, I was behind the wheel, joyriding around the grounds in a specially armed and armored Toyota 4Runner, complete with gun turret, up the road to the Young Turks' Play-house, a smaller palace, high on a hill overlooking Baghdad. It was a fraternity house for young killers—a gym, big screen TV, PlayStation, bedrooms galore with mattresses on the floor, and not much else. It was time for us to leave, but as we were saying our goodbyes, we were jolted by the unmistakable rumble and blast of a bomb going off. It was a pretty big blast, although not that close, but they asked us to come back inside and wait until they had a chance to check it out. After about ten or fifteen minutes, a sleek young man wearing a black, crewneck, long-sleeve shirt came over and asked us in a hushed voice if we wouldn't mind waiting in another room. The silky man, Doc, escorted us to his office/operating room/pharmacy. It had the feel of a big den in a modern castle but instead of books, the walls were lined with industrial-sized shelving holding Costco-size jars of various drugs. Leather easy chairs sat next to a doctor's examining table, with movable lights and trays and cabinets. Six Young Turks were already in the room and told us not to worry about the bombing, which was a relief. Doc walked over to the door I was standing near and threw the dead bolt. "Odd," I thought. He glided across the room to another door and bolted that one as well, almost ceremoniously. He was making a bit of a show of it, and it certainly had me curious. What is it that we need to lock in? Or lock out? He walked back across the room to me, and said, "As your host I would like to inform you that . . . the bar is open. While it's true that there is an absolute ban on alcohol in this country, we happen to be pretty good at making things happen. I have beer, wine, Chivas, Dewars, some nice vodkas, and Jägermeister. What can I get you?" I got the picture. We were going to party, fraternity style. Henry of Harvard was right in his element. I, responsibly, said that we didn't want to stop them if they needed to respond to the bombing at the bottom of the hill. They said that it was a hotel that was hit and insisted that fire and rescue would take care of it for now. "We'll probably have to go out later, once they find out who did it."

"Then I'll have a scotch."

The evening that followed is a collage of stories and incidents which somehow found a branch to hold onto in a brain flooded with alcohol. It was a night of decadence, danger, machismo, fast friends, sex, drugs, and rock and roll. Like hanging with great friends in a great New York bar, but with guns and a license to kill. They were letting off steam, getting drunk with Marv from *Home Alone*, and spoke freely about the job requirements of being a killing machine. Every day they climbed mountains or went scuba diving or jumped out of a plane and killed people, just like we played when we were young, all that heroism and killing, but for real. Gino was short, pugnacious, to-the-point, and fearless, a seasoned veteran of many operations and on his way to being a commander if he wanted to. He said his motto was, "Kill to Live," and that the Iraqis didn't scare him because they shot like they were scared, hiding behind a wall and just sticking their guns out and spraying them around. He acted out "sissy-shooting," looking like Pee Wee Herman, and said he had the advantage because, "I just keep coming at them," swinging his rifle into place to show me how deftly he closed in on his target. "I'm trained on them. So as soon as they show themselves at all, blam, I'm ready."

A handsome, cocky young man named Mike said his motto was "Kill for Fun." This one I can't shake, because from his point of view, that probably seemed about right. Chevy was the only woman, taller than any of the men on the team, like a seventh-grade class where the boys haven't had their growth spurt yet. She told us that the first time she jumped out of a plane, she was so excited she hit her head on the short exit door and almost knocked herself out. She laughed at herself. Aaron was a tough warrior but hadn't shaken the experience of having to kill a young boy as he approached Aaron's truck with an AK-47 in his hands. I tried to talk to all of them about their families, but they didn't seem to want to talk about that much. At one point, there was a knock on the door and these killer soldiers suddenly looked like teenagers, hiding the liquor when mom and dad come home early. It turned out not to be the commander, but rather four more members of the team, just back from patrol. There was an intense energy radiating from them, the adrenaline of having just been out there doing God knows what. They joined the party.

One of the other guys had been quietly making Henry and me bracelets from parachute cord. That was his thing. He made them for everyone. Another one of the guys we hadn't met piped in with a story of seeing weapons at an Iraqi wedding procession and shooting up the party. It was hard to take it all in, the confusion that must cause to a person's soul. I walked by a group playing darts and Chevy handed me one of her darts to throw for her, and believe it or not, bull's-eye! The room went nuts! Wax on, wax off, bitch! Between this, the coin-slamming incident, and just being Marv, I was a God to these fine, young, drunken people. Doc, the bracelet guy, and Gino took turns calling their wives and put me on the phone, introducing me as "the real *Home Alone* guy!" I thanked them for lending us their husbands and wished them Merry Christmas. I took the opportunity when I was talking to Gino's wife to lobby for the idea of them all moving to LA and Gino becoming an A-list stuntman, vowing to introduce them to my friends and connections. He would have been awesome at it, although for all his skills, I don't know if he was trained well enough in the art of bullshit to survive Hollywood.

Aaron had the brilliant, drunken idea of having me perform surgery on him, right then and there. He showed me a bump on his hip the size of a tangerine, a fatty tissue build-up under the skin, and said, "I want you to cut it out. That would be so cool, to have it cut out by Marv." Turning to the doctor he asked, "He could do it, right? It's not that hard."

Doc thought about it for a second and said, "Yeah, he could probably do it."

My drunken thought was, "What an opportunity! How many chances will I ever get in my life to perform elective surgery on a willing patient under the supervision of a doctor outside the legal reach of the malpractice laws of the United States?" Aaron lay down on the table and Doc brought over the operating equipment. He drew with his finger across the four-inch round bump on Aaron's hip. "All you have to do is make an incision across the top. Once you get it open, take the scalpel and just kind of cut the fatty lump away from the under part of the skin. You do that all the way around and then you close it up. I could stitch it up if you're not comfortable doing that." Aaron was egging me on to do it, a way to prove to me and the gang that he was so tough that he wouldn't even feel me slicing him open and cutting out a piece of him, while also challenging the "movie star" to see if I was brave enough to do it. I came to my senses, thank God. I stood down. I surrendered. I was weak and he was strong. He never backed down from being ready to be cut, and of course Doc never said anything that doubted that Aaron could take it. The responsibility to back off was up to me not to do something so drunkenly reckless as amateur tumor surgery. But I have regretted it ever since. It would have been so fucking cool to have done a real fucking surgery!

I knew it was time to leave when I saw Henry going off with Chevy to the bathroom, wearing night vision goggles and carrying a machine gun. I didn't know what was going on in there, but I knew we should go before we caused some real damage. We all headed out to Major Fun's Jeep, exchanging hugs and email addresses. There was gunfire in the distance, so the Young Turks decided to escort us back to the airport camp and "then maybe drive out and see what's going on." I got the sense they were about to put in a full night's work. As a farewell gift, Doc handed Henry a huge baggie full of unmarked prescription pills, ostensibly to help him sleep on the plane. "Don't take more than two at a time. But two of those and a beer and you will sleep the whole trip." (At the rate of two per plane trip, the baggie contained enough pills for about 150 round trips.) We raced through Baghdad, with Major Fun showing considerable driving skills, and went back to our tent to try to sleep and digest not only the burgers and beer, but these new hard facts of war that I had ingested over the course of one strange evening.

We got up hungover, scarfed up some shitty breakfast food, and made it to the departure area of the airport, where there were at least a thousand soldiers, all waiting. It was a great opportunity to finish my Handshake Tour and hand out the last of the letters from my Malibu mates. I got a feeling what it must be like to run for office, introducing myself to strangers and finding a personal connection with so many individuals, so many faces and so many, many stories. Henry and I strapped into seats made of netting against the wall of another C-130, this one filled with Humvees and soldiers. The pilot performed a stomach-bending, spiraling, tactical takeoff, which strained not only the chains holding the Humvees in place, but the Pop Tarts that were about to pop out of my guts. Up, up, and away, and in an hour and a half it was over. We had left Iraq, left the war zone, and I could feel the passage of time. Like my wedding and the birth of my children, I knew that this trip would divide my life into before, during, and after, and I had crossed over into the forever after.

It was surreal to end up back in the hotel in Kuwait with the butler. Even though we had only been in the war zone a short time, we felt like we had "survived" and treated ourselves like sailors on leave. My brilliant son had booked our trip home through Amsterdam for three days, what he had dubbed "The Hookers and Hash Tour." It was a smashing success, and of course ended up being all hash and no hookers. The Van Gogh Museum, The Rijksmuseum, Anne Frank's House, and canals everywhere. We rented bikes, smoked a lot of pot at bars, ate and drank three meals a day of the finest food and spirits, floated in isolation tanks, met beautiful Dutch people, saw the freak show of the Red Light District, and stayed in a beautiful little apartment. It was way too short and way too fun. When I got back to Malibu, I kissed Laure with the best soldier-returning-from-war kiss I could muster and hugged Sophie and Ella for an uncomfortably long time. I went to each school and did an assembly, showing pictures from the trip and my stolen piece of marble, answering questions, telling them how much their letters meant to the troops, and completing this unique mission and honor I had been given, to be the conduit of love and gratitude between the soldiers fighting the fight and the people in whose name they were fighting it.

SUGAR TITS AND ME

Garry Marshall was a show business hero of mine. A brilliant comedy writer who created *Happy Days*, *Mork & Mindy*, and other hit TV shows, he then transformed himself into a top film director with *Pretty Woman*, *Flamingo Kid*, and *A League of Their Own*. Garry's passion was theater, and he owned the beautiful, 130-seat Falcon Theatre in Burbank. So when he said he wanted to produce the West Coast premiere of *Barbra's Wedding*, I was beside myself with excitement. He told me how much he loved the play and asked if I would consider being in it. The role of Jerry Schiff was obviously written as my pathetic, self-loathing alter ego, and he thought it would be quite something to see me play it. It was a great part (if I do say so myself) that I had acted out in my head everyday while I was writing it, and I decided to see what it would be like to actually play it. We cast Crystal Bernard as Molly, hired a terrific young director, and had a wonderfully successful run. I loved playing the part; it was emotional and cathartic, and every laugh we got, I got a double dopamine hit—one as actor and one as writer. Getting to perform in a first-class production of my own play in front of Garry's show business friends, giants of Hollywood, was the cherry on the cake of this adventure I had created for myself out of thin air, with the inadvertent help of Barbra Streisand.

Speaking of Barbra Streisand, Malibu was getting crazier and crazier. It had been discovered, with McMansions popping up all around, and I was getting more and more claustrophobic. Where I used to have electricians and car mechanics as my neighbors, now I had Kid Rock and Cindy Crawford. The fireman across the gully passed away, and his son, who became the realtor-to-the-rich, turned their humble home into a McMansion monstrosity, with construction going on for years. On the other hand, I was fundraising for the Malibu Foundation, and networking my ass off, especially with wealthy potential donors. The parties we went to were over the top. Christmas parties with acres of real snow (in Malibu!) including sledding hills, piles of caviar, free-flowing booze, and hot chocolate bars. A private concert with the legendary Tom Jones performing in the backyard. An afternoon with an enormous crowd in an authentic Bedouin tent, chanting with some guru introduced by Tony Robbins himself. But the craziest night of all was when we went to television producer Mark Burnett's house for an intimate dinner, just twelve of us, and who should be sitting across from me but none other than Barbra Streisand herself and her handsome husband James Brolin. And sitting next to them was Donald Trump, who was starring in Mark's show, *The Apprentice*. Mr. Trump was thrilled to see me, since we had "starred in *Home Alone 2* together," and spent the evening bragging to me about the ratings for *The Apprentice*, which was the Number One show on TV, going into minute detail about the different demographics that were watching. He was just another boring actor, needy and egotistical, and having quality time like this with him did nothing to diminish my first impression of him, from back in the day in New York when he was a tabloid playboy, living off his daddy's money. Who knew he was presidential material?

But the chitchat at the table got bizarrely awkward when Mark focused the conversation on me for a moment, saying he had heard I had written a play, and asking me what it was about. My face burned red with embarrassment. The whole night I had been on edge, not knowing if Barbra and James had ever even heard of *Barbra's Wedding*, let alone knew I wrote it, and feeling guilty about the jokes I had written at their expense, especially Mr. Brolin. So I responded by saying the play was "about marriage and how tough it can be." He pressed for specifics, but I gave him back only generalities. I was looking at all of them to see if they were fucking with me, but they weren't. It was just regular show business small talk to them and I, like Mr. Trump, was just another actor talking about his play. I changed the subject as soon as I could, but Laure and I were stunned when we got back in the car. What are the chances that I would end up at dinner with Barbra Fucking Streisand and have to explain my play to her directly? And that having dinner with the future president of the United States would be the least interesting part of the evening?

The biggest celebrity in my real life at that time was Mel Gibson. Robyn and Mel were so generous to the Malibu Foundation, giving a one-million-dollar donation that gave the organization long-term stability. Mel and I did another fundraising show together and had a blast onstage making each other laugh. When he produced his first TV comedy series, *Complete Savages*, he asked me to direct, which gave us a chance to work together.

He bought a Gulf Stream G5 jet, and I was touched and amazed that he invited me, out of everyone, to go with him on its maiden flight—flying to Las Vegas for the day to play a round of golf and fly home. It was crazy, just the two of us on that plane, with leather seats and sofas, two stewardesses, and all the food and drink you could consume. Mel felt guilty about buying it, worried that his dad would think it was a ridiculous waste of money, and I somehow found myself advocating that the plane was a good thing to buy. We played a round of golf at the fanciest course I have ever been to, with caddies who rode ahead in golf carts to find the ball you shanked into the woods or rough (which came in handy because we were both terrible golfers). Then we got back on the jet and home in time for dinner. The carbon footprint of that trip probably equaled a family-of-four's energy consumption for a year.

But a problem was brewing. Mel had just directed *Passion of the Christ*, which caused a worldwide, phenomenal, box-office, and cultural explosion. It was also drawing worldwide condemnation for the anti-Semitic stereotypes it portrayed. I held off seeing it as long as I could because I preferred being in the dark, but one day my dad and I went to a matinee. Mel was in the press arguing that there was no anti-Semitism in the film, that it was just "historically accurate," at least according to the New Testament as he interpreted it, and I tried to give him the benefit of the doubt. But the hooked-nosed Jews, their bloodlust, and their culpability in the killing of Jesus was the same anti-Semitic bullshit I had been hearing since elementary school, and I was disturbed that Mel was giving that hateful crap so much media attention. But truthfully, what was even more disturbing was Mel's bloodlust, the way he fetishized the torture, wounds, and pain in close-up after close-up, over-dramatizing it to a ridiculous degree. At least in *Braveheart* there was a complex story to justify the gore in some way, but this film was *only* about suffering. It was disgusting to watch, and a pretty terrible, one-note movie, and I was at a total loss as to what I would say when I saw him again. But before long, Mel had the famous drunk-driving incident in which he called the arresting officer "Sugar Tits" and ranted that "the Jews are responsible for all the wars in the world." When I saw that on the news, I felt very bad for him. He is a very twisted guy—raised by a fucked-up, racist father and crippled by religious guilt, while also being the "Sexiest Man Alive" and a hugely talented artist— I can't begin to imagine what that must be like. I didn't want to let him off the hook, but I wanted him to know I was there for him, that I wanted to help him dig his way out of the terrible hole he had put himself in. I left him a funny voicemail message from "Rabbi Stern," asking if he wanted to talk, although I don't know if he thought it was funny because he never called back, and I have not spoken to him since. He soon got divorced, and Robyn and Laure remained close, so there has never been a way to reconnect. But if Mel is reading this book, Rabbi Stern sends love and peace to you.

My life was changing. I had been a dad since I was twenty-four years old and by forty-five, I had two kids in college and the last one getting ready to do the same, so I no longer had any day-to-day responsibility for them. We convinced my parents to sell the old house in Chevy Chase and move to Malibu, where they bought a sweet little place overlooking the ocean, in a mobile home park about a mile from our house. It was great to have them in the mix of our family life, although at times it felt like a never-ending episode of a family sitcom, with my parents bursting into our house unannounced, judging and commenting on my life choices and making sure I never got "too big for my britches." I spent weeks at a time at the cattle ranch, hiking our property and learning its nooks and crannies. It was profound to find myself deep in the mountains, like a dream of being in Eden, alone with nature. Or at the top of our mountain at sunset, looking out over pasturelands and orange groves, with the Sierra Mountains in the distance, actually living the American Dream.

O beautiful for spacious skies
For amber waves of grain
For purple mountain majesties
Above the fruited plain

Even though my Quad was my horse, I impressed my cattleman (and myself) with how good I was at herding cows, so thankful that I was getting to act out the *City Slickers* fantasy for real. I felt like myself there. And the ranch needed me. There was a house to be painted, porch to repair, single-wide trailer to restore, drainage and erosion to take care of, pest control, brush to clear, and the endless other chores that go into keeping up a ranch. Laure had been given a horse from a friend, and so there was, of course, shit to dispose of, hay to stack, an arena to groom, and on and on. I even grew to love working in the 105-degree heat in the summer, drinking gallons of water and sleeping like a baby when it cooled off at night. The fame thing was tricky in a place like this. A trip to Home Depot inevitably ended up in a photoshoot with the employees. The intrusions made Laure crazy, but to me, it felt like the civilian extension of my USO Handshake Tour, bringing the Power of Marv to the far-off reaches of Central California, and answering those same burning questions—"What the hell are you doing here?" and "Was that a real spider?" The only time anyone crossed a line was when some of the neighbor kids thought it would be funny to prank The Wet Bandit and broke into the single-wide trailer while we were away. They stuffed rags into the sink drain, turned on the water, and flooded the whole trailer. I'm not sure if the wasted money or the wasted water pissed me off more, but it showed the Power of Marv had a dark side as well.

But sculpture had taken over my days, and my life. It felt empowering to get up every day and go to the little house and work, not beholden to anyone to cast me or fund me. By now, I had filled the little house with crazy, huge, papier-mâché pieces— a man doing a one-handed handstand, a swimmer in mid-flight off the high-dive, a man bursting through a painting. I started making more durable pieces with plaster-cloth, plumbing pipe, and exterior paint that could live outside and placed them around the property—a surfer riding a huge wave, a fat man jumping over a picket fence. I loved the physical labor and problem-solving of making them. I tried to come up with new poses I hoped would make the audience laugh, learning how to make these seemingly impossible poses stand securely on their own and make the viewer smile at the visual trick. It gave me the same artistic satisfaction as the performance art I had been involved with, communicating a story to the viewer, even if the sculpture was only one frame of film. People started seeing my stuff and, through word of mouth, I got offers to buy some of my work, which, for a fledgling artist, was such a validation.

Henry moved back to LA, and we helped him look for an apartment while he applied to law school and worked at a nonprofit. He was going to need a little help with his rent, but before that happened, I had an epiphany—instead of spending money renting a place for him, why didn't I give him the little house and spend that money to rent a sculpture studio for myself? I found a funky, industrial space on La Cienega Boulevard in Culver City, a one-thousand-square-foot space behind a mom-and-pop computer repair place. My place was an old refrigeration storage space with a roll-up door, corrugated metal walls, and thick, commercial refrigerator doors dividing the place into three separate rooms.

Besides the space itself, the best thing was that my block was becoming the hippest art scene in LA, with galleries popping up in weird spaces like an old gas station or industrial storage spaces like mine. The galleries created a lot of foot traffic, especially when they had regular art walks, so not only did I have a space to make my art, I could open my doors whenever I wanted to and try to sell my art as well. I thought if I could sell enough to pay for my rent, I would be truly winning. I loved commuting every day and getting out of Malibu. My friends started coming over and hanging out. There was a great bar on the street and always new art to see at the galleries, although I was the only person on the block actually using my space as a working studio. I used the front room as a gallery, the back space as my work area, and the small space for a hangout area, and it worked perfectly. For the first year, I made more life-sized, dynamic, plaster sculptures and sold a bunch. I also started using the space to showcase other artists, giving them The Iceboxx, as it was now being called, for shows of their work and at the art walks. We did play readings and shot a little film there, and I loved having my own gallery right in the middle of the Art District. But most importantly, it made me take myself seriously as an artist. I wasn't hiding anymore in my little house and garage. The coolest gallery owners in LA were my neighbors, coming in to see what I was working on, and it lit a fire under my ass.

The God of Sculpture is Rodin. I visited the Rodin Museum in France and was moved to tears by the people he created and the stories he told in a single gesture or pose. His bronze sculptures are huge, with the size and weight of them impacting the viewer just as much as the characters. I felt if I wanted call myself a sculptor, I would have to move past the Pop Art I was making and teach myself how to make sculptures like his. But how the fuck do you make a bronze sculpture? Get a piece of bronze and hammer it until you get a face or a hand? I did my homework, learning that bronze sculptures begin as sculptures in clay. A mold is made of the clay sculpture and then a bronze casting is made from the mold, using the lost-wax process, the same way bronze sculptures have been made since Egyptian times. I had forgotten how much I love clay. As a teenager, I built a potter's wheel in our basement and sculpted a few small busts for fun, but I really didn't know much about sculpting the human form. My drawing skills are truly at a toddler level, and I am always blown away when someone can draw people realistically, with accurate proportions and perspectives, tricking the eye into seeing three dimensions. But there is no need for those skills when you're sculpting with clay because you are creating humans in actual three dimensions, and right off the bat I was able to shape the clay into the exact form I wanted. I could feel in my hands if a nose was too big or a finger too short. Clay is very forgiving. Unlike pottery clay, sculpting clay is oil-based and never dries out, so if you make a mistake or change your mind, you can add on more or take some away until it is just how you want it.

I bought a book on anatomy and a hundred pounds of sculpting clay and dove in. I made a half-life size young surfer, working long and hard to get the musculature and facial features right. I made a life-size young woman, her dress flying as she runs, balanced on one foot. These were also my first opportunities to work with a foundry and go through the whole process of creating a bronze sculpture—making the molds and wax castings, pouring the molten bronze, welding the pieces back together, adding patina and polishing it until it is finished. Like a movie crew, I now understood the crafts and laborers needed to produce the final vision. And seeing the strength of the material and the engineering possibilities, I got inspired to create even more out-of-balance poses than I was already making. Casting a sculpture in bronze is not cheap, so the financial investment in a piece was also a factor, and now I committed myself to selling my pieces to make my money back. I started sculpting smaller pieces too, making things that were more affordable to people coming through The Iceboxx Gallery. I made a ton of mistakes, but overall I was pleased with what I was doing. I was barely breaking even, but creatively I was on fire in a way I had never experienced before. Even though I made my living in the performing arts, for the first time in my life, through sheer will and hard work, I could finally call myself an artist.

PRESIDENT OBAMA
MAKES ME CRY

Henry had finished law school and was working in Washington, DC for Henry Waxman when the country voted in Barack Obama. Through his connections and my family-friendly fame, I got an invitation to participate in the White House Easter Egg Roll and meet the president of the United States, with Henry as my date. It was deeply emotional and joyous for us, being at the White House, the People's House finally free of Bush and Cheney, with our first Black president working for a more just America inside its walls. I read books to groups of children on the lawn, mingled with military families, signed autographs, and took pictures. When it was time, we were escorted through the White House to the president's quarters by a military escort and then into the Blue Room, where President Obama, Michelle Obama, and their daughters were waiting to meet with us for a few minutes. They were all *Home Alone* fans, and the president thought I was "a funny guy." The kids asked about the spider and paint cans, and Michelle was as charming as a person can be. I was on autopilot because it does not get any more out-of-body than a moment like this. We had our picture taken as a group (which was later sent to me, signed by the President and Michelle) and said our goodbyes. Our military escort took us into the rotunda outside the room, where there were a hundred or so people mingling. Henry and I stood there in shock, having just hung out with Barack and his family, when a voice cut through the din of conversation. "Daniel Stern! Daniel Stern, come over here." Henry and I turned to see Joe Biden waving at me. The vice president was standing with his wife Jill and Michelle's mother, Marian Robinson, who lived upstairs at the White House. They were laughing and having the time of their lives, enjoying the Easter festivities, and brought us right into the conversation. Mr. Biden was a huge fan of *Breaking Away* but knew so many of my other movies, which was crazy. Mrs. Biden was as warm and welcoming as could be, and when they found out Henry and I had visited Iraq with the USO, they were even more engaged with us. Mrs. Robinson told us that sometimes living at the White House felt claustrophobic. She laughed as she explained that she had finally figured out how to sneak out of the White House but had not yet figured out how to sneak back in. The experience, especially sharing it with Henry, felt like the culmination of a political era in my life. When I got on the plane to go home, I was embarrassed that I could not control my sobbing—with joy, relief, and gratitude—in front of the other passengers.

By this point, I was acting when I was inspired by a part, a director, a paycheck, or a location. I directed a play, *American Buffalo*, in Portland so that Laure and I could live near Ella for a couple of months. I shot an HBO show, *Getting On*, with Laurie

Metcalf, just because I loved her so much. I did a Hallmark Christmas movie for a nice paycheck, where Laure and I rented a breathtaking house on Vancouver Bay. Drew Barrymore asked me to be in her directorial debut, *Whip It*, which was a blast, especially the night Jimmy Fallon took us on an underground bar crawl through Detroit, meeting up with the White Stripes and getting incredibly hammered in a pop-up bar in some abandoned building. I spent a month living on a farm in Malta, shooting a film but mostly spending my days smoking hash, swimming in the Mediterranean, and making a couple of papier-mâché sculptures just for fun. (When I left, I gave the sculptures to my driver, who kept the sweatsuit and pajamas that I dressed them in but threw out the sculptures themselves. Everybody's a critic.)

I made my Broadway debut, costarring with Laurie Metcalf again in a powerful, Alzheimer-themed drama called *The Other Place*. What a joy to act with her every night and watch her performance get deeper and deeper. She is one of the most brilliant stage actresses ever, and it was the honor of a lifetime to dance with her on that stage. I acted in and directed a new TV series called *Manhattan*, which was a 1940s drama about the building of the nuclear bomb. Laure and I brought the dogs and the horses, rented a farm in Santa Fe for five months, and had the time of our lives. I had never directed an epic drama like this before and loved leading the crew to make a visually spectacular show filled with world-class performances. The bonus of this adventure was that Santa Fe is a major art destination, and home to a world-class bronze foundry called Shidoni. I set up a studio in the garage and did two sculptures while I was there, learning so much from their master craftsmen. The triple bonus was that I connected with a high-end gallery there on the famed Canyon Street, who agreed to represent me and show my work. Having my sculptures in such a classy gallery was a real confidence booster.

I had The Iceboxx Studio for five years and had established a legitimate career as a sculptor—galleries in Palm Springs, Santa Fe, and Venice carried my work as well as The Iceboxx. My work was in art magazines and interior design publications. I did art fairs in Palm Springs and Beverly Hills, created and maintained a website, and everything else that goes with being a small business operator. (Oh, and the sculpting too.) But I wasn't used to selling myself. I always had an agent in show business to tell people how great my work was and how much it would cost to buy my services, and I hated having to do that for myself in this new world, especially because I didn't really need the money. Then I discovered Public Art. I competed with other artists to create an original work of art that would be displayed on the Waterfront Park at the Port of San Diego. Each winning artist would be given a ten-foot-tall flagpole to create a work of art with, and those poles would line the waterfront walkway. I won one of the slots when I submitted a small model of one of my original poses, a man doing a one-handed handstand, this time on top of a flagpole. Getting chosen for that put me on the map, and I started getting offered other Public Art projects. It was the perfect job for me, and I grew to love it. When a city hired me to celebrate their heritage through one of my sculptures, I would dig into their history and attend the city's town hall meetings to listen to the citizens about what aspects of their city were important to them. I worked with the arts commission, city planners, and even the city's safety and construction departments when it came time for installation. It was the perfect combination of public service and art.

Grinding in traffic every day to The Iceboxx was starting to eat me up. I loved the space and being in the cool Art District that was growing all around me, but my style of art was not the avant-garde stuff that the galleries on my block sold. My acting fame caught people's attention, but I felt I was intruding into the cool kids' party with my Rodin-inspired work. I didn't need or enjoy the foot traffic in and out of my studio, especially since most of my commissions were public art projects. I had lost interest in selling myself or my art. So I was wide open when an artist friend from Malibu told me about studio space near Ventura. It was the same distance from Malibu as Culver City, except that instead of driving down the Pacific Coast Highway into the hell of LA, the commute was up the PCH along the beautiful coast and farm fields. I checked it out and fell in love. An elementary school had been converted into an art colony, each classroom turned into an art studio, with the auditorium serving as a gallery and store. On top of that, the artists had set up community outreach programs to teach art in schools, held monthly art fairs, had professionals running the gallery, and the rent was half of what I was paying in Culver City. The move to the new studio gave me a gigantic creative boost. I felt that I had proven myself as a professional artist in the coolest art district in the world, and now it was time to just focus on the work itself, to try to be the best sculptor I could be. It never ceased to amaze me that I ended up sculpting in a kindergarten classroom, just like the one I dreamed about, making papier-mâché with my teacher, Mrs. Burton, that started me sculpting in the first place.

Laure and I fell in love with Ventura and the farm fields surrounding it. We started snooping around with a realtor, looking at lemon farms and avocado farms, educating ourselves about water issues, fruit-pickers, tree-trimmers, sprayers, and everything else that goes into running a farm like that. We were in no rush to take on such a big move and change, and still wrapped up in Malibu, but we were getting ready to move on. We had done what we set out to do—raise our family and commit to helping our community as best we could. I was now the chairman of the Art Task Force for the city, with a goal to create a new official

Arts Commission that would oversee public art and education in Malibu. I had loved it all—coaching, teaching, community organizing, even fundraising—but our kids had grown and gone, and it was time for the parents of the next generation of kids to take the reins, do the work, and keep things going to pass on to the generation after that. I had stepped up to become the president of Malibu Foundation in an attempt to wean the organization of its dependency on Laure and transition it into an organization that could function well without its founders. Over my term as president, we recruited new board members, reinforced the staff of the Boys & Girls Club, expanded our connection with the national board, and tried to assure the strength and longevity of all that we had helped build. When Laure and I were comfortable and confident that everything was in good hands, we announced that we would resign from the board and become emeritus board members. Like our kids going off into the world, this twenty-year dream was up and running, and we were so proud and exhausted. Boys & Girls Club of America saluted us with a service award, and the Malibu community gave us a wonderful farewell party. We were touched and honored. Little did we know just how honored we would be.

Not only did the community recognize the contribution that Laure and I had made, but so did President Obama. That's right, my old friend Barack. Our community nominated us for, and the President bestowed upon us, the President's Call to Service Award, the nation's highest honor for volunteerism. We were given a plaque and the special pin you wear to show this honor, although I am still afraid to take it out of its case. He also included a letter to each of us, thanking us for dedicating our time and service, and congratulating us on all we had achieved. I might not have an Oscar or a Tony, but in my family, there can be no higher honor than to get recognized for public service. Laure and I were brought to tears by this huge surprise. It touched us in the deepest possible way. We had done our work out of our love and commitment to the betterment of the youth and families in our community, not for any public recognition. I had never even heard of the President's Award before. But man, did that feel special. (And it still does!) Laure and I had been together for most of our lives and had long ago bonded with each other through our marriage, our children, and our home. But creating the Malibu Foundation for Youth and Families, which is still growing and thriving, with Boys & Girls Clubs branches at every single school in Malibu, created a new kind of bond for us—sharing a vision for building a safe home for all of the kids in town to call their own, and then bringing it to life. We finally felt like our work in Malibu was done. So now what?

THE PLAY IS THE THING

And so begins the last chapter of this book. (Or maybe it's the first chapter of the next one?)

2016 was the year wherein one life ended and this new one began. At this point, Ella was a paramedic, riding at breakneck speed through the streets of Portland, delivering babies on the side of the road, bringing overdose victims back to life, carrying a child who had their face bitten badly by a dog, and other absolutely crazy shit you can't even imagine. She had already been accepted to medical school, was in love with a great young man, and they were getting married in October 2016. By then, Sophie was already married and was crushing it with her music. She toured with her band, Sophie and the Bom Boms, and was an outstanding performer and singer, thrilling audiences with her shows. She also had a songwriting deal with the infamous Dr.

Luke and was writing songs for Britney Spears, Kesha, Conor Maynard, and many other pop stars.

By now, Henry was legislative counsel to the legendary California State Senator Fran Pavley, using his degree to help write groundbreaking environmental laws. But Senator Pavley's term limit of twelve years ended in 2016, and she asked Henry to run for her seat. He had always played in the political arena, although never as a candidate, but it turned out he was built for the job. And so was Laure. None of us had any experience organizing a political campaign, but we did know how to fundraise, which is unfortunately the most important part of politics. We turned the little house into campaign headquarters. Everyone in Malibu knew Henry and Laure and their contributions to their community, and they were supportive of their hometown boy seeking such a high office like state senator. Billy Crystal, Rob Reiner, Paul Reiser, and so many of our show business friends knew Henry from when he was a kid, and his nickname was "Mr. President" because he was so smart, caring, and charismatic. Henry hired Senator Pavley's campaign people and Laure raised money. Henry went from debate to debate and fundraiser to fundraiser, a happy warrior offering real solutions to the problems of environmental justice, drought issues, clean energy, fracking, and so many other seemingly unsolvable issues. I did what I could, going to events and talking him up, but Henry didn't need my help and neither did Laure, so mostly my job was to worry. In June 2016, Henry won the Democratic Primary, fending off other well-funded challengers in a somewhat ugly campaign. (Although what political campaign isn't ugly?) The district leaned Democrat, but he had a fight on his hands to win in November, and we went into fundraising mode again to raise the money needed to compete. Henry and Laure were a well-oiled machine, but I was beginning to crack.

On the outside I was saying, "I love Malibu! I have worked as hard as I could, my wife has given a big chunk of her life to make this a better place, and now our son wants to serve the people of this city. There is no better place on earth." But on the inside I was saying, "Fuck Malibu! I hate this fucking place. Too crowded, too entitled. Ripping up its natural beauty to build monstrous homes and have parties? Fuck this place!" I was torn apart by the dueling voices and dealt with it by going to the ranch and my studio as much as possible. But on the Fourth of July weekend, I finally snapped. I always tried to be away during holidays in Malibu because that is when the entitled assholes really come out to play, but this weekend a friend was getting married, and I had to stay for the wedding. We got home after midnight, and when we pulled into the driveway, the music blaring from our neighbor's house was as loud as if you were at a disco. And it wasn't even Kid Rock's house this time. It was the real estate mogul, the son of the fireman who embodied Old Malibu, now disrespecting his neighbors, as well as nature, in such an arrogant way. I was fuming mad. It was my worst fear come to life, the final killing of the Malibu dream I had for our family. Henry and Laure tried to calm me down, but I became unmoored. By one in the morning, I was out of my mind. With the disco bass beating into my brain, I finally called our neighbor to tell him to shut it off, but only got his answering machine. I called our other neighbors, who were incredibly pissed off that this was going on, but no one could get in touch with the real estate asshole because it turned out he had rented the house to Bono (yes, that Bono), who was having a birthday party for his daughter. Henry and Laure made one more attempt to stop me, both feeling the headline of me being arrested for going crazy at a trendy Malibu party might not be good for Senator-to-Be Stern, but I was too far gone by then. I called the police and told them that there was an unlawful party going on and that I was going over there to shut it down and I hoped they would join me. I hopped in my truck, drove around the block to the house, parked the car in the middle of the street, and headed in. The security guys at the door recognized me and since I was still wearing my suit and tie from the wedding, assumed I must be on the list, so I got in with no problem. I had not been in the McMansion the real estate narcissist had put up in place of the modest home his parents raised him in, and the absolute gaudiness of the place slowed me down for a beat. It looked like a hotel—slate walls, dim lighting, waterfall. The open lobby area had a bar in it, where cool people in black clothing mingled. At the far side of the lobby was a balcony, which overlooked a lit stairway leading down to the pool area where most of the party was taking place. It also happened to look into *my bedroom!* I lost it.

I started ranting, "Shut the fucking music off!! Families with children are trying to sleep, and instead we all have to listen to this shitty music all night long?! Shut it off! You don't even live here, you fucking pretentious assholes! To celebrate Bono's daughter's fucking birthday at one o'clock in the morning? Shut it off!" (Or something like that.) At first it was hard for people to understand what was going on, so I had to keep getting louder and louder. Security finally came in as I descended the stairs, blocking my way but not wanting to get in a fight with a "guest." Also, I am six-foot-four and can look pretty insane and scary when I lose my shit, and I was at full tilt. The police came quickly, thank God. They shut down the party, calmed me down, and mercifully let me go on my way, empathetic to how out-of-control and inappropriate that party was and how justified my anger was. I drove back to our house, where Laure and Henry were worried sick, and broke down. "I can't live in this place anymore. I hate it here so much." The most beautiful place in the world, that we had worked so hard to sustain and preserve, had been ruined beyond repair. They won. "I give up."

Two months later, we found the perfect farm in Ventura. Forty acres of tangerines, lemons, and avocados, a house big enough for family to stay with us and even a small guesthouse. With Sophie's album coming out, Ella's wedding, and Henry's election all happening at the same time, we didn't even tell the kids that we had put a deposit on it. They were all having incredible adventures in their lives, which is everything a parent could hope for, and this was a new Laure and Danny Adventure, the first one without the kids in a very long time. By November, Ella was married, Sophie was pregnant, and Henry was a senator, winning his election on the same day my old buddy Donald Trump became the president (talk about mixed emotions!). When we finally told the kids and my parents about the farm, they were thrilled for us. The farm owners let us bring everyone out to see the place, and they were excited that it was going to be ours. Unlike my first time on our cattle ranch, I did not start a stampede, mostly because this farm didn't have cows. But it was drizzling that day, lush and wet. Too wet, actually, because when I drove us all out into the orchard to see the beautiful fruit trees, I somehow managed to get the car stuck in the mud. It was about a mile from the house, and I had to hike back to get a neighbor to pull us out with his tractor. My ninety-year-old parents sat calmly in the car while my children laughed at how ridiculous it was that I took us out there without knowing what I was doing. But they should be used that by now. That's how I roll.

About a year after we moved in, the Woolsey Fire burned through Malibu and my parents had to evacuate their beach side trailer and shelter with us. The stress, the fear, and the eight hours stuck in traffic on the PCH was a lot. The first night they stayed with us, my dad had severe shortness of breath, and I took him to the hospital. He came out a week later, but Laure and I realized that even when Malibu reopened, which wouldn't be for weeks, it would be too dangerous for them go back and live on their own—too isolated for my dad's worsening condition, and too much stress on my mother to be his full-time caretaker. They loved and needed their independence, but eventually we convinced them to move into our guesthouse, where they would be totally separate from us but right there if they needed us. They were both Philadelphia city kids, and living on a farm, right across from the ducks and chickens, both confounded and delighted them. My dad was in and out of the hospital for a year, and just after they celebrated their sixty-fifth anniversary, my dad went into sudden decline. My sister flew down, my brother came out, my kids and nieces and nephews and even my dad's best friend from DC were all there when he passed away in his bed. Watching him pass from this life to the next was transformational for me. (As well as for him!)

I loved my dad with every fiber of my being. He was so fun, so smart, so loving, so emotional, and so fucked up too, a role model for me as well as a cautionary tale, which I guess could be said about most fathers and sons. He worked his whole life trying to make other people's lives better and safer and more just. We buried his ashes under a beautiful tree near the guesthouse so that he is always near us. My mom still lives in the guesthouse, and what a blessing that has been. All of her kids, grandkids, and great-grandkids visit her constantly, and the people who work on the farm love and respect "Ms. Cynthia" deeply, making sure she always has fresh lemons, avocados, tangerines, eggs, and her newspaper brought in from the street. Laure loves her like her own mother, showers her with food, coordinates everything from electricians to doctors, as well as being tech support. Mom loves us all back so freely and shows us how a great life is lived. She has been in and out of the hospital herself a few times, adding to my list of things to worry about, but the opportunity to have so much time with her at this point in our lives is one of the many unforeseen joys that this new life on our farm has brought me.

We have lived here for six years as of this writing, and it is everything I hoped it would be, and more. Between the farm and the ranch, I spend 100 percent of my time in the beautiful countryside of California as a Gentleman Farmer. Of course, I let the real work go to the cattlemen, orchard managers, and Laure—you know, people who actually know what they're doing. But I am free to make as much tangerine juice as I want, clean horse stalls, lay irrigation pipe, pick avocados, collect eggs, herd cattle, and give tractor rides whenever I feel like it. I still like acting when I am inspired by a part or a project and I should probably direct at least one more film before I die, just for the personal challenge of it, although the job itself might kill me. I have spent my entire life on movie sets, which is crazy, but what is crazier is now I have graduated into being the "wise old man" on set. The crew calls me "Mr. Stern," tell me their favorite movies of mine, and sometimes look at me like I must have looked at Jack Palance, Robert Redford, and Roy Scheider when I had the honor of working with them, older guys you loved in older movies, still standing and doing it.

I put up an art studio in the middle of the orchard, and my daily commute is now on our dirt road through a forest of avocado trees. Sculpting has become more than a job or an art form to me and moved into something more spiritual. For the moment, I have stopped showing my work in galleries or seeking public art projects. I have been selling myself and my art my whole life, the product always being my creativity, so I am trying something new—doing the work for the sake of the work and not for those kinds of commercial goals. My hours alone in the studio, pushing clay this way and that way until it comes to life for me, have given me time to understand the Tao of Sculpting. There is the moment of inspiration, when the pose and the story flash in my mind. Then I imagine how to physically make it, and what the viewer would feel when they see it. Then, just the work—cutting the foam, welding the pipe, laying the clay, climbing the scaffold, and all of the physical labor it takes to make an eight-foot-tall totem or a couple dancing. Doing the work is what separates the fantasist from the achiever. I respect the commitment I make to myself to see these things through to the end, even though the world would continue just fine if I didn't make it. The physical labor is good for me. I am an animal and I need to move. But the deepest lesson sculpting has taught me is the necessity of seeing things from all angles. When I am working on a face, I can carve the nose so that it looks perfect, but as soon as I take a step to my left and see it from a new angle, I see that the bridge is too long. Another step to my left shows me another flaw and when I look at it from below, it isn't even recognizable as a nose. It takes time and focus to keep re-examining something, but if you do it long enough and clearly enough, you will eventually get as close as possible to the truth, the best nose you can possibly make. Don't fool yourself and think things are perfect, or that you fully understand the situation, if you have only looked at it from your immediate point of view. Take one step to your left and see what it looks like from there. Get on your knees and look at it from that perspective. And while you are there in that moment looking at the nose, look at the ear too, and everything else you can see from where you are, because you will never be there again. The light, the angle, the time of day, and your frame of mind will never be in this exact position again. So take in the moment and explore everything you can see and do right now. Find the flaws and fix them right now. Find the beauty from this angle, and feel satisfaction at your creation and understanding. If you tell yourself you will come back and fix the problem later, you are fooling yourself. Why clutter your mind with the nagging thought that you need to find this perspective again, and do the repair work later? Just finish the work in front of you and move on to the next thing. The way I sculpt has shown me how to see my life, and the world. There are so many perspectives in this world of eight billion people (and countless other creatures, large and small), and I need to always have the humility to remember that I don't understand the big picture at all, not even close.

Lately I have been writing a musical with CeeLo Green based on my old movie *C.H.U.D.*, a film adaptation of *Barbra's Wedding*, a black comedy Christmas movie, and a couple of TV series, but all of those need producers, actors, designers, crew people, and a big pile of cash to get them from the page to you, the audience, and I know the chances for each are slim. Writing this book has been another personal challenge that I did not expect to undertake, and it has been quite a learning experience. Everything else I have written has been fiction, where I ask myself, "What can happen?" Writing this book, the consistent question is "What *did* happen?" and it has been a fascinating exercise, reassessing my life at sixty-five. I highly recommend it. Lucky for me, the story doesn't end here. But the book does. So with only a page or so to go before I can call myself a book writer, I guess I need to wrap it up with a few choice words of wisdom, a final message, the moral of the story. Unfortunately, I don't have any of those.

If I have a cause, it's empowering children and young people. I was raised to be confident in my abilities as well as understand my limitations, and I have made my life choices accordingly. From my first solo trip across Philadelphia at age four, to canoe camp, hitchhiking as a preteen, and up through my decision to drop out of high school and move to New York on my own at seventeen, I was led to believe that I could handle myself in adult situations. And I could. My biggest hit movies have had the same message—if a kid is raised to believe they can handle themselves in an adult situation, they usually can. Keeping our kids safe while also helping them expand their world should be our Number One goal as a species. By making sure each child has the knowledge they need, a mentor to learn from, and the critical thinking skills to be able to make good decisions and navigate the crazy world we have brought them into, we assure the healthy survival of the human race. None of it means anything if we don't invest everything we can in our kids.

Save your money! If you are lucky enough to be making money doing what you love, save it! Especially for artists. The goal is to make a living doing what you love, have control over your life and how you spend your time on Earth. Life is long and you are going to need money the whole time, so hold onto it tight. I have talked about money in this book. That is the other half of fame and fortune. I hope it hasn't been gross to mention how much money I made on individual projects, but it is important to paint a picture of the money part of show business too. Saving money bought me the freedom to spend my time the way I want to spend it, and when you get down to it, there is nothing more valuable than how you spend your time. To me, this is the next step in Young People Empowerment. Invest your money and time into yourself, your talent, and your dream. No excuses!

My life took an amazing turn with *Home Alone*. Playing Marv Merchants was a ton of fun, but the lasting impact it had on my life is immeasurable. How many people in the world are stopped by perfect strangers who tell them, "I love you. My family loves you. You bring us joy. You are a part of our family holiday tradition," and all of the other wonderful things people say to me all the time? My face is on T-shirts, kids' toys, dog toys, shower curtains, and tattooed on people's bodies. Justin Timberlake himself dressed up as me for Halloween! The kids in Iraq, monks in Japan, tribespeople in the Alaskan wilderness, presidents of the United States—literally everywhere I go, people recognize Marv, connect with me, and share a smile or a kind word. I have spent years trying to understand Marv's superpower and how to use it for good. I hope the gratitude I feel towards all the fans of my movies comes through on these pages, although the Power of Marv still scares me, and I don't leave the house that much. The love and attention people show me overwhelms me a bit and throws me off-balance from my regular life and self-image. But it is the blessing of a lifetime to be able to meet anyone, anywhere, under any circumstance, and without doing anything, have an immediate positive connection and elicit a smile. I did get a new lease on life during the COVID19 pandemic and mask mandates, when, for the first time in decades, I felt I could walk around stores and fly on airplanes unrecognized and people watch, instead of being watched by people. I am going to pretend to be immuno-compromised for the rest of my life!

On his ninetieth birthday, surrounded by his family and friends, my dad, not one for speechifying, speechified. He said he had thought about it and, looking back over his time on Earth, he had concluded that the most important thing in life is . . . work. He said that of course he loves his family, but his work touched a lot of people, made their lives better, and made the world better. He loved being in the trenches with workmates and, if you add it up, had probably spent more time with them than he had with his family. Dad loved being the contrarian, and the family gave him the proper amount of shit for not picking his family as his most important accomplishment. But I could tell he was only half kidding, and I have been trying to balance that in my mind ever since. My family are the most important people in the world to me. My kids have amazed me every day of their lives. My parents, my siblings, in-laws, uncles, aunts, grandparents, cousins, nieces, and nephews are my blood, literally and figuratively. My grand-kids are delicious and tickle the old parts of my brain, when I was being a dad to little kids—nurturing, playing games, teaching. I am giving myself the time to waste whole days doing nothing but playing with them, and those are truly the best days of my life. And I love watching my kids figure out how to be parents. Seeing them grow into these new roles and responsibilities is a continuation of the miraculous journey of being a parent, as the circle of life continues. But my work has also made me who I am. The people I have worked with, the opportunities I have had, the art I've created, the audiences I have touched, the places I have traveled, the lessons I have learned, and the chances I have been given to serve my fellow man have shaped me into the other half of who I have become.

Of course, this is all a moot argument because the absolute most important factor in shaping my life is Laure. Literally none of it would have happened like this if not for Laure. She believed in me, loved me, made our family, and made our home. She does all our financial work, all travel arrangements, takes care of children, grandchildren, and parents, runs the farm, runs the ranch, sells the house, buys the house, cooks the food, fixes computers, feeds the animals, knows the neighbors, gets the truck fixed, and rubs my back in bed at night so perfectly it feels like all is right with the world. So I guess that is the real answer in the work versus family debate, and I am sure my father would have said that about his wife if we had pressed him. But his point still has truth to me—my family and my work are the two sides to my world, and both hemispheres are needed to make my world whole.

As all good book writers do, I will end on a Shakespearean quote, even though I have still never read one of his plays. But this one I actually understand, and it hits home. "The play's the thing." Play. That is what I have been doing my *entire* life:

playing as much as I possibly could. I take playing very seriously and always have. It is "the thing," after all. Playing baseball, football, basketball, tennis, golf, bowling, ping pong, anything where I can throw or chase a ball. Playing Cowboys and Indians, Sharks and Jets. Playing Army. Playing trumpet, and then playing guitar. Playing music in my studio all day long. Playing cards, Risk, chess, Barbies, swimming pool basketball. Acting in plays, playing many parts, playwriting, directing plays, writing screenplays. I have played enormous theaters and my films have played all over the world. Playing with my children. Playing with other people's children. And now playing with my grandchildren. I have tried to play "the game" and "play ball" but usually end up just playing the fool in those situations. Like every one else, I am playing for time, hoping to keep playing on, and always seem to be playing it all by ear.

"WHAT ARE
THE CHANCES?"

Okay, one last thing before I go. As you now know, I have the craziest luck in the world. If I had a catchphrase, it would be, "What are the chances?" It started on the day I was born, with the town's beloved doctor dying immediately after delivering me. As a kid I had chicken pox twice, even though you are only supposed to be able to get it once. I was struck by lightning, not once but twice; not a direct hit either time, but instead hitting a nearby tree. Both times, I felt electricity pulse through my body and the metal fillings in my teeth buzzed for days afterward. When I moved to California and I got my new driver's license, the number was the exact same number as our telephone number when I was a kid growing up in Maryland. What are the chances of that? I played left field for three innings in the Hollywood All-Star Game at Dodger Stadium and, as one of nine fielders, did not get one ball hit to me. But when I stayed to see the game, wouldn't you know it, a foul ball came right to me while I was sitting in a crowd of forty thousand people. I am still pissed that it hit my hands and I missed it, but still, what are the chances?

But the craziest life-changing coincidence involves the house at 64 Plochmann Lane in Woodstock, New York. This was the house that Laure and I had put escrow money down on back in 1986, when we had sold our first little co-op apartment and were going to move there. At the last minute, we decided to move to LA and got the escrow money out, even though we loved that house and the possibility of the life it would have given us and our kids. Cut to fifteen years later. During this time, my brother had withdrawn from the family. He had no contact with any of us, except once in a while he would email my mom. In this time, he had gotten married and had a kid. It was a painful wound in our family to not have David in the mix, although we came to discover that this kind of break is common in a lot of families. One day my mom told me she got an email from David saying he and his wife, who were living in New York, had been on vacation in Woodstock and, even though it was their first time there, on a whim, they bought a house and moved there.

"Woodstock? Dave moved to Woodstock? Where is his house?"

"64 Plochmann Lane," she read from his email, and my jaw hit the floor. That was the same house we bought!

"Am I remembering the address of that house correctly?" I wondered. I ran it by Laure and she thought it was the same house. Was Dave fucking with me? How would he know that that was our house? He was twenty years old at the time, and our families never knew the address anyway. David bought 64 Plochmann Lane? I had to see for myself. When I went back to New York for a wedding, I rented a car and drove up to Woodstock. Any chance that I was misremembering the address was dismissed when I saw the mailbox, pulled down the beautiful long, driveway through the woods, and came upon the house we had fallen in love with all those years ago. I knocked on the front door. No answer. I knocked again. Still no answer. I tried the front door, and it was unlocked, so I opened it. There was mail on the floor and addressed to my brother. Holy shit, it was true! Dave bought the same house I did! All of a sudden I heard, "Hello?" and my brother appeared on the balcony overlooking the entranceway. I will never forget the look on the poor guy's face, seeing the one person in the world he did not want to see, standing uninvited in his house, the one he had moved to to get away from it all. I apologized profusely and told him why I was there. He was blown away by this almost biblical coincidence and before long, Dave was back in the fold of the family, his deep connection to all of us undeniably presented to him in the weirdest coincidence of all time. Talk about God moving in mysterious ways. As with most of my life, I am left asking the question, "What are the chances?"

ACKNOWLEDGEMENTS

This is the Acknowledgements Section, where I am supposed to thank everyone who has contributed to making this book. I was going to take this golden opportunity to finally use the Academy Award acceptance speech I have been waiting in vain to use for the last forty years, since my chances of winning an Oscar are getting slimmer by the day (in direct opposite of my waistline,) but upon further review, I thought better of it. As much as I would like to thank my dialect coach, personal trainer, personal chef, key grip, best boy, Covid compliance officer, VFX department, boom operator, weapons wrangler, foley artist, and gang boss, they really had nothing to do with the making of this book. (Although I would like it noted that no animals were harmed during production of this work, except my dogs, who did not get walked nearly enough for the last few months.) And even though I explicitly do *not* want to thank the Academy, there are a few people I would like to acknowledge for their support and assistance.

If you end up hating this book, it is my agents' fault. There I was, minding my own business, when Ryan Martin and Scott Kaufman approached me with the idea of publishing my story, so this whole fiasco is their doing. They somehow convinced Jarred Weisfeld, the publisher at Start Publishing, that he could sell enough copies of this book to pay for all of the ink and paper that go into making one of these things, so thank you Jarred for prioritizing putting my story into the public square over your children's college education. David Krintzman, Michael Diamant, and Aileen Gorospe are the crack team of lawyers who have been my sherpa guides into the publishing world, and their understanding of the statute of limitations on a variety of potential felonies has been invaluable in the editing of these stories. Rene Sears has been the editor of this book and has shouldered the weight of the work, trying to make English sense out of all the words I put into every sentence and thought and bringing clear-eyed, clarifying, illuminating, simplifying, elucidating coherence to sentences that have too many words in them and seem to run on and drift into other thoughts but always able to bring them back again, like the swallows of Capistrano returning in the spring to where they had once come from, but who was unfortunately on vacation when it came time to write and edit the Acknowledgement Section of this voluminous volume. She has been the English teacher I never had. Ashley Calvano is an up-and-coming editor at Start who has been instrumental in keeping me on track and focused on the light at the end of the tunnel. With a full head of steam, she has kept the trains running and supplied all the technical bells and whistles to get us to the end of the line. (Although she could not prevent this train wreck of a metaphor.) Jennifer Do brought her artistry to making the book cover. She was a life-saver, since my original idea was deemed "too costly," and the Pope didn't seem that willing to let us do a photo shoot at the Vatican anyway.

My brother David is the writer in the family and his encouragement and support means everything to me. I had originally hoped he would write the book for me but instead, he instilled a false sense of confidence in me, sent me on my way, and dodged the bullet of being trapped in a room with me for months listening to me drone on about myself. (Speaking from experience, it was hell.) Well-played, bro. Well-played. I want to thank all my friends who read early drafts of this (or pretended to) and agreed to write a blurb for the book. It has been quite embarrassing to have them all be asked to write nice things about me. On the other hand, it is just a blurb, which isn't really asking a lot. (Blurb is a very odd term by the way. It sounds like a mash-up of blurred, burp, herb, and turd, which, come to think of it, describes my writing process pretty well.) I have already dedicated this book to my family, friends, and fans in world-class poetic and inspirational words (see Dedication Page) but I am new to the rules of book etiquette and want to stay on everybody's good side, so in this section I want to acknowledge this group of people again. Let me say to you all with acknowledgement, "Look at you. There you are."

I guess the last thing I would want to acknowledge in this book is the Power of Love. (I have not been able to find a place in the book to say this so I figured I would place it at the bottom of the Acknowledgement Section, which very few people will read anyway.) It astounds me to realize that all life on planet Earth is powered by love. Every living thing, from a tiny mouse to a human being, survives on love and the primal need to be connected, protected, erected, respected, projected, and perfected. I get so busy during the day sometimes (like spending three hours with a rhyming dictionary for that last sentence) that I can forget this simple truth. And so I want to acknowledge that the greatest power in the world is love, and my wish for the reader is to have as much of it in their lives as is humanly possible.